Moresby, John

Discoveries and surveys in New Guinea and the d'Entrecasteaux Islands

Moresby, John

Discoveries and surveys in New Guinea and the d'Entrecasteaux Islands

Inktank publishing, 2018

www.inktank-publishing.com

ISBN/EAN: 9783747781098

NEW GUINEA & POLYNESIA

DISCOVERIES & SURVEYS

IN

NEW GUINEA

AND THE

D'ENTRECASTEAUX ISLANDS

A CRUISE IN POLYNESIA AND VISITS TO THE PEARL-SHELLING STATIONS IN TORRES STRAITS OF H.M.S. BASILISK

BY CAPT[N.] JOHN MORESBY, R.N.

WITH MAPS AND ILLUSTRATIONS

LONDON

JOHN MURRAY, ALBEMARLE STREET

1876

DEDICATED

TO

SIR FAIRFAX MORESBY,

ADMIRAL OF THE FLEET, G.C.B., D.C.L. (OXON.)

KNIGHT OF MARIA THERESA,

BY

HIS SON.

PREFACE.

It seems desirable to state, for the information of the general reader, that the line of New Guinea coast, first placed on the chart by H.M.S. "Basilisk," had never been visited, and was actually unknown as to its conformation (as far as I have been able to discover any record), up to the period of her first visit in 1873, between the wide limits of Heath Island and Huon Gulf.

None of the navigators who did good service in the South Seas and on other parts of the New Guinea coast, neared the coast-line laid down by the "Basilisk" within these bounds, a fact as singular as it is interesting.

By the courtesy of the present hydrographer of the Navy, I have been able to take from a chart, constructed in his department, the tracks of my predecessors in these waters, from which the appended table has been compiled, which will show the reader that up to the advent of the "Basilisk" in 1873, this portion of the coast had been avoided by common consent, with a sort of fatality; strange, indeed, when we consider the extent of coast-line thus lying unknown, and the position held by the great island ot New Guinea on the habitable part of the globe.

TABLE

Showing the nearest points of approach attained by former ships to the unknown coast-line of South-East and North-East New Guinea, since surveyed by H.M.S. "Basilisk," between the limits of Heath Island and Huon Gulf.

NAVIGATOR.	NEAREST POINT OF APPROACH.
SOUTH-EAST COAST.	
Bougainville (A.D. 1768).	Some 40 miles south of Heath Island.
D'Urville (A.D. 1840).	Some 16 miles south of Heath Island, or some 20 miles from the New Guinea coast.
NORTH-EAST COAST.	
D'Entrecasteaux (A.D. 1793).	Some 28 miles east of the now known eastern extremity of New Guinea, at which distance it is not visible. Second approach—(240 miles farther to the westward) to an estimated distance of 25 miles from the land, and from a point which he named Richie Island, but which was found to be part of the mainland.
Captain Simpson, R.N. H.M.S. "Blanche." (A.D. 1872).	Some 34 miles from East Cape, the nearest point of the mainland of New Guinea, and 21 miles E.N.E. from Moresby Island, the outermost of the group of large islands into which the south-east extremity of New Guinea is now known to be broken up. See Admiralty Chart, Papua, sheet 7 (A.D. 1875).

Captain Owen Stanley, R.N., whose valuable survey on the south-east coast is a source of pride to English seamen, never passed round the east end of New Guinea, or we should have had a shorter story to tell; or rather perhaps no story at all. His work lay in the other direction; he commenced his New Guinea survey about three miles south-west of Heath Island, and then ran westward.

On this *great blank* of coast-line, some 340 miles in extent (as the crow flies, save for the curve of Milne Bay) from Heath Island to Huon Gulf, the only positions laid down were the two solitary ones by D'Entrecasteaux in 1793 (situated 170 and 220 miles to the westward of East Cape), as seen from his second and nearer point of approach. They were named by him respectively "Cape Sud Est," and "Richie Island;" both these positions, however, were incorrect. Cape Sud Est was placed by D'Entrecasteaux in latitude 8° 45′ S., and longitude 148° 18′ E. (see Admiralty Chart, Coral Sea, sheet 2, A.D. 1869), whereas the only cape-like projection of the land existing here, one to which we have now transferred the name of Cape Sud Est, is in latitude 8° 41′ S., and longitude 148° 33′ E., a discrepancy which shows an error of some seventeen miles.

The position assigned to Cape Sud Est was further found by us to fall on a range of high mountains, sixteen miles inland.

The north-east point of Richie Island, D'Entrecasteaux's second position, was placed by him in latitude 8° 7′ S., and longitude 147° 54′ E. (see Admiralty Chart, quoted above). No island exists here, and the north-east point of the supposed island falls some twelve miles inland, and some eighteen miles from the cape which we have named Richie, on the "Basilisk's" chart. D'Entrecasteaux, in sailing past this coast, had doubtless caught two glimpses of high land in the interior, and very naturally mistaken them for portions of a coast-line.

In its own place I shall refer to the valuable work done by this old navigator beyond the limits of the "Basilisk's" special survey.

From Huon Gulf to Astrolobe Bay, the "Basilisk's" voyage ceased to be one of discovery; and her work between those limits consisted in the making of needful corrections on the existing chart of the coast-line, which was very little known.

It is not on record that any ship before the "Basilisk" had ever passed from south to north New Guinea, without first going some 240 miles to the eastward, to avoid the great Louisiade reefs, which stretch that distance east. She has found a safe ship channel through these reefs, and opened a highway for commerce.

The "Basilisk" has placed on the chart more than

140 islands and islets, of which 25 are inhabited; and has added many excellent harbours and safe anchorages to our knowledge.

I specify the limits within which our task has lain, with an anxious and painstaking distinctness, which will, I know, be appreciated by my late shipmates; and I attempt in the pages that follow to show how far we discharged it.

The results of our labours have been generously received by those who understand them, but we wish our friends at large to know exactly what we have done—no less—no more; and to know that we have honestly tried to do the good that seemed to lie within our power.

J. MORESBY.

THE GLEN, QUEENSTOWN,
15th December 1875.

CONTENTS.

CHAPTER I.

CHAPTER II.

CHAPTER III.

CHAPTER IV.

CHAPTER V.

CHAPTER VI.

CHAPTER VII.

CHAPTER VIII.

CHAPTER IX.

CHAPTER X.

CHAPTER XI.

CHAPTER XII.

CHAPTER XVI.

CHAPTER XVII.

CHAPTER XVIII.

SUPPLEMENTARY CHAPTER.

LIST OF ILLUSTRATIONS.

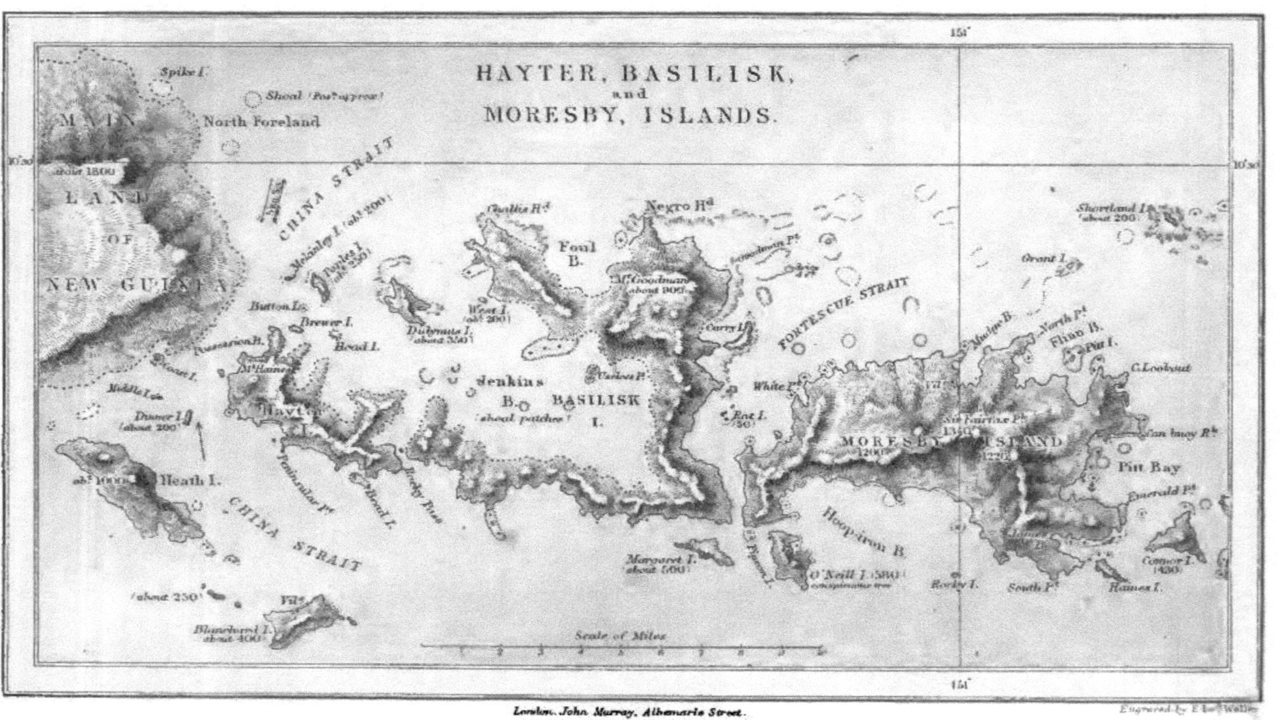
HAYTER, BASILISK,
and
MORESBY, ISLANDS.
MAIN LAND OF NEW GUINEA
Spike I.
North Foreland
CHINA STRAIT
Button Is.
Brewer I.
Bead I.
Heath I.
CHINA STRAIT
Foul B.
Negro Hd.
West I.
Jenkins B.
BASILISK I.
FORTESCUE STRAIT
White Pt.
Rat I.
MORESBY ISLAND
Hoop-iron B.
Margaret I.
Pigeon I.
Grant I.
Shortland I.
North Pt.
Fitzroy B.
Pitt I.
C. Lookout
Pitt Bay
Emerald Pt.
Rocky I.
South Pt.
Haines I.
Scale of Miles
London. John Murray, Albemarle Street.

NEW GUINEA.

CHAPTER I.

LEAVE SYDNEY—FIRST VISIT TO BRISBANE—INSIDE THE BARRIER REEF—THE "PERI," AND HER STORY—THE SETTLEMENT AT CARDWELL—FITZROY ISLAND, AND A WOODING PARTY.

"Of making many books there is no end," and I have no desire to add to the number of books produced without sufficient motive; but I trust that the work done by H.M.S. "Basilisk," in waters hitherto untracked, on shores hitherto untrodden, and amongst races hitherto unknown by Europeans, will be held to call for some account.

I will try to take my reader to new ground, on the coasts of New Guinea, and to some of the lovely adjacent islands of which we were the discoverers; but I crave leave to make a digression to Polynesia, even at the risk of saying a little that has been better said by others.

On January 15th, 1871, H.M.S. "Basilisk," a steamship of 1031 tons, 400 horse-power, with five guns, and manned by 178 officers and men, left Sydney, under orders to proceed to Cape York, with horses and stores for that settlement, and to spend three months in the cruise. The Cape York cruise was not generally thought an inviting one, and we were somewhat loath

B

2

to leave civilisation and the kindness of our Sydney friends; but it offered variety, and a hope of interest,—above all, a possibility of doing some useful work.

We reached Brisbane on the 22d, and there, in conversing with Lord Normanby (to whom we all owe gratitude for the kindest hospitality), and the Hon. A. Palmer, Colonial Secretary, my ideas as to profitable work to be done in northern waters began to take definite shape. It was no small advantage to obtain an insight into the views of two such men, possessed of a perfect knowledge of the cumulative forces which have wrought out the present aspects of Australian affairs, and much foresight of the future; and this I hoped to turn to good account as opportunity offered, as far as it should lie parallel with the routine of the service and my duty.

Having taken on board the horses and stores for Cape York, and filled up our coal, we took leave of Moreton Bay and the mangrove-covered shores of Brisbane river on January 28th, and left finally for our destination.

The voyage from Brisbane to Cape York is now a common one, and is performed by two routes, one leading inside, and the other outside, the Great Barrier Reef. We took the inner one, which is now coming into general use, being shorter than the other, and of course more sheltered. These advantages will in time outweigh the difficulty of a somewhat more intricate navigation, and cause it to be all but exclusively used.

It is generally known that the gigantic Barrier

Reef runs north and south for 1200 miles, at a distance varying from seven to eighteen miles from the Queensland coast, and that it is supposed to have originally been joined to the Australian continent as a shore or fringing reef. It is submerged in parts, generally to a shallow depth, and traceable only by the surf that breaks on it, out of which a crowd of "nigger heads," black points of coral rock, peep up in places; but here and there it comes to the surface as a sandbank or vegetated island, or, breaking its continuous line, leaves a channel or gateway open to the sea, in which the plumb-line goes down to a bottomless depth. The water inclosed by the Barrier Reef is everywhere studded with islands, islets, coral banks, and hidden reefs, which would render its navigation dangerous but for the admirable surveys of Captains Owen Stanley and Francis Blackwood, by the help of whose charts, and using caution, this intricate bye-way of the ocean may be safely taken. No one, I think, but the responsible navigator of a ship, using this route, can sufficiently admire the skill and resolution of its first great explorer, Captain Cook. Reading his voyages here, on the spot where he pioneered the way, and considering his difficulties and his power of resource, I recognised his greatness as I had never done before. Unless a strong monsoon is blowing, the sailor moves inside this great breakwater on a perfect summer sea, over calm translucent water, whilst he sees the surf, and hears the roar of the Pacific, thundering against its everlasting wall outside.

On the 5th of February we were slipping through a sea like glass, blue as the sky that hung over, and watching the great lazy water-snakes at play on the surface, all of us languid from the intense heat, when the masthead-man reported "Sail right ahead!" and waked us up in a moment—it was such an event to see a sail. We almost hoped it might not belong to a kidnapper, for the law was not then in a state to protect captors; but she looked very like one—a small fore and aft schooner—as she rose to our glasses. There was something puzzling about the slovenly set of her sails, and she had a heavy water-logged look as she swayed slowly with the long smooth undulations of the sea. We hoisted the ensign to see what she would say to us, but there was no response, so we steered to pass her close. There were signs of strange neglect in the weather-beaten sails and slackened ropes as we neared her, and not a soul was moving on board; but just as we were thinking her abandoned, two or three wild-looking creatures, Solomon Islanders, rose up in the stern, and then we saw that others lay on the deck as if asleep. Lieutenant Hayter, and Mr. Bently, the gunner, went with two boats to board, and these men pointed muskets at them over the side; but what men! they were living skeletons, creatures dazed with fear and mortal weakness. As our crews boarded, other half-dead wretches tottered to their feet, fumbling too at rusty, lockless muskets, and our men disarmed them gently. They were dreadful to look at—beings in the last stage of famine, wasted to the bone; some were barely alive, and the sleeping figures were dead bodies fast losing the shape of humanity, on a deck foul with blood. We tried to show that we would not hurt them, we gave them water, and it was awful to see their eagerness to drink. Our men vied with each other in their rough cares, but the help came too late for one—one dark Melanesian soul passed away from the blood-stained deck, to find the mercy from God which man had denied. There was no water on board, no food, no boat by which they might have saved themselves. The hold was full of the sea; and the ransacked cabin, the blood, the planking splintered and scored by axe-strokes, told of a tragedy. Having given our first succour to the living under Dr. Goodman's direction, we turned to pump out the hold, and to bury the dead. The bodies, six in number, were wrapped separately in a decent canvas, and weighted, insufficiently as it proved, and the pumps ceased clanging on board the "Peri," and our men stood bare-headed as an officer read the words, "we commit their bodies to the deep, in sure and certain hope of the resurrection to eternal life." The poor remnants of mortality when launched overboard did not sink, but floated away beyond our sight, mute witnesses to heaven of a foul wrong.

The story of the "Peri" proved to be this:—A noted kidnapping vessel, the "Nukulow," had brought a cargo of some 180 kidnapped natives to Rewa River, Fiji, some two months previous to our falling in with the "Peri." At Rewa they were disposed of, by being hired out to planters at the rate of ten to fifteen pounds a-head, paid to the owners of the "Nukulow," and about eighty of them were transferred to the "Peri" for conveyance to various islands of the Fiji group, in charge of three white men, and a Fijian crew. On getting to sea insufficient food was served to the natives, who were quite unsecured, and they clamoured for more, on which some rice was issued; but one of the white men, angered by the clamour for food, was heartless enough to throw the rice overboard as the natives were cooking it, and the maddened creatures rose at once and threw him over after the rice. The other two whites and the Fijians followed; and the savages, thus left to themselves, and wholly unable to manage the ship, drifted helpless and starving before the south-east trade wind for about five weeks, accomplishing a distance of nearly 1800 miles, through a sea infested with coral reefs and full of islands; finally passing either over a submerged part of the Barrier Reef, or through one of its narrow openings, to the place where the "Basilisk" found them. Thirteen only were then alive out of the eighty natives who had sailed from Rewa. We took these survivors to Cardwell, thirty miles distant, which was then, excepting Cape York, the most northerly point of civilisation in Queensland, and there, under the humane care of Mr. Brinsley Sheridan, the police magistrate, they recovered strength in time, and were afterwards taken by us to Sydney, whence they were carried by one of H.M. ships to their various islands in the Solomon group.

Cardwell, a lately-made Queensland settlement, stands at the head of Rockingham Bay, in latitude 18° 15′ S., and longitude 146° 5′ E., in a clearing made in undulating and richly tropical country, and the anchorage lies before the settlement. The southern part of the bay is flanked by the lofty Goold and Hinchinbrooke Islands, of which the highest point, Mount Bowen, is 3600 feet high. The inner passage, between Hinchinbrooke Island and the mainland, is an exquisite piece of scenery, overshadowed by the frowning foliated peak of Mount Bowen on the one shore, whilst from the other the densely-wooded lower mainland stretches away till it meets the dark range of the Rocky Hills ten miles inland.

Cardwell has few recommendations as a commercial port. The most available approach to the anchorage is difficult, and too shallow to be used by ships of heavy draught. Vessels drawing but 16 feet of water must lie two miles off the shore, but a pier is being built which will partly obviate this difficulty. The place consists of a line of tiny wooden houses running parallel to the beach. In front of Mr. Sheridan's house young cocoa-nut trees, planted by him as an experiment, are growing vigorously, the only ones, strange to say, to be found in North or East Australia, although they grow on Cocoa-nut Island, only about 20 miles off Cardwell. The houses belong to Government officials; and there are two general stores, and two houses of entertainment, for gold-diggers on their way to and from the Etheridge gold-digging, some 120 miles north-west of Cardwell.

Various tribes of Australian aborigines roam about the vicinity, and not unnaturally regard the white men, who are rapidly dispossessing them of their homes, as mortal enemies. They show this feeling by committing murders and outrages, and suffer terrible retaliation at the hands of our countrymen, who employ native troopers, commanded by white men, to hunt down and destroy the offenders when the opportunity offers.

The "Basilisk's" stay at Cardwell could not be prolonged, so, leaving Mr. Sabben, navigating midshipman, and four men in charge of the "Peri," with orders to wait our return, we stood away to the north.

Eighty miles north of Cardwell, and only some three miles from the mainland, lies Fitzroy Island, small, but lofty and well timbered, affording every facility for wooding and watering, and possessing a fine open bay on its north side, with a good anchorage, which is sheltered from N.W. winds by its position with regard to the high land of Cape Grafton on the mainland. I had determined to lay in a good stock of wood there, so as to economise our coal for any future emergency; so, on reaching the island, we anchored under the shadow of its wooded centre hill, abreast of a deep channel, where a mountain-stream cleaves through the alluvial soil at its base. The greater force of the sea has heaped up a coral beach across the outlet, and formed a small brackish lagoon, from which the water filters slowly into the sea. The trees are thick on the hill-side, but at the head of the bay we observed that they stood more open, amongst rank grass and huge rocky boulders, and thus offered better scope to our woodcutters. Our men accordingly laboured all day there under a burning vertical sun, felling and lopping the trees, whilst a smaller party took water off to the ship. It was very hard work, and we were new to it then. We little imagined that many hundred tons of wood were to fall to our axes hereafter. The men, led by Lieutenant Hayter, worked with cheery good humour, and turned the occasion into a sort of holiday, but nobody was sorry when the word was passed at sunset—"Knock off work! hands to bathe! and a party to haul the seine!" Enjoyment commenced at once, and the calm water became alive with officers and men enjoying its delicious coolness after the exhausting work of the day. Our party hauling the seine soon drew it in with a silvery freight, and almost ere the fish had gasped their last they were broiling on the embers of a large wood fire, and all hands crowded round for supper. The officers who had been shooting returned with but ill success, the cockatoos and parrots with which the island abounds being too wild and cautious to let themselves be approached within gunshot. I have always noticed that whilst hawks, finches, ducks, and most other birds inhabiting places unvisited by man are at first easily reached, and fall ready victims, birds of the parrot kind are always wild from the first.

On the following day, February 9th, after getting

the wood on board, we left Fitzroy Island and proceeded on towards Cape York, anchoring each night to avoid the dangerous reefs which lay in our course.

Nearing Cape York, the great Barrier Reef approaches to within five or six miles of the Australian coast, and the narrow navigable channel between the reefs becomes more tortuous, for islets and sandbanks thicken.

We often looked for turtle on these banks and islets, but mostly in vain; for between the months of December and March light winds prevail, and the natives come from the mainland in their fragile canoes and betake themselves to these off-lying islets to fish and take turtle, and we nearly always found ourselves forestalled. At other seasons strong winds prevail, and the natives do not venture from the land. Our shooting parties on the islands were more fortunate, and succeeded in making good bags of pigeons and doves; our men amusing themselves the while on the coral reefs like children; splashing knee-deep in water after the fishes that darted about in all directions, breaking off the coral that branched from below in every variety of shape and colour, picking up the beautiful courie, cream-coloured with black spots, and other shells, from the tiniest to the huge clam with a hinge like that of a jail door. But shooting and exploring had always to terminate before evening fell, for the crowds of vicious mosquitoes that then darkened the air would have driven the boldest from the islets and reefs.

CHAPTER II.

CAPE YORK AND THE SETTLEMENT AT SOMERSET—CITY OF THE WHITE ANTS—BOAT EXPEDITION TO ISLANDS OF TORRES STRAITS—A CAMP OF AUSTRALIAN ABORIGINES—SEARCH FOR THE DANGEROUS ROCK OFF SADDLE ISLAND, AND FIND IT.

On February 16th we reached our destination, Cape York, and anchored off the settlement of Somerset. This extreme northern point of Queensland was first settled in 1866, under the supervision of Sir George Bowen and Commodore Burnett, R.N., who thought, from its geographical position, that it would become another Singapore in importance. These anticipations have not been realised, and the party of Royal Marines which guarded the settlement has been removed. There are but six white settlers now,—the Government police magistrate, and his boat's crew; the other fifteen or twenty men resident here are native troopers and pearl-shell divers; and most of the wooden houses are falling into decay from the ravages of the white ant. The gardens cultivated by the marines have now grown wild, and the small cleared spaces before the inhabited wooden houses, alone are free from primeval forest or bush.

We landed the horses we had brought up by swimming them on shore, although the sea abounded with sharks—the noise they made, and the splashing of a boat's oars behind them preventing an attack, so that we landed all safely, to the delight of Mr. Jardine, the police magistrate, who needed them to follow the cattle of the settlement, which are constantly escaping through its broken fences into the bush.

Somerset is situated on the northern extreme of Queensland, where it dips in a series of steep hills, covered with dense tropical forest, to the waters of Albany Pass. This strait which separates Albany Island from Somerset is a narrow slip of water, about seven miles in length, and from half to three quarters of a mile wide; free from rocks or shoals, and possessing a comfortable depth of water for anchorage, but is not a good channel for ships, as fierce tides sweep through it, and the uncertainty of the winds between the high lands renders it dangerous of approach to a sailing vessel. The anchorage is off Somerset, in a small bay, between two points of the mainland, and is narrowed by a coral and sand reef, which extends from the beach, so that not more than half-a-dozen ships can lie there together. From the landing-place, now in ruin, where you step or wade ashore, according to the state of the tide, the path leads through bush, and a luxuriant growth of ferns and creepers, which has usurped the place of the fruit and vegetables of the Royal Marines' gardens, to Mr. Jardine's house, which stands on the brow of a steep hill some 150 feet high, overlooking Albany Pass. It is a simple wooden bungalow, surrounded by the usual verandah, and standing in a small cleared space, with a stock-yard for the cattle, and a few wooden huts for the native servants, and others in the rear. On a similar hill, half-a-mile distant, are built the white police quarters, and a storehouse for every article of consumption required. But they are fast falling into decay under the attack of the white ant, and no attempt is made to arrest the ruin, for the inhabitants are absorbed directly or indirectly in the pearl-shell fishery, and a feeling also prevails that the site is a bad one, and that before long the settlement will move to one of the Torres Straits islands, whence ready and safe communication can be held with the commerce of the world. Thick Australian bush runs up to the rear of the settlement, opening here and there into glades, where cattle can find pasture. About one mile from Somerset, at the eastern entrance to Albany Pass, the land is low, flat, and bare of trees, and there the Termites, or white ants, have established themselves in a gigantic city, consisting of many hundreds of ant-houses. These dwellings, which are built of red clay, vary from one foot to sixteen feet in height, with a diameter equal to the height, and are irregular cones, covered with smaller cones and turrets. At a distance this termite city looks like a military encampment, and was very puzzling to us when we first saw it on entering Albany Pass. It is strange that insects should build such palaces, and the human being who inhabits this country take no example, but remains incapable of constructing the smallest hut.

Our orders permitted us ten days' stay at Somerset, of which three only would be occupied in refitting, and taking on board some coal which was lying on the beach, so I began to think of making a boat expedition to the islands in Torres Straits, to which many reasons inclined me. A dangerous sunken rock, not marked on the chart, was known to lie off Saddle Island, directly in the course recommended by the Admiralty charts, through the great north-east channel of Torres Straits. Two vessels had already been wrecked on it, and I wished not only to find this rock, but also to fix the position of other reefs now becoming dangerous, because of the increasing traffic in Torres Straits.

I had been informed that illegal acts were being perpetrated at the pearl-shelling and bêche-de-mer stations, on islands which had never as yet been visited by a man-of-war; that the imported native divers were detained there beyond their stipulated period of service, and so ill fed as to be driven to make raids on the supplies of the native inhabitants—a situation calculated to provoke all sorts of evils. I desired to examine into this state of affairs, as also into the condition of certain Polynesian missionary teachers lately established by the London Missionary Society on Cornwallis Island, who were reported to be in peril from the natives, and needing either protection or removal. Lastly, it seemed desirable to visit as many as possible of the islands lying in Torres Straits, off the south coast of New Guinea, three or four of which had already become seats of the pearl-shelling and bêche-de-mer industries, so as to gain some general ideas as to their character, products, and inhabitants, and the peculiarities of the surrounding navigation. The time at our disposal was very short for the accomplishment of such purposes, so we determined to make the most of it, and on Sunday 18th left the ship in two boats: Lieutenant Hayter, Mr. Jones, sub-lieutenant, Mr. Waters, midshipman, Dr. Haines, Mr. Bently the gunner, and four seamen, in a boat belonging to the police-magistrate; and Navigating-Lieutenant Mourilyan, Mr. Pitt, midshipman, and Mr. Mudge the boatswain, with me in the pinnace, Mr. Chester, formerly police-magistrate of Somerset, being our pilot.

We passed out at the west end of Albany Pass, entered Torres Straits, and stood north under sail, hardly clearing the Pass when we met with heavy squalls; but the boat made good way, and we did very well until, getting into some heavy tide-races, we shipped a quantity of water, and had rather an anxious time. This over, matters mended a little, and hoping for better weather, we pressed on.

As night wore, the squalls came down with unexpected fury, and the blinding downpour of rain, and heavy confused sea, made our position a trying one. It was as easy to go on as to retrace our way, and we could not even keep the binnacle light burning to see how we were steering. To add to our discomfort, nearly every one was sea-sick. I had many an anxious thought as to our safety, and that of the other boat, and longed for the day; but when day broke it did not help us much—the weather was as thick as a hedge; we had no idea as to our whereabouts, we were surrounded by reefs and rocks, the boat was labouring heavily, and shipping water fast; but I hoped that the breeze was beginning to blow itself out. Suddenly, whistling and seething, down came a white squall, looking innocent as a babe after the inky black squalls that had persecuted us all night, but big with mischief; we just saw the water ripping towards us in time to get the after sail in, but ere we could touch the foresail the wind had struck us, and the foremast was broken, and the sail in the water.

After this it cleared a little, and we made out our position as some twelve miles to leeward of where we had supposed, and found that we had providentially passed through a belt of coral islets and reefs, on any one of which it would have been destruction to have struck. Mr. Hayter's boat was nowhere to be seen, but we knew that she was lighter and higher out of the water than our pinnace, and had been expressly built for service in these seas. I thought it probable that he would stand on to our destination, and be perplexed at not meeting us there; but the state of the weather, and our disabled condition, left me no alternative; we jury-rigged the boat, and put about. Jenkins, the coxswain, contrived to light a fire, when no one else could, and give us something hot to drink, which helped us to throw off the effects of wet and cold.

A fearful afternoon succeeded, with wind and heavy sea, and incidents of squalls, tide-races, and coral reefs, that kept us in constant peril, and over all, the relentless rain fell in a deluge; but the men's spirits never flagged, and that fine seaman, Mr. Mudge, showed his quality then, as he did on many a future occasion. At sunset the wind went down. We lowered masts and sails, and after some hours of weary pulling, got under the shelter of a mountainous island, and anchored in a little bay, smooth as a mill-pond. It was raining heavily still, but rest and safety made us forget that, and we slept soundly. Once or twice I started awake, mistaking the rushing of a cascade on shore for the sound of rising wind, but all was calm. We roused up early next morning, breakfasted on a piece of biscuit and a glass of rum and water, had morning prayer, and started for the ship. It was still raining, but the wind was down, and we had a good strong tide behind us. During a lift in the thick weather we caught sight of Mr. Hayter's boat at anchor under the lee of a small island, and he of us, and this wrung a hearty cheer of relief from both crews.

The "Basilisk" was a welcome sight, for I had felt doubtful of ever putting my men on board her again, but we were much disappointed by this failure of our first effort.

On the 21st, finding that the work of fitting out the ship for sea was progressing well, I rode out with Mr. Jardine to visit a camp of North Australian

C

aborigines, within a few miles of Somerset. The encampment, if such it could be called, consisted of nothing but a row of leafy branches stuck in the ground, under the lee of which the savages crouched for shelter from sun and wind. These poor people are evidently of the very low type of humanity which all writers assign them, a black straight-haired race, with an animal expression of countenance; the young men, tall, lithe, and able looking; but all who had even touched on middle-age, wretched, decrepid creatures, with bones almost starting from the skin. These poor people did not appear to have any occupation or amusement; the men were lolling listlessly about, some smoking; and the women, sad, haggard-looking beings, were roasting roots and small fish on embers, watched by a tribe of children who kept anxious eyes on the food. The only weapons we saw were spears of the least cunning shape, waddys, and clubs.

It is strange that these people have never learnt to cultivate the earth and build houses, but remain content to wander about, living precariously on wild fruits, grubs, a little chance fish, and such animals as they can spear, whilst their Papuan neighbours, in the near Torres Straits islands build good huts, supply themselves with constant vegetable food, and have fine canoes for fishing.

The tribe came on board the "Basilisk" in the evening, and treated us to a corroboric. The dancers, who were all young men, were decked with fillets of leaves, and moved in harmony with the idea they intended to convey, such as the "Pursuit of enemies," "The struggle," "The victory," accompanied by much clapping of hands from the women and older men. Their dances afforded a measure of the narrow range of their habits, and fell far below the really pictorial efforts which were afterwards made for our amusement by the Warrior Island natives.

Our first attempt to cross the Straits in the boats having failed, I had now to consider how far I should be justified in risking H.M. ship in the dangerous navigation of Torres Straits without authority, especially as two years previously H.M.S. "Blanche," in a somewhat similar attempt, had been almost totally lost on a coral reef a few miles from Cape York, and had only been saved by good seamanship. The limits of the Australian station, which have since been altered to embrace the whole of New Guinea, then extended only to a few miles north of Cape York, and to carry out my intention of visiting the pearl-shell stations close to New Guinea, I should have to take the "Basilisk" inside the limits of the China station. Knowing, however, that the pearl-shelling establishments, lying outside the limit line of the station, called for inspection, I determined to incur this responsibility.

Torres Straits, which divide New Guinea from Australia, are about 200 miles long, with a least breadth of 80 miles between Cape York and the opposite coast of New Guinea. At this part the depth of water nowhere exceeds twelve fathoms, the average being from eight to nine fathoms, elsewhere in the Straits the depth is somewhat greater, but rarely exceeds twenty fathoms. The entire area of the Straits is strewn with coral reefs and sandbanks, and with islands, the larger of which are of volcanic origin, well wooded, some of them seven or eight hundred feet, and varying in size from four or five to thirty-five miles in circumference. The smaller are low white islands of coral formation, scarcely raised ten feet above the sea-level, covered with small vegetation, but rarely possessing cocoa-nut, and never bread-fruit trees, both of which grow so luxuriantly on all the other South Sea islands.

Through these reefs and islands a tolerably safe channel has been admirably sounded out and surveyed by Captain Francis Blackwood, of H.M.S. "Fly," in 1843-5, but the northern shores of Torres Straits, and the islands adjacent to the coast of New Guinea, had not been surveyed, and in some cases had not been seen, by Captain Blackwood or his officers, since whose time no man-of-war had approached them. A few miles to the west of Cape York a series of lofty volcanic islands, succeeded by lines of coral reefs, with very narrow channels for ships between, lie like giant stepping-stones between the hills of Queensland and the low mangrove shores of New Guinea, and suggest the idea, which examination confirms, that at one time in the history of the world New Guinea and Australia were one land.

We left our anchorage at Somerset on Thursday, and steered for Saddle Island. Near this island, which is twenty miles from Cape York, a dangerous rock, as I have mentioned, had been reported as lying directly off it, in the fairway through Torres Straits. As we dropped anchor before this fertile and hilly, though uninhabited island, Torres Straits, lately so tempestuous when we attempted to cross in the boats, lay like a sheet of glass, unruffled by even a cat's-paw; but I hoped that something of a breeze might stir in the morning, ere the sun got power, so as to ruffle the water a little over the rock, and guide us to its position; but at daylight there was no breeze—not a sigh—the sea lay like oil, glaring back to the vertical sun. We got out four boats and swept the water for the rock, dropping our leads for hours, but had no success, and time being short made no longer delay, but left for the pearl shelling station on Brothers' Island, twenty-eight miles to the north. Three days afterwards, however, we made a second search, and, when almost in despair of finding, Mr. Jones in the little dingy suddenly hoisted the ensign to tell us that he had carried away the honour from the other boats, and touched the rock with his lead. His success was received by us with acclamations, for we had all become interested in the search, and felt a satisfaction that all sailors will understand in unmasking a danger which lay in wait for our brother seamen. We anchored the dingy over the rock, and hoisted the ensign in her to make a mark distinguishable from a distance, and Mr. Mourilyan and I took a round of bearings and fixed the position. This dangerous rock, or bank, has but six feet of water over it, and rises up only half-a-mile from the track taken by all vessels passing through the Straits.

CHAPTER III.

VISIT THE BROTHERS' ISLAND, AND FIX THE POSITION OF A REEF THERE—PEARL-SHELLING—POWERFUL TRIBE AT WARRIOR ISLAND—A SWIFT TIDE—A CORROBORIE—TRIBE VISIT THE "BASILISK"—SCENES IN CAPTAIN COOK'S VOYAGES VISITED.

Having fixed the position of the reef off Saddle Island, we steered for an island which lies about sixty miles north of Cape York, and twenty from the coast of New Guinea, called by the natives "Gabba," and by the pearl-shellers "The Brothers," from the circumstance of its possessing two high hills bearing a fanciful resemblance to each other. This island is one of the principal pearl-shelling stations in Torres Straits, and is situated almost in the centre of those fisheries. It had not, to our knowledge, ever been visited by a man-of-war, though it had been seen and its position fixed by the officers of H.M.S. "Fly," twenty-five years before; and it lay not only in unsurveyed waters, but also beyond the limit of the Australian station. A few hours after leaving Saddle Island we passed this Rubicon, and broke into the waters of the China station, with an anxious desire on my part that the assumption of such responsibility might be justified by success.

As we neared The Brothers, we observed a large detached unknown reef lying off it, and therefore approached with much caution, finally securing a good anchorage, about half-a-mile off the north side of the island, which is surrounded by these great submerged coral reefs, some of which are twenty or thirty miles in length, with a breadth sometimes as large, on which, but principally in the narrow ruts and channels which intersect them, lie the valuable pearl-shell oysters. The newly-discovered reef was carefully surveyed by Mr. Mourilyan, and now bears his name.

The great pearl-shell fisheries of Torres Straits are principally worked by Sydney capital and owners, Queensland and Victoria being but partially represented. Two modes were till lately used in obtaining divers; one was for the small schooners used in the trade, after shipping as many native divers as could be had at Sydney, to go to the islands—generally the Loyalty, Solomon; and New Hebrides groups—and hire islanders to fill up their complement. Under these circumstances, the natives were generally much wronged in the bargain made with them; induced to leave their homes under promises of short service and good wages, which were made to be broken, as they were kept for years beyond the time agreed on, in a state of veritable slavery. This means of securing the needful labour was shown guiltless indeed, however, beside the other, which was nothing more nor less than an organised system of kidnapping, attended at times with atrocities, that it blanches the cheek and makes the blood run cold to hear of. The islanders were induced to go on board the ships as visitors on various pretences, and then seized and fastened down; or else captured from their canoes whilst fishing, and, without being allowed one parting word to their relatives, hurried off to slavery. The schooners having thus by hook or by crook collected some forty or fifty natives, steered for the fishing-grounds in Torres Straits, and anchored off the island chosen for a station. The inhabitants of these Torres Straits islands are black Papuans—like those of the opposite New Guinea coast—a fierce and warlike race, armed with powerful bows and arrows. But they have been taught by the pearl-shellers, who have been politic in respecting their rights during the eight or nine years of the existence of the fishery, to know the value of friendly intercourse. Low corrugated iron buildings are erected by the pearl-sheller on the island chosen, or, as in some cases, the Papuan huts are used, and the provisions and materials needed for the prosecution of the fishery are stored there, in charge of a white, or English-speaking native storekeeper. Five or six large open boats form the fishing fleet at a station, each carrying a party of eight or ten divers, commanded by a leading man from the schooner as coxswain. The divers, who live either in huts erected for them on shore, when not engaged on the reefs, or on board the vessel, are generally absent from headquarters in the boats for one or two weeks together, on parts of these gigantic submerged reefs which encumber the sea for many hundreds of square miles in Torres Straits, and return when they have filled up with shell. At the time of this visit we found that only in rare instances had even the form of an agreement been entered into between the masters of the pearl-shelling vessels and the divers; and that in numerous instances the divers had been obtained by force or fraud, and were now improperly detained year after year, earning enormously for the owners, but receiving little for their labour save food, tobacco, and some bright calico for clothing. The daily bill of fare for the divers, as officially supplied to me by a white man in charge of a station, was this—for breakfast, two small pannikins of rice, each about the size of a large breakfast-cup; for dinner, one pannikin of "sharps," *i.e.* an inferior kind of flour, which is converted into doughboys; for supper, the same allowance as for dinner. They had no tea nor molasses supplied to them, nor any other food; but it was said that they could go out on the reefs and catch fish. Salt meat was in store, but was only issued to the white men, and to the man who is rated captain of the boat, who was allowed some three times a week. At the close of the year, when the setting in of the north-west monsoon makes the passage to Sydney easy, the schooners take their cargo of thirty or forty tons of pearl shell on board and sail for Sydney, where it is valued at £150 to £180 per ton.

A proportion of the South Sea Islanders who had brought this treasure up from the depth of the sea used to be taken back to Sydney, on these visits; but the poor savages, soon spending their small earnings there, were generally glad to ship on board the schooner again, sometimes in the belief that they were to be carried back to their native islands, as was frequently promised them, and but too often in vain. Due north of The Brothers, the high peak of Cornwallis could be seen about twenty miles off, and occasionally, when raised by the mirage, the low wooded outline of Sybai island, lying about four miles from the New Guinea coast, not marked on any chart, and only recently brought into knowledge by the pearl shellers. One of our objects had been to rescue some native missionaries, said to be ill treated on these islands; but the information collected at The Brothers disproved the statements made, and giving up the idea of visiting Sybai, we proceeded direct to Warrior Island, about thirty miles distant to the east. Warrior Island is a contrast to lofty, volcanic Brothers, being nothing but a vegetated sandbank on a coral reef, not more than two miles in circumference, with a salt water lagoon in the centre, and covered with scanty bush, nevertheless, it is the home of one of the most powerful tribes in Torres Straits. These natives in former years attacked a man-of-war becalmed near the island, and were with difficulty beaten off, hence the name of the island. It may appear strange that so inconsiderable a spot should be a greater power than islands in the Straits twenty times its size; but Warrior Island commands the fishing of the great coral reef which now bears its name, and is thus enabled to maintain a large population, and to employ its many canoes, which have proved a very aggressive navy, until the advent of the pearl-shellers, which has turned the minds of their owners from thoughts of war to those of trade for axes, tobacco, turkey red, and European food.

The approach to Warrior Island is full of difficulty, not so much because of the uncertain position of the reefs as from the fierce tides pent in by them, which sweep with great velocity through the deep narrow channels. Unaware of this, we approached in fancied security, but being caught by one of these fierce tidal streams, were suddenly swept close to an outlying portion of the Warrior Island reef. The anchor was immediately let go, but with a bad holding ground, and the tide running five knots it failed to hold, and we dragged swiftly along the edge of the dangerous reef. Providentially, the tide did not set on the reef, but ran parallel to it, which gave us some breathing time; and whilst anxiously endeavouring to hold our position by riding with a long scope of cable, and steaming ahead to stem the tide, we found ourselves swept into comparatively quiet waters, where the ship rode safely to her anchor. A survey the following morning showed that we had been swept into a horseshoe curve in the reef, past which the body of the tide rushed without entering.

There was no mistaking the genuineness of the welcome given us by Mr. Bedford, who was in charge of this, the largest, and, I may add, best-conducted, pearl shell station in the Straits. He hailed us as the first naval officers who had ever landed on this tiny islet, and told me of the lively recollection the natives still retained of the attack made by their forefathers on the man-of-war, from which they had claimed the victory, inasmuch she had sailed away from them. As I looked at the formidable war canoes, fifty and sixty feet long, hauled up on the beach, and the powerful men ready to man them, all armed with six-foot bows, requiring muscle as strong as that which shot at Agincourt to draw them, and send the poisoned arrows true to the mark at eighty yards, I felt that they might easily have proved awkward customers to an old-fashioned sailing man-of-war.

The station belonged to Messrs. Merriman, of Sydney, who, it appeared, were honestly anxious to do the right and just thing towards the South Sea Islanders and other natives in their employ, but could not always control the actions of the masters in their vessels, so difficult was it at that time to obtain labour from the South Sea Islands without transgressing on the rights of the islanders. Mr. Bedford, ready, rough, kindly, and a skilful organiser, had commanded a body of thirty South Sea Islanders here since the previous year, assisted by two white men as cook and carpenter, and amply supplied with boats, storehouse, and huts for the fishers. He had been left alone on the island whilst the vessel went to Sydney and returned, and during its absence had induced forty-four of the Warrior Island natives to associate themselves with him, and man two of the boats under a chief in each. The competition between these boats and those manned by the South Sea Islanders was now very keen, and Mr. Bedford gave the palm to the Warrior men, who generally succeeded in obtaining more shell than their rivals. Such was the ascendency obtained by him over these people, that just before our arrival they had held a meeting and solemnly elected him a chief.

Inspecting the store-rooms, which contained provisions, axes, knives, bright calicoes, tobacco, and other articles of incalculable value to savages, I remarked, with surprise, that nothing was secured with anything stronger than a clumsy lock, but Mr. Bedford assured me that even this was a needless precaution, as none of the islanders would steal from him.

I was unfortunate in not meeting the South Sea Islanders, as they were absent fishing, except one or two who were sick. One of these was a poor fellow who had been fearfully torn by a shark whilst diving for pearl-shell, and was now a hopeless cripple for life, the sinews of the thigh having been divided, but he was quite cheerful, and Mr. Bedford told me that he would be taken care of, and never suffered to want.

The divers go down in four and six fathom water, in localities abounding with sharks, but are very rarely attacked, probably because so many dive together as to alarm the sharks. I only know of one other accident having happened, by which a woman was similarly injured. The women, as a rule, are considered more dependable divers than the men.

The pearl-shell oyster of Torres Straits is a magnificent oyster, weighing from three to six pounds, in some instances reaching a weight of even ten pounds. The divers frequently bring one up under each arm. The oysters are opened at once, when taken into the boat, and the fish used as food; the pearls, if any, falling to the share of the crew, but the pearls are few, small, and of poor quality.

After dark Mr. Bedford proposed that we should see a corroborie, which he promised us should far exceed the performance of the aborigines at Cape York, and sent messages to the chiefs, whilst I sent on board the "Basilisk" to summon all our people who could be spared; and in a short time the tribe had assembled in front of the station, where nearly all our officers and a large number of men had gathered to see the sight.

It was a striking one, for a huge wood fire threw a broad light on the tall naked figures of the savages, and painted them sharp against the darkness. The old men and women crouched in a ring, and enclosed the dancers, droning out a slow chant, to which they clapped in time, and beat rude drums, always quickening as the dancers quickened. These gave us a battle dance, and chased their enemies with guttural cries, tossing their bracelated arms, and heads decked with long cassowary plumes, as they rushed; their eyes flashing, and the whole body alive with fierce excitement, till they looked more like evil spirits than men. The dance was a perfect study from reality; they made signs of all their actions of war, drew the bow and threw missiles, and bounded on their enemies at last and slew them, with a semblance that was frightfully like reality. Better things were the picture dances representing scenes in daily life, such as spearing the dugong, fishing, love making; and the last and most graceful of all was one which illustrated the coming of the north-west monsoon, and the consequent planting of yams, taro, and sweet potatoes—a poem in a dance. Nothing more perfectly graceful could be seen than their movements, as, rapidly gliding round the fire with swaying bodies and inflected limbs, they showed how the wind blew, how the ground was turned up and the seed sown, and ended with a joyous dance. We were never fortunate enough to see any dance amongst the Malay race, except the few meaningless steps which we sometimes enticed the bolder youths to perform when on board, perhaps because our movements in East New Guinea were too rapid to give the natives time to subside from the excitement which our visit caused into their normal state of work and play.

The following day was Sunday, and deluges of rain prevented us from holding divine service. I was anxious to make the most of the disposable time, and as we could not stretch our time so as to visit the remaining pearl shelling stations, I determined to get the Warrior Island natives on board, and impress them with a sense of our power, that they would be likely to spread in their intercourse with other tribes in the Straits, as this might prove a sort of protection to wrecked or isolated white men. Mr. Bedford went with me to the village and used all his powers of persuasion, and I seconded his efforts by giving the people beads and trinkets, and making signs that they should have plenty to eat if they would accompany me on board the "big war canoe," but we found them very unwilling, and evidently alarmed lest evil should happen them. Mr. Bedford's influence at length so far prevailed, that nearly all the young and able-bodied men of the tribe set out with us for our boats, which lay a mile off, on the opposite side of the island; but as they walked their courage oozed out, and with all our whipping-in we only brought about twenty of the bravest off.

The jokes and good humour of our blue-jackets somewhat allayed their fears as the distance increased between them and the land, but they stepped on deck as frightened as sheep. A few trifling presents were given them, and they were regaled with abundance of sweet hot tea, which is their delight, and soon became reassured, and began to express wonderment at the number of white men and the bigness of the ship. We put them on the bridge, and fired shot and shell, and they screamed and shouted with amazement. Some stopped their ears and crouched down, but the boldest stood upright beside us, and expressed their wonder with a loud "coo-ee!" as they saw a column of spray thrown up by the shot at 3000 or 4000 yards distance.

After supplying them well with tobacco and biscuit, we sent them on shore, proud and happy, to be envied by the timid ones.

At Warrior Island I met two of the native mis-

D

sionaries from the Loyalty group, who some nine months previous had been landed with three other teachers and their families on Saibai and Cornwallis Islands, to begin a mission work for the London Missionary Society, which would extend to the coast of New Guinea.

Every impartial man must heartily and thankfully admit that vast benefits have resulted from missionary enterprise in the South Seas; but no human arrangements are perfect, and I have no fear of being misunderstood if I say that in some cases zeal overruns prudence, and new stations are occupied before a proper staff has been organised or means of support ensured. The English missionaries, however, show all the pluck and tenacity of Englishmen, and although their first efforts may result in failure for a time, the good cause is fought for till success is won.

A case of what one would incline to call rashness came now to my notice. Here were two South Sea Islanders, instructed only since they had reached manhood in the truths of Christianity, and holding them like children in a simple illogical way, brought up by the missionaries in a state of dependence, indolent by habit and constitution, and they had been suddenly transplanted from their home and semi-civilised associates, a thousand miles hence, and placed here amongst these fierce Papuan warriors, of whose language and habits they knew nothing. Two clergymen, the Revs. S—— M'Farlane and A. W. Murray, had brought them to Cape York, and from thence taken and stationed them at Cornwallis and Saibai, giving some tomahawks and trade to the chiefs to propitiate them, and purchase the ground on which the teachers were to build their huts.

The teachers were provided with a small stock of provisions and trade, and were then left to their own devices, the clergymen returning to Sydney. As long as the trade lasted, and they could purchase food, for supplies of which they were soon entirely dependent on the natives, all went well; but when the Papuans found that the burden of supporting these missionaries and their wives and children would be thrown on them,—people, too, with whom they could hold no converse, and who had no recommendation in their eyes except that of being protected by white men,—they naturally refused to accept the position. Painful scenes accordingly took place; they used to bring food to the teachers and take it away again when no payment was offered in return. The unfortunate creatures were thus ready to starve, but for the liberality of Mr. Bedford's employers, who permitted him to supply them free of charge. The teachers had now come to Warrior Island from their station at Cornwallis, about thirty miles distant, principally to get medicine and nourishing food for their ailing wives; and a collection was made on board the "Basilisk" on their behalf, which enabled them to return with lightened hearts. These poor teachers did not pretend that they exercised the slightest influence over the Papuans, but they hoped in time to learn the language and become useful.

The time permitted for our stay in Torres Straits having elapsed, we returned south inside the great Barrier Reef, calling on our way at some of the only historic spots the Australian colonies possess—places connected by some incident with the history of Captain Cook's voyages. The first of these was Lizard Island, so called by Cook because the reptile abounded. Here, about fifteen miles off the mouth of the Endeavour River, where his little vessel had been all but destroyed on a neighbouring coral reef, he remained two days; each day ascended its peak, 1200 feet high, to look for an opening in the great Barrier by which his vessel, when repaired, might gain the open sea, and each day returned disappointed by hazy weather. It is well known that Cook then thought it impossible to trace the Australian coast any farther inside the Reef. He found a passage through to the open sea in the end, and was rejoicing in safety, when a calm ensued, and his ship, swept on by the combined influence of swell and current, would have been dashed to pieces on the outside, had not Providence launched her back again through a narrow opening, which he well named Providential Channel, into the still waters inside. From this point he again traced the Australian coast to its final northern point.

After much difficult climbing I stood at last on the bare windy top of Lizard Island, and gazed on the scene which had met the eyes of our great sailor just

102 years before; thinking with a new wonder on the skill, indomitable energy, and courage he had shown in matching his frail, lonely vessel against such odds. I do not think our country remembers as she should, the debt of gratitude she owes Cook for writing the home-names on so large a portion of the map of the world. We anchored off the mouth of Endeavour River on the evening of the 5th of March, so as to pass some dangerous shoals in the vicinity by daylight. The spot where Cook hove down and repaired his vessel, the "Endeavour," was just as he had left it; for though a few passing white men have occasionally visited it, they have left no trace. I had Cook's picture of the place in my hand as I landed, and had no difficulty in steering my boat to the exact spot on which the "Endeavour" was beached. Since our visit, the report of gold found at the Palmer diggings, some 200 miles inland, has brought a rush of settlers to the place; a township, appropriately named Cooktown, has formed itself at the entrance of the river, and having made the rapid growth characteristic of most Australian towns, already musters a population of 10,000 people; has three banks, a daily newspaper, and all the appointments of a full-grown city.

CHAPTER IV.

RETURN TO CARDWELL—FATE OF THE "MARIA" EXPEDITION—WE RESCUE THE SURVIVORS—NATIVE GUNYAHS, AND KINDNESS OF THE BLACKS—EDIBLE ANT EGGS—FIND, AND NAME GLADYS' RIVER, MOURILYAN HARBOUR, AND MORESBY RIVER—RICH COUNTRY ROUND THEM FOR SUGAR GROWING—SAIL FOR SYDNEY—NEWCASTLE COAL MINES.

WE returned to Cardwell, and arrived there March 9th, when Mr. Sabben, the officer I had left in charge of the "Peri," came on board with tidings of the wreck of a brig on the great Barrier Reef; having, besides her crew, seventy-five spirited young men from Sydney on board, who had attempted a prospecting expedition to New Guinea. They had clubbed together, at the rate of ten pounds a-piece, and bought the "Maria," a crazy old brig of 167 tons, as ill-found aloft as she was leaky below; and had fortune favoured, might have reached New Guinea, for all went well for a fortnight, and they had come within 400 miles of the desired coast. There their misfortunes commenced, for they met the north-west monsoon, accompanied by heavy gales, lost spars and sails, and were driven south again, with the ship's hull strained and leaking badly. The men, pent in such narrow quarters, were so incongruous in character as to be incapable of acting together in a difficulty, and they had no leader: added to this, the master of the vessel was utterly worthless as a navigator. After many divided councils, it was resolved to steer west, pass inside the Barrier Reef, and make one of the North Queensland ports; and acting on this intention they gained the inner waters safely. Instead of anchoring at night and waiting for daylight to pick their way through the labyrinth of reefs which surrounded them, they pressed recklessly on, and struck on Bramble Reef, early in the morning of February 26th, about thirty miles east of Cardwell, and twenty from Hinchinbrooke, on the south side of Rockingham Bay. Scarcely had the luckless vessel fastened herself on the rocks, than the master, whose incapacity had caused the disaster, basely deserted the vessel before day broke, taking six men with him in the best boat, which would have held twenty, pretending that he was going for assistance.

The mate left in charge now became madly excited; the vessel was filling rapidly, and but two boats remained, which were incapable of holding a third of the company. Two rafts were constructed, and barely launched, when the vessel heeled over, slipped from the reef, and sank in deep water to her lower yards. Thirteen men struggled on to the larger raft, twelve gained the smaller, and some clung to the rigging; the rest were drowned, with the exception of a few men in the second boat, who had gone to pick up the third boat, which had broken adrift before the sinking of the vessel. These boats returning, took some men off the rigging, and leaving nine to perish there, made for the land fifteen miles off.

The captain, not knowing his position, took his boat past Cardwell, and landed at Tam o' Shanter's Point, at the north of Rockingham Bay, where he was attacked by the natives, and met his fate, being murdered, with three of his men. The other three, though badly wounded, escaped, and hiding in the bush by day, and creeping out at night (when the blacks fear to stir abroad), reached Cardwell, forty miles distant, where the other boats also arrived after five days' wandering.

Mr. Sheridan, on hearing their story, chartered a steamer which happened to be lying in the bay, and sent her to the scene of the wreck, from which she returned with a report that all on the masts had perished, and that no rafts were to be seen. Navigating-Midshipman Sabben, present in charge of the "Peri," then left in a gig, with two men-of-war's men, and six shore volunteers, all well armed, to recover the boat taken by the natives from the murdered captain, and reached Tam o' Shanter's Point at 4 P.M. on the 5th. On landing he found the captured boat drawn up amongst the scrub, her masts stepped, and preparation made to burn her. He hauled her into the water, and his men began to cook some food, their first for twelve hours. Suddenly there was a yell, and about 120 natives, making hostile demonstrations, rushed from the mangrove bushes 300 yards off the boat, and made for her; Mr. Sabben and his men ran also, gained her first, and opened fire on the blacks at eighty yards, who returned it with a volley of spears, and took to their heels after a while, leaving eight dead and eight wounded behind them. Mr. Sabben then left for Cardwell with his gig and the captain's boat, and after pulling all night, had to beach the boats for a couple of hours till a heavy sea and head wind had somewhat subsided, when he went on, and landed his men at Cardwell at 8 P.M.

On our arrival, Mr. Sabben came and reported his execution of this service to me, and Mr. Sheridan met me with a magisterial requisition for assistance, rendered necessary by the fact that various murders and acts of violence had been committed by the blacks of late near Cardwell. It concluded in these words—"If some immediate action is not taken, no boat will be safe on the coast, and I am afraid that the settlers outside the town, or even the town itself, may be attacked by the savages." I therefore aided him to send his black troopers and their officers to the scene of the latest murder—that of the boat's crew of the "Maria" (there to inflict a decisive punishment), by embarking them on board the "Peri,"—sending with them three officers and twelve men of H. M. S. "Basilisk," under the command of Lieutenant Francis Hayter. It is needless to say that I felt it very painful to take such a step, but in Mr. Sheridan's opinion as well as my own it was necessary, not only for the sake of justice, and in the interests of all white men who might hereafter be placed at the mercy of the tribe, but to secure the safety of Cardwell itself. The tribe was surprised before daylight,

—several unfortunate blacks were shot down by the native troopers, who showed an unrestrained ferocity that disgusted our officers; and the camp, in which some clothing and effects of the four murdered men were found, was destroyed. This work of justice over, the party returned to Cardwell, bringing with them a little native lad about six years old, whose father had been shot. The boy, afterwards christened John Peri, soon became a great favourite on board the "Basilisk." He died in England, where he had been sent for education by the kind act of Mr. Hayter, three years afterwards, of disease of the lungs.

I had a hope that some survivors might even yet be found on the rafts, so, directly on despatching Mr. Hayter and his party, the "Basilisk" left again in search of the rafts. Calculating the effect of the winds and prevailing currents, I concluded that the rafts, unless stopped by some obstruction, would strike the mainland sixty or seventy miles north of Cardwell. We therefore steered at first to examine the banks and islets which lay in the supposed line of their drift. Finding no traces, we stood in for the Queensland coast, anchored off Cooper's Point, and sent our boats north and south to examine the whole coast minutely.

After the boats had left, Mr. O'Neill, our paymaster, suddenly called out, "I see white men on the beach!" and our glasses soon confirmed the truth of his discovery. I stepped into a boat, taking some food and wine, and pulled rapidly for the beach. As we neared the beach we were rather alarmed by seeing that the white men had disappeared, and that a number of blacks were standing in their place, and our men gave way with a will that sent the boat flying through the water. Just as we landed, the white men rose into sight again, and we afterwards learned that they had fallen on their knees behind a rock on seeing us, to give thanks to the Almighty for their deliverance. Eight emaciated half-naked creatures met us, and clasped our hands, and told us that they only were left alive of the thirteen belonging to the larger raft. There was no need to tell of the sufferings they had gone through, their wasted, ulcerated bodies, and the feeble voices with which they tried to raise a cheer, told plainly that we had only saved them just in time. The wine we had brought gave them a little strength, and they crawled along with us to the native camp in order that I might see for myself how well the natives had cared for them.

Many rocks cropped up through this sandy beach, and it was bordered with scrub, behind which rose steep hills covered with Australian firs, wild banana trees, and smaller vegetation. In some places the bush was quite impenetrable, being composed of various kinds of canes, some of a thorny nature, and vines and creepers, some of which ran nearly to the top of the tallest trees.

In a luxuriant glen, at the foot of these hills, after about five minutes' walk from the beach, we came to the gunyahs or huts of the blacks, standing in a cleared space, surrounded by gigantic trees, a contrast indeed to the poor shelter of branches with which their Cape York brethren content themselves. These gunyahs, which were oval in shape, and about five feet high, and eight or nine long at their greatest diameter, were made of rows of long pliable canes, secured to the ground at one end, and bent in a bow towards each other, and tied so as to form a succession of arches, thatched over with palm leaves and the bark of trees. One gunyah, which we were told was for the unmarried women, was considerably larger, being fully seven feet high and fifteen feet long at its greatest diameter. The floor was strewn with clean rushes, and it had quite a comfortable appearance. In one or two of the smaller gunyahs the shipwrecked men had been lodged, and precariously fed with wild fruits, and small quantities of fish by the kindly blacks, whose diminutive size and skeleton-like appearance showed how hard a struggle they themselves had for existence. Their weapons and fishing gear were of the rudest kind, and consisted only of light spears tipped with hard wood roughly pointed, shields, and huge unwieldy swords, about five feet long and four inches broad, with a handle small out of all proportion, being not more than three inches in length. For fishing they had hooks made of hard wood, lines of twisted fibre, and funnel-shaped baskets for catching shrimps. Having expressed to these good-natured savages, as far as signs could go, my gratitude for their humanity, and a promise of sending them a present, the shipwrecked men and the blacks said good-bye to each other in a manner more affecting than I had supposed possible. The latter seemed to rejoice that the white men had found their friends, whilst they grieved to part with them. They embraced them, weeping bitterly at the water's edge, and remained on the beach gazing after our receding boat. Immediately on reaching the ship I sent the blacks a bag of biscuit and other presents. The eight rescued men were soon clothed from our wardrobes, the doctor attended to their sores and ulcers, and a hearty meal did much to revive them. They told us that they had left the wreck on the morning of February 26th, without a drop of fresh water, or a particle of food on their ill-constructed raft, with only one oar, and without a sail; a tent was afterwards converted into a sail, but soon lost. For the first day the smaller raft kept company, but after that they saw it no more. Their distance from the mainland was about twenty miles, and the first day passed tolerably well, as they were buoyed up by the hope of reaching land, but during the night the wind and the sea rose, and they lost sight of land, and grew disheartened, all but one or two brave fellows who seem never to have despaired. The morning sun of the 27th cheered them all for a time, but the weather became worse; their make-shift sail and solitary oar were washed away, and they drifted past some islands about five miles distant. Despair now seized the majority, and two men became insane. The second night closed on them in a miserable plight, the lashings of the raft had become so loose that she continually rolled over and over, throwing the occupants into the water, and when morning broke it was found that the insane men and two others had been drowned. The rest turned to manfully, and split some planks into paddles, but could not reach the shore, along which they drifted at a distance of about two miles; a third man now lost his senses and died raving mad. A third night closed in on these unfortunates, and a fourth man became insane; but two companions, Foster and Coyle, the former son of an ex-prime minister of New South Wales, kept up heart, and were the salvation of their comrades. Some time after midnight the raft grounded on a sandy beach, and its eight surviving occupants reached the shore, and slept on the beach till daylight enabled them to look for food. Strange to say, although from the time of their leaving the "Maria," not a morsel of food or drop of water had passed their lips, they did not feel hungry or thirsty. The system was doubtless supplied with moisture through the pores of the skin, as the men were immersed in water the whole time; but it is difficult to account for the absence of hunger. They found some wild fruits, which partly restored their strength, and coming to the remains of a fire left by the natives, searched about, thinking the blacks might have left something eatable, and Coyle presently picked up the stem of some bulbous plant and bit it, but instantly dropped it, gasping out "water." Foster hobbled off to a small creek and brought him a shell full of water, with which he washed his mouth, but for about an hour he suffered agony from an intense burning in the mouth, and could scarcely speak for the rest of the day. They now met some natives, and finding them kindly, kept with them to the end of the twelve days, wandering with them up and down the coast, as they shifted their quarters in search of food. Part of the food consisted of ant eggs, which the natives bruised in water, and strained through a porous basket into the hollow of a rock. The pulpy matter was first eaten, and the water then drunk. It was white as milk from the juice of the eggs, and had a pleasant acid flavour. Having thus saved the survivors from the larger raft, I felt full of hope that we should save some from the smaller; but it was not so to be: the crew had already met its fate, and a sad one.

On the day that we rescued these men, Lieutenant Sydney Smith, in charge of a cutter detached to explore the coast from the point where the "Basilisk" had anchored to the southward, found the remains of the small raft on the beach, not more than six miles from the spot where the larger had struck, but separated by a good-sized navigable river, which had prevented (providentially, as it appeared) any communication between their respective crews. Shortly after passing this fine stream, which we afterwards examined and named "Gladys' River," Mr. Smith found the bodies of two white men, one as if asleep, in an attitude of peaceful repose, with the head resting on a folded coat, and the other lying on the edge of the surf. In the pocket of one a lady's embroidered handkerchief was found, and near these bodies were the remains of the raft. Two more days were devoted to careful search along the coast for many miles, but no traces of living men could be found. A few miles to the southward the naked body of one of the castaways was found. He was but a few hours dead, and had evidently been murdered by the natives, the skull being beaten in. Still further search, afterwards made by Navigating-Lieutenant Gowland, of the New South Wales steamer "Governor Blackall," discovered six more bodies farther to the south, which showed that those who had landed from the smaller raft had endeavoured to reach Cardwell by walking along the beach, but, meeting hostile natives, had been murdered.

Thus ended this unfortunate attempt to reach New Guinea; an attempt which is but one proof, out of many, that Australian instinct points to the possession of this great island. Many attempts to establish a footing in New Guinea may fail, but the instinct is a true one, founded on natural facts and needs, which time will prove to be imperative.

During this search for the shipwrecked men we were fortunate enough to bring to light a harbour on the Queensland coast, only 60 miles north of Cardwell, the existence of which had been previously merely guessed at. Navigating Lieutenant Mourilyan and I, passing in the galley between two headlands but 120 yards apart, were hardly able to believe our eyes, when we saw a land-locked sheet of water spread before us, apparently capable of holding hundreds of vessels, with a river falling into it. Further examination proved that the greater part of this harbour is too shoal for anything larger than boats, but that there is sufficient deep water for several large ships to moor in safety. The mud banks which encumber the rest of the harbour seem easy of removal by dredging, as space may be required. The want of any secure harbours on the Queensland coast rendered this discovery important, and had it been made before, this position would doubtless have been chosen as the site of the settlement made at Cardwell. The country inland of Mourilyan Harbour, as we named it, has since been surveyed by G. Elphinstone Dalrymple, Esq., who says that it is a magnificent scrub-land, fit for the growth of sugar; that the extent of the available sugar land may be roughly estimated as between 300,000 and 400,000 acres, and that this fine tract of country is tapped by the river which falls into this harbour.

Mourilyan Harbour (as we named it), is thus one day likely to become the seat of a prosperous community. At the south head of the harbour, Moresby River empties itself. It is a stream of good width, nearly as large as the Brisbane River below Brisbane, with 7 feet of water over the bar at half flood, and carries a depth of 8 to 12 feet for about 14 miles above the harbour. It flows sluggishly between low banks, which are covered with mangroves, but open out eventually into the rich scrub-land described. The soil on the hills which surround the new harbour is declared to be very rich, and suitable for the growth of coffee and nutmegs.

We returned to Cardwell on March 15, and the steamer "Governor Blackall," sent by the New South Wales Government to search for the survivors of the "Maria" arriving, the rescued men went on board her, and the "Basilisk," taking the "Peri" prize, with the kidnapped islanders on board, in tow, sailed for Sydney on the 17th March.

At the Percy Islands—uninhabited wooded islets some 40 miles from the Queensland coast—we stopped to water, on our way down. The anchorage was bad; and the water, at the time of our visit, ran but slowly over a rocky ledge. With hammer and chisel we cut the rock, so as to let all the water fall into the mouth of the watering hose, but only succeeded in getting six tons in twelve hours. On the largest of the Percy Islets the sea has broken through the outside rocks and formed a land-locked basin, which yielded a plentiful supply of fish to our seining party.

On March 22d we reached Keppel's Bay, where a small supply of coal was waiting us, and whilst taking this on board visited the rising town of Rockingham, 40 miles up the Fitzroy River, which is a fine stream, but has a sluggish current. At Rockingham we were fortunate enough to meet the ladies of the neighbourhood at a ball held for a local charity, the sight of whom was refreshing indeed to eyes fresh from savagedom.

March 27th saw us once more at anchor in Moreton Bay, where we were received with much kindness by the governor and Mr. Palmer, who complimented us on the services they considered us to have rendered the colony. The "Peri" being now within the jurisdiction of the Brisbane prize court, Lord Normanby and the ministers wished to take legal possession of her; but on the plea that evidence had been produced to show that she might belong to the Fijian Government, they allowed us to take her to Sydney. We reached Sydney on April the 6th, and there an owner for the "Peri" came forward and proved his claim, and the vessel, lately the scene of such a terrible tragedy, was handed over to him. The natives were shipped on board H.M.S. "Cossack," and returned to their own islands, in the Solomon group.

On our way to Sydney we called at Newcastle, 80 miles north, to replenish our coal cheaply, by getting it direct from the mines, and whilst there I visited the extensive coal mines which lie 10 miles from the port. The extent and value of these great coalfields cannot yet be calculated, the greatest depth reached being only 300 feet. It is a singular fact that all the fossil remains, and impressions of wood and foliage found embedded in the coal-strata of Australia, are the same precisely as those which now exist in life, and that no trace is to be found of an extinct fauna and flora.

CHAPTER V.

LEAVE SYDNEY FOR ISLAND CRUISE—NORFOLK ISLAND, AND ITS SEMI-ENGLISH RACE — KEPPEL'S ISLE, AND ITS FINE NATIVES — LAVA BREAKWATER, LAKE AND THREE ISLETS AT NIUA—FEAST WITH THE CHIEF—CEREMONY OF THE AVA AT FOTUNA — UPSET IN THE SURF — ROTUMAH, AND ITS SAILORLY NATIVES.

THE increasing atrocities connected with the labour traffic amongst the South Sea Islands had at this time drawn universal attention, and it was felt that the English flag must no longer be disgraced by barbarities, too often wrought under its shelter, in procuring the natives. The system of enforced labour, which followed their capture, was also seen to be a form of slavery, and, as such, not only inconsistent with all human rights, but capable of having its normal evils exaggerated to the last extreme by circumstances of isolation, distance from law and authority, want of organisation, ignorance, brutality, or incapacity in the overseers. Efforts had been made by various commanders of H.M. ships to bring matters to a crisis by capturing vessels against which the most flagrant cases could be proved, and running the risk of a legal trial at Sydney. Some such cases were brought before the humane Chief-Justice of New South Wales, Sir Alfred Stephen, but he was obliged to rule that, as the law then stood, the only acts under which they could be tried, were those existing against piracy and slavery, and that the plaintiffs not being able to deny that the unfortunate islanders had received or been promised some compensation for their work, and that their period of service was ostensibly limited by time, had failed to establish a charge. To meet this evil the Kidnapping Act of 1872 was passed, and under its provisions the crime may be said to have virtually ceased, though isolated instances may even yet occasionally occur. At this time the Act was not in force, and when, in May 1872, H.M.S. "Basilisk" sailed under orders to visit many groups of the South Sea Islands and check kidnapping, she went, like her predecessors, to work with eyes open but hands tied. There were many possibilities, however, of our performing good service in the cruise, besides that of capturing kidnappers. Hydrographical knowledge might be somewhat increased; islands, as yet unvisited, might be explored, and found to offer inviting homes to fresh swarms from the English hive; the pleasure of the prospect, a sight of the loveliest islands of the Pacific, was undoubted, and stirred the most apathetic amongst us. Having taken on board a deck load of coal and provisions, and provided ourselves with beads, knives, and other trifles for presents or barter with the islanders, we left Sydney on May 14th, and steered for Lord Howe's Island, about 400 miles east of Sydney, uninhabited except by a few people, who live on garden produce, and supply passing whalers. A heavy gale, however, blew us to leeward, and when it abated, I considered it unwise to expend coal at the beginning of our long cruise in an attempt to reach the island under steam. The gale had also shattered us aloft, leaving our foreyard and foretop sail-yard hanging each in two pieces. This accident had been caused by the ship being taken suddenly aback in the night, when the officer of the watch was knocked senseless by a blow on the head from the trysail-sheet block at the critical moment, and about three minutes elapsed before the necessary orders could be given, in which time the mischief was done. Through the heavy wind and rain, in pitch darkness, illumined constantly by blinding lightning, Mr. Mudge, our gallant boatswain, led a party of seamen in the difficult task of getting down and securing the great broken spars which swayed heavily from side to side with the violent motion of the ship. Our chief engineer, Mr. Slade, aided us much afterwards in repairing the broken foreyard. Wooden fishes were rejected, and the spare iron radius bars of the paddle-wheels used instead, and bolted through the yard to each other—a ship-shape, neat piece of work being made, that we were all proud of, whilst the yard was stronger than ever. On the third day after the mishap we were once more a-taunto, and on May 26th reached Norfolk Island, the home of the descendants of the mutineers of the "Bounty," and anchored on the north side of the island, in Cascade Bay. We were known by the islanders to be the "Basilisk," and my father's name being dear to the inhabitants, they gathered in nearly their full numbers at Cascade landing, and gave us a hearty and affectionate welcome that was appreciated by us all. Shaggy ponies were provided, and we climbed the steep hill by a rough bridle-path to the summit, when a ride of about three miles through a rich, open, undulating country, dotted with herds of well bred cattle, brought us within view of the settlement on the opposite side of the island. Here we found the venerable, but still hale and active pastor of the island, the Rev. G. H. Nobbs, awaiting us; and whilst the officers and men were eagerly taken possession of by various inhabitants, I became his guest.

So much has been written of Norfolk Island since it exchanged its convicts for the most gentle and well-reported of Anglo-Polynesian race existing, that I will not add to it here. The briefest stay amongst the Norfolk Islanders convinces one that the passive virtues abound amongst them, but that a development of mental muscle is needed to make them systematically energetic, industrious, and persevering.

The following day I went to the Milanesian Mission College, three miles distant, to gain information from the Rev. —— Coddrington respecting kidnapping amongst the many islands visited by him in the course of his duty. At this Mission College youths from all parts of Milanesia are trained to become missionary teachers; and many of them being very intelligent, it occurred to me that I might gain some knowledge from them and the missionary clergy, which would be useful in our island cruise.

I slept that night in the room but lately occupied by

the martyred Bishop Pattison, surrounded by many books—the only luxury he appeared to have allowed himself; for the small iron bedstead and scanty furniture were in keeping with the simple habits of his life. At first the place seemed so pervaded with his presence that it felt like a profanation to sleep there, but after a while I remembered that we were just about to try and avenge him in the way he would best have loved, by putting down the kidnapping which had caused his death, wherever we could hunt it out.

The harmonious singing, and devout manner of the native youths in the chapel, struck me very much. I gained considerable information from them—some of it sad and startling indeed. One lad from the Solomon group told me, with truth in his face, that he had seen his own brother's head cut off by white men belonging to a schooner which ran down his canoe. Another, a Christian native of Florida, one of the Solomon Isles, had seen five islanders beheaded by the crew of a brig. The heads of the murdered men were doubtless to be used in bartering for slaves or sandal-wood, with chiefs who rate their greatness by the number of skulls they possess.

It is difficult to believe that such atrocities were common—but the evidence compels belief. I made an early start to return on board next morning, but so heavy a sea was rolling in at the landing-place that it was impossible to embark. A fierce gale sprang up; and the ship, now mounted on a great wave, now lost to sight in a trough of the sea, had to put out for safety, and leave us all behind. The gale did not abate till the third day, and the sixth day arrived before the "Basilisk" was again able to make the island. But for our anxiety for the ship, no time could have been spent more enjoyably than was this, in riding, and walking with the kindly islanders, and joining in their evening amusements at the public room; and we found one useful piece of work to put our hands to. Wishing to set an example of industry, as well as meet the islanders in good fellowship, I pointed out to the chief magistrate and Mr. Nobbs, that the flagstaff on the hill, blown down some time since, by which alone clear communication could be held with passing ships, ought to be replaced; and having their consent, I got a party of islanders to go with Mr. Maben, our carpenter, to the bush, where a straight tall pine about 70 feet high was selected and felled, which was then brought by sheer strength to the signal hill. Our seamen, with Mr. Mudge, prepared the rigging, and the islanders dug a deep hole, and by our united efforts, after three days' work with very imperfect tools, the flagstaff was made, and erected.

June 1st, the "Basilisk" having returned, we bade a regretful adieu to the Norfolk Islanders, who for six days had entertained us hospitably, putting all they had at our service, with a kindliness and simplicity that we shall never forget.

Good wishes and presents were exchanged, and then with a favouring breeze we went on our way.

The ship had suffered somewhat in the heavy gale

that had driven her to sea; had lost an anchor and chain, and one man had broken his arm, and another his collar-bone by a severe fall. Indeed the gale was described by those on board as something terrific.

After a tedious passage we sighted Keppel and Boscawen Islands on June 21st, but it was dark before we could close the land, so we tacked and stood off for the night. Next morning we ran between the two islands, hove to about a mile from the reef which surrounds Keppel, and feasted our eyes on the green paradise which rose from the still blue water before us, two wooded peaks rising abruptly from a rich flat, 400 feet, into air as blue and still; a white coral beach glistening below; and little native huts peeping out like birds' nests from between the trees. Keppel Island is but some four miles long by two and a half broad; but being of coral and volcanic origin combined, it has variety, and the beauties belonging to both origins; the bold volcanic heights, and the coraline bright beach and verdant flat. On strictly coral islets you see no trees but cocoa-nut, bread-fruit, and small palms; but here they were mixed with forest trees, as on volcanic soils, and the light greens thus broken up with deeper tints.

Visitors have spoken in such enchanting terms of these coral and volcanic isles, that we were prepared to be disappointed. I can only say that some of these emerald gems, shrined in by the summer sea, with sparkling beach, leafy shades, and a wealth—a waste of fruit and flower, seemed to me like scenes in a dream of peace and beauty. We landed at once, to make the acquaintance of the islanders, and see if, in appearance at least, they were worthy inhabitants of their Eden; fully armed, for we knew nothing of their disposition —the latest account of the island dating from 1832. Judge then of our pleasure when we saw a group of fishers on a reef, young men and women, break up, and after some talking and pointing, move towards us, instead of flying. We beckoned, and the young folk came running, and clustered round us, without a sign of fear—shaking our hands, and uttering sounds of welcome. I must confess that we English seemed to grow suddenly shorter and more thick-set as we stood amongst them; but what wonder! Some of these men, lithe and strong as Apollo, with short curled lip, and keen eye, were models for a sculptor. The colour of these fine people is not unpleasing; a clear brown, with a slight copper tint; indeed it became agreeable to us after a time, by contrast with our own sun-dyed faces.

Their stature, even that of the women, is far above the average, and their limbs are so symmetrical as to give an idea of undeteriorated physical perfection. The noble head is well set on the slender throat, over a massive shoulder, and every movement of the body, from the turn of the head to the poise of the shapely foot, is full of grace and strength. Our new friends wore the "Ti-ti," a short grass petticoat, ornamented with long feathers, and bright ribbons of sea-weed, and a few white shells, which set off their forms to advantage. The skin of the girls was soft as satin from the constant use of cocoa-nut oil, and their dark eyes were full of expression, as they smiled, perhaps with lips a little too full for the strict idea of beauty, at our attempts to make them understand.

We soon discovered that one of the men could speak a little English, and began to talk; and this native presently undertook to pilot our boat into the lagoon. He took us two miles along the reef to a very narrow opening, and we shot between high coral walls over a translucent depth of nine or ten fathoms, through which you could see the coral glimmer below, into the lagoon, a lake of quiet blue water, backed by a dazzling white beach, on which cocoa-nut trees and rich greenery came crowding down. We landed, and took a short path, through grateful shade, to the village, accompanied by our fisher friends, who told us that they were all Christians, and that a missionary, a native of Tonga, lives on the island and instructs them. The village lies in a grove of cocoa-nut, bread-fruit, and shady trees, amongst which its pretty elliptical houses nestle at irregular distances. The church stands in an open space, a building 130 feet long, 30 wide, and 35 high. The frame is supported by immense uprights of the bread-fruit tree, the roof is high-pitched and thatched, the sides are covered with cocoa matting, spaces being left for windows, and both ends are quite open. All the houses are similarly built, on a small scale. The church was beautifully clean, as were all the houses, and tastefully decorated with shells. We spoke to a German, the solitary white man living on the island, and he told me that the kidnappers had once attempted to cozen these people, but found them too enlightened to be trapped. In every house that we entered fresh clean mats were spread for us, and we were offered bananas, mammy apples, and fresh cocoa-nut milk; and all was done with a natural politeness that charmed us. We stood away for Niua or Good Hope Island that evening, bearing with us pleasant thoughts of the nut-brown maidens of Keppel's isle.

Sunday night brought heavy rain and squalls, which kept us on the alert nearly all night, but Monday broke fine, and we ran down under sail to Niua, an island in lat. 16° 5′, and 176° W. We were seen at once, and some canoes, well carved and polished, came off. The natives hesitated at first, but finally some came on board, and I took one as a pilot and started for shore, followed by two boats containing a number of our officers and men. Niua is a purely volcanic island, rising steep and wooded from the surf, and fronted us with a rampart of black lava cliffs that seemed to forbid our landing. Our pilot pointed to a place where a mighty stream of lava had run out 200 yards into the sea, and cooled down, and our boats went in and lay under the lee of this natural breakwater in safety; but a rougher landing-place I never saw, and we had to continue a tiring scramble over broken masses of lava that strewed the ground at every step, until we got well up into the bush, where it had become pulverised and mixed with vegetable matter. There it was pleasant walking enough, but our shoes had by this time been cut to pieces. The island is about six miles long by three in breadth, and seems from its shape and the deep soundings about it to be the summit of a buried volcanic mountain.

Fire and lava break from various parts of the surface within every period of two years. The last outburst came up through a house ; the owner, who barely escaped with terrible burns, having had no warning. The soil is so scanty and the lava rock so hard that the people are obliged to raise the surface of their burial-places artificially, and no fresh water, save rain, can be obtained; but the island is luxuriantly productive; and the inhabitants need never fear a drought, for they are supplied with milk by millions of cocoanuts, the most delicious of all drinks when fresh. The most singular natural feature in the island is a lake about six miles in circumference, which lies in a bed formed by a vast extinct crater, between picturesque, wooded, hilly shores, and bears on its bosom three lovely islets, covered with ferns, palms, and rich vegetation. As I stood looking down from a height of 400 or 500 feet, Niua itself seemed but a speck of green afloat on a world of waters, and the lake a morsel of silver dropped in its centre.

The water is brackish, for the sea percolates through the narrow neck of land which encloses the lake on one side; but there is a spring on one of the islets, which, though brackish, is drinkable. Niua forms part of King George of Tonga's dominions (the

Friendly Isles), and is Christianised; but the habits and manners of the people, who do not seem so fine a race as the Keppel islanders, are still aboriginal. A walk of four miles through a shady tropical forest brought us to the village, where the chief, an intelligent-looking grey-headed man, barefooted, but dressed in a black coat, bought in one of his annual visits to Tonga, received me with great respect, in a space overhung by the huge projecting eaves of his "Talking-House." Some hundreds of natives were assembled to do us honour, and sat in a semicircle on the grass, in a clearing in front of us, preserving perfect silence. It was a pretty sight to see the rows of islanders dressed in the picturesque "Ti-ti," over which the girls had thrown scarfs of white tappa, seated on the emerald grass, with a belt of sunny trees behind. Oval huts lay snugly nestling all round, amongst the bread-fruit trees that grew in great masses of shade on the rich flat, broken to the south by blue glimpses of the sea; on the north a wooded and cultivated hill shut in all. The chief gave us a grand banquet in South Sea Island fashion, under the eaves of his reception or talking-room, consisting of roast pig, bread-fruit, and an enormous land crab—which land crab is a dish for a gourmand. It feeds only on the nuts which fall from the cocoa-nut tree, the hardest of which it cracks with ease, and thus acquires a delicious flavour. No spirit of any kind is allowed on the island; but the milk of the fresh cracked cocoa-nuts was perfect nectar to us thirsty folk. I strolled about the village after the feast, and entering the church, was much touched by visible signs of the reverence with which these simple people worship the Creator. Indeed, the feeling of reverence comes over the mind as powerfully in one of these little island churches as in any cathedral at home. There is, of course, no thought of bygone saintliness and valour, as at home, where time-stained marble and tattered colour witness mutely from the walls, and appeal to all that is good in us; and this want is felt by the visitor as in all young countries; but his mind turns to the future, and that is full of hope. Whilst on the island we gained some valuable information relative to kidnapping from a German, here as at Keppel, the only white man resident. Thirty men had been kidnapped from Niua five years before our visit, not one of whom had since been heard of; and a near island, one of the Union group, which had contained a population of fifty or sixty souls, had been depopulated by one act. The master of a barque, under Spanish colours, had decoyed all its inhabitants on board, under pretence of teaching and making missionaries of them, and had secured and sailed away with them.

The wind was north-west, in the heart of the south-east trade, when we left Niua on the 26th, and we had not coal enough to steam, but coaxing the old "Basilisk" to make the most of the light variable winds, we sighted Wallis Island in the middle watch of the night of the 28th. We stood on till eight A.M. and then hove-to, about a mile off its surrounding

UEA ISLAND
OR WALLIS I^s.
Mataloa
Mua
Nukuofo
Nulmtea I.
Allier B.
Houi-Kolou Pass
(Principal entrance)
1 2 3 4 5 Sea Miles

reef, where we were boarded by a native pilot, a splendid-looking old man. I do not know of any instance in which a reef surrounds an island more completely than here. A ring of water from two to four miles wide is perfectly inclosed between Wallis and its reef. We might have taken the ship through the entrance, and anchored within, but were content to land in the boats, in which we shot at once from the deep heave of the ocean to the stillness of a sleeping lake, whose broad expanse is dotted over with tree-covered islets, some of which are very lovely. The island, which is of coral-volcanic formation, is about nine miles in length, of an irregular shape, and rises to a height of 700 or 800 feet. It has a population of about 3800 souls. The landing-place is on the south-east side of the island, and here we were met by the French priest in charge of the Roman Catholic mission, a kindly, well-informed man, who seemed very proud of his large stone-built church, which, he told us, had taken ten years to build. We visited the church, and found it filled with gaudy religious pictures. The priest told us that for many years the island had been the scene of fierce religious wars between the Protestant and Roman Catholic natives, till the former were defeated, on which the latter faith was established.

The natives differ from the light-coloured Polynesians of Keppel and Good Hope Islands, and incline more to the dark Milanesian type. Their huts were small, and not clean; and the women seemed careless of their appearance. Wallis Island, lying only 400 miles north of the Fiji group, possessing secure anchorage for ships, and abundant supplies of fruit and vegetables, should, I think, be taken into our new Fijian colony, on the ground that every colony, if possible, should be put in a position to develope and protect its own future. In the hands of an enemy at war, it would offer a strategic position of great value, to be used in operations against Fiji.

The priest told us that no kidnapping had taken place at Wallis Island, though several labour vessels had attempted it.

Fotuna, forty miles south of Wallis Island, consists of two rugged and precipitous islands, of coral-volcanic origin, of which the central peak is 2000 feet high. They are broken up into yawning fissures and perpendicular rocks, so that there seems no room for cultivation except on the south shore, where the coral asserts itself, and some level ground is found. Little cultivated ravines also run up between the spurs of the hills; and from the top of the highest peak to the edge of high-water mark, one dense growth of tropical vegetation prevails. The larger island is seven by five miles in extent, and has a population of about 1300 people, governed by two kings; the smaller is only about two miles by one in extent, and not permanently inhabited. We hove-to off the principal village, from which some canoes came off, and, picking out a pilot from one of them, I pushed off in the galley for shore, followed by Lieutenant Hayter, Dr. Haines, and other officers, in two boats. On nearing, we found that a flat coral rock ran out a long distance from the beach, with so heavy a surf breaking on it as to prevent the approach of boats. I therefore sent the two boats back to the ship, left the galley outside the reef, and stepped into a canoe. My native rowers watched for the intervals of smooth water between the breakers, then paddled with great rapidity, and beached her safely, and I was soon surrounded by a crowd of gesticulating, noisy natives. Lieutenant Hayter, fearing lest evil should befall me, came hurriedly on shore, followed by other officers, but we soon saw that the crowding was only the result of curiosity and excitement. We walked for about two miles through a succession of villages, scattered amongst groves of bread-fruit trees, and, passing by the little Roman Catholic church, ascended by steps cut in the rock, to a high coral plateau, once the site of a native fort, where the priest has his dwelling. Here the king met us, nowise to be distinguished from one of his subjects, but evidently fully recognised by his people. As we conversed with him, by the help of the priest, a bowl of ava was prepared for our drinking, in the following way:—Some young men brought the ava, a species of root, dried in the sun, and the ava bowl, very capacious, and beautifully clean, and then sat down in two rows, and biting off large pieces of the ava, chewed it till their mouths were full of pulp, which was thrown into the bowl, and water added, the whole was stirred up, and then passed through a strainer of vegetable fibre, and this done,

one of the young men stood up, and pronounced in a loud tone, "The ava is ready!" This announcement was followed by the salute of a loud clapping of hands from all the natives present. A cup-bearer and a talking-man then came forward; the former filled a cocoa-nut shell with the liquor, and the young men asked in a kind of song, "Who is this for?" "The king!" replied the talking-man; on which his majesty received, and quaffed off the cup, amid much cheering. The cup was again replenished, and, "Who is this for?" asked, and I was named. I had foreseen that Fate had this honour in store for me, and with no small effort had made up my mind to taste the ava. The flavour was more like that of a mild mixture of rhubarb and magnesia than anything else; but two or three of our young officers drank a draught right off, and the French priest seemed quite to enjoy it. The ava acts on the system somewhat similarly to opium, and is doubtless valued for this soothing property. Having ascertained that no kidnapping has taken place here, also that many of the islanders ship on board passing whalers, and never return, we took leave, with expressions of friendship on both sides, in token of which I was presented with some beautiful tappa cloth. At the beach the surf had so much increased that it was only by the influence of the king that we could get a canoe to take us off to our boats, which lay outside. Dr. Haines and I waited till the last trip, and then tried our luck, but hit the surf at a bad time, and were swamped, and rolled over and over in a second. Alas for my tappa, and our new-laced coats! After bailing out, and putting things to rights, we tried again, and failed, till our rowers, finding the canoe filling, jumped overboard, and, with a skill and strength perfectly marvellous, towed and guided us through the boiling surf—the doctor and I paddling for our lives all the time.

The trade-wind visited us at last; with a flowing sheet we sailed that evening for Rotumah, 300 miles to the west, and on Wednesday the 3d sighted it. We did not possess any chart or plan of this island; but a good anchorage was reported, and we met a native coming out in his canoe, who showed it us, under the lee of a coral reef, and near two small islets. Rotumah is fertile, but the inhabited and cultivated part is only a narrow fringe bordering on the sea-shore The interior, as with many of these South Sea Islands, being a mass of dark dank tropical jungle, with no path or track through it.

Whilst our men were watering, I gained information from the missionary, Mr. Osborne, a fine manly Englishman, and found that, thanks to the missionaries, Rotumah has not suffered from kidnappers. The Rotumah men, who belong to the light-coloured Polynesian race, have such a reputation for ability as boatmen and seamen that they have been hired at high wages by the masters of the kidnapping vessels to aid them in capturing the South Sea Islanders, and some fifteen have been killed at various times by the poisoned arrows of the natives they were seeking to capture, which served them right. The people of Rotumah are taught by English Protestant and French Roman Catholic missionaries, of whom the former has by far the larger flock: the two parties have agreed to differ in a peaceable manner. I visited Mr. Osborne, the English missionary, and found his neat house and schools for native children all that could be desired.

Hearing that some vessels were anchored in a bay six or seven miles distant, Mr. Mourilyan and I went over in the galley, and found that one of the vessels was a labour vessel, just come down from the Line Islands, where she had been boarded by Captain Moore, of H.M.S. "Barossa." Her papers were all right, so I was compelled to pass her, as he had been. The others were legitimate traders.

CHAPTER VI.

MAKE MITCHELL'S GROUP, OF WHICH THE EXISTENCE WAS DOUBTED—DIRECTIONS FOR LANDING—A DESERTED ISLAND—A VILLAGE BY MOONLIGHT—HAMMOCKS FOR EVIL SPIRITS—HUDSON ISLAND AND RED CORAL SHORE-REEF—ISLAND OF GRAN-COCAL NOT TO BE FOUND—CHERRY ISLAND AND ITS SWIMMERS—DUFF'S ISLANDS OF SANTA CRUZ GROUP—NATIVES APPEAR FIERCE AND FORBIDDING—POISONED ARROWS—CORAL BREASTWORK—GREAT WAR CANOES—SUNSET AT NUKUPU.

On the night of July 30th our course lay close to the position assigned by some navigators to a cluster of islands south of the Ellice group, named "Mitchell's group;" of which others denied the existence; whilst the chart was doubtful. I had been assured by several old traders in these parts that there were no such islands, but thought it prudent to give the order—"leadsmen in the chains, and a bright look-out to be kept for breakers," before I turned in at midnight. At two o'clock in the morning the officer of the watch reported "land on starboard bow." We hove-to, and at daylight our eyes rested on Mitchell's group, real enough, and on a crowd of canoes coming off to look at us. Getting a pilot, we went away with the boats as usual to communicate, but there was no passage for them over the reef, so Mr. Mourilyan and I betook ourselves to canoes, the most slender beautiful things we had ever floated in. My rowers, as good-humoured as possible, smiled, and showed their white teeth as they paddled with much judgment, and landed me without a wetting; but my poor companion was capsized and had a roll in the surf, from which he soon re-appeared in a dripping state on the bottom of the boat, much to my relief, though there is no real danger in these upsets, for the natives of all the South Sea Islands are perfectly amphibious, and consider it a point of honour to save you. In my experience they are as much pleased by your frank trust in their skill as Englishmen would be.

The Mitchell group consists of a cluster of about ten islets, situated on a coral reef, which surrounds a shoal lagoon, extending about five miles north and south, and two east and west. The principal village, and the best landing-place, are on the W.S.W. side of the cluster, and may be known by a neat white church built of coral rock, which, when almost off the islet, may be seen through the trees. The natives belong to the light-coloured Polynesian race, but are somewhat darker than the Keppel islanders, and number seventy.

We landed at the principal island, and found the people strikingly clean in appearance and quiet in manner. They have been Christianised by the efforts of a native Samoan missionary, who found them easy docile converts. From a German, and a native who could speak broken English, we learned a sad story. These harmless people had numbered 450 souls in 1857, all living in peace and plenty. In 1864, the German was absent for a short time at Samoa, and on his return he found but fifty worn-out people and children remaining—the rest had all been swept away by kidnappers. Three large barques, under Spanish colours, had appeared off the islands, from which an old man had landed, who told the natives that they were missionary ships, and invited them on board to receive the holy sacrament. All the able-bodied men went on board in simple faith, and were immediately made prisoners; again the old fiend went on shore and told the assembled women and children that the men had sent for them, and they were also beguiled. The tragedy thus complete, the ships bore away, it was supposed for the guano islands of Peru; and not a word has ever reached the islands as to the fate of these lost ones from that day. It was sickening to hear the tale told on the spot which had seen all this sorrow. Two of the men, one of whom we saw, had contrived to jump overboard, and swim six or seven miles back to the island.

The whole surface of these flat coral islets is like the clean white-sanded floor of an old English kitchen. The cocoa-nut tree springs up everywhere, but in the spots where yams and taro are grown the sand is hollowed out, and a pit formed, from one to two hundred yards long, and of varying width, into which decaying cocoa-nut leaves and refuse are thrown, till a rich soil is formed. I was much interested in these people; they are prepossessing and kindly, and their houses, mats, and persons, are pleasingly neat. The church is a little gem, built of coral stone, and by their own labour. Fine specimens of the operculum (the stony lid by which the South Sea Island whelk closes the aperture of its shell) are found on the reefs here, and, when polished and set, make handsome bracelets for ladies.

The Ellice group consists of a large number of tiny islets, scattered between 5 and 10 degrees south latitude, and 175 and 180 east longitude, and is but little known, having only been seen by passing vessels till quite recently. English Protestant missionaries have established themselves on most of the islands, and the German oil traders have a white agent stationed on nearly every one to collect cocoa-nuts and cocoa-nut oil, against the periodical visits of the small schooners, which take them to Samoa for shipment to Germany. All the islets of this group are of coral formation, and are so low as scarcely to be raised ten feet above the sea level, but are covered with cocoa-nut and bread-fruit trees.

All day long, on the 14th, we were trying to find an inhabited island in the Ellice cluster, from which all the scattered Ellice group takes its name. I landed at one village, and found it a deserted village indeed —many houses, many graves, but no inhabitants, save the tenants of the graves. It was depressing to miss the life and sound that met us everywhere else on our arrival; it is always saddening to see the ownership yielded back to nature, and ruin creeping over a spot that has once been warm with the affections of human life. We feared that kidnappers had been here, but knew there was a chance that the villagers might have migrated for better fishing.

During the night a current swept us twenty miles away from the islands. We regained our position next day, and saw a canoe paddling out, from which we learned that the only inhabited islet of the Ellice cluster lay nine or ten miles dead to windward. There was nothing for it but to row this distance in the galley—a heavy pull against a fresh breeze. We rowed our best, officers and men, but it was nine in the evening before we reached the village. Once inside the usual inclosing reef, we saw the full size of the lagoon it shelters—a lake some eighteen miles long by nine wide, which is a most unusual size. Bright white moonlight steeped the shore as we landed, making visible every leaf and frond of the trees and undergrowth that fringed it. The pure white coral surface shone like silver in the opens, flecked with soft shadows from the trees, and across it a warm yellow glow came from the cocoa-nut oil burning in the pretty oval huts. Here was life at last, and that was cheering; and then what loveliness!

I paused for a moment to look at the mingling of the two lights. It gave the sort of radiance that Corregio has in his "Notte," where the cold clear light of morning comes stealing through the doorway from the eastern hills, and flows over the yellow lambent flame, thrown upward from the body of the infant Christ to the faces of his adorers. The little huts are open on all sides, and the dusky forms of their owners soon began to emerge like shadows. It was like a scene in a dream—the sheet of moonlight, the graceful trees, the perfect stillness, the roar of the surf, like a silence, it was so measured—all seemed unreal, and ready to dissolve.

The island is about seven miles in length, and only a hundred yards wide at its greatest breadth, so that the whole air is always full of the thunder of the surf to windward. The natives greeted us kindly, and we went up to the house of the only resident white man. As we talked with him, nearly all the people of the island crowded round outside, but they behaved with good taste, and did not even speak aloud. They are Christians, taught by a native missionary, and number only 140 souls now, more than half the original population having been carried off by kidnappers. The lonely white man we found here was making a living by trading in cocoa-nut oil, supplied him by the natives, and appeared quite happy.

The wind, which had been against us, was fair for our return, a welcome help; and we reached the ship at midnight, and immediately bore away for the cluster of coral islets named Nukufuti, or De Peyser's Isles—also comprehended in the Ellice group. We learned that the island containing the graves was used as a cemetery, and only resorted to at certain seasons for fishing and the gathering of cocoa-nuts. Myriads of cocoa-nut plants covered these islets, in all stages of growth. Some, just bursting the shell, were shooting forth slender fern-like leaves; others, more advanced, were sending their small roots downwards through the shell to find the soil—the shell still containing moisture needful for the growth of the young tree. Older plants had discarded the shell, and were throwing a clump of graceful leaves upward, to the height of a man, but showing no sign of a stem as yet; and from this they ranged up to the full-sized tree. A description of one of these South Sea Islands will nearly serve for all. At Nukufuti we found the usual circular coral reef, with islets scattered along its inner edge, which were densely covered with cocoa-nut trees. A ship channel leads through this reef, and a brig lay within at this time, bound for Sydney, with oil. No white man lives here, but an intelligent chief governs well, and has foiled the attempts of the kidnappers. There are native missionaries here, and the church and school-house, large coral white-washed buildings, are models of neatness. All the officers landed here; and it was a sight to see them coming off afterwards, laden with mats, fowls, and pigs, tramping down a mile of flat coral reef up to the ankles and knees in water, to the canoes, which lay waiting on the moonlit water to take them off to our boats.

On the 17th we communicated with Egg, or Netherland Island, a crescent-shaped reef, with the horns of the crescent lying about two miles and a half north and south of each other. The 200 inhabitants were all Christians, and had escaped the kidnapper; their village stands on an islet on the southern horn. We sighted the northmost island of the Ellice group next morning, to our surprise fully forty miles out of position. This island differs from the others of the group in having no guarding reef, and no companion islands near it. It stands alone in the ocean, scarcely raised above its level, and is simply a huge flat-topped coral rock, two and a half miles by one and a half in extent, which rises perpendicularly from fathomless depths, and is crowded over with cocoa-nut trees. It is only saved from being washed over by the sea by a narrow shore reef, on which the great surf expends itself. We pulled to the edge of the boiling surf and met canoes, which landed us without a wetting, and were received on the beach with the most intense curiosity by the natives, who had never seen a man-of-war before. They are a well-looking, dark, straight-haired race, and number 417 souls, a large population for so small an island, but their food is abundant; an unlimited supply of cocoa-nuts, fowls, pigs, flying-fish, skip-jack, and sharks. Native missionaries have been two years at work here, but half the people are as yet devil-worshippers, and adore the evil spirit under the form of cocoa-nut leaves, skip-jacks, and wooden posts. Every heathen family has a small devil-hut, in which a tiny grass hammock is slung for the evil spirit to sleep in, and where offerings of fresh nuts are brought him every morning; many of these huts were in full use, but we were pleased to find others forsaken. The people looked very picturesque dressed in their sole garment the Ti-ti, and seeing that I admired it they gave me one made of the bark of the cocoa-nut tree beaten out and cut into ribbons, which were dyed with red ochre. They are governed by a king and a chief, and both these potentates, fat ugly-looking men, received us with much ceremony in their "talking-house," a building with a high pitched roof, which comes down within three feet of the ground, the space left between the roof and the ground being perfectly open all round. They sat cross-legged on the ground, and listened with most attentive faces, whilst I told them, through the resident white man how glad I was to find they were kind to white people; that every man-of-war that followed the "Basilisk" would therefore be friendly to them, but that if they ever behaved otherwise, a ship would come and punish them. After this we shook hands and talked generally, and they presented us with nuts, fowls, and fruit, in return for our gifts of fish-hooks and looking-glasses. Their mode of procuring fresh water is curious. They cut the coral rock to a depth of twenty feet, and make an opening wide at the top and narrowing into three small holes below, which fill with a brackish water as the tide rises. They have not any other supply, but do not need it, as they have an unlimited supply of cocoa-nut milk.

On the 20th we communicated with Hudson Island, in latitude 6° 30′, longitude 176° 40′ E. The description of the foregoing island will serve equally for this; but here the fringing shore reef is composed of red coral, which looks beautiful when the receding surf allows its bright wet tints to show. The poor people, who are Christians, but go about nearly unclothed, received us very kindly—one man actually kissing me with every sign of affection. Leaving Hudson, we sailed in search of an island named Gran-cocal, the existence of which is both affirmed and denied, but could find no trace of it, though we sailed right over its alleged position.

At St. Augustine, the last of the Ellice group visited by us, the people are all devil-worshippers, and have never suffered any missionaries to come amongst them.

The village is on the east side of the principal islet, off which a broad shore reef of reddish coral extends, springing up like a wall from the depths of the ocean. On this the surf beats with terrific violence, and runs up in a mass of white foam to the beach beyond. The natives bring thin frail canoes to the edge of the reef, and hold on, lost in foam, till a lull occurs, and then they launch and paddle for their lives, rising like feathers over the next gigantic surf. Mr. Bentley and I went in the galley to the edge of the surf, but it seemed as impossible to land safely as to go down the Falls of Niagara and live. At intervals the surf, it is said, subsides, so as to allow boats to land. The islanders seeing, came off to us, and thus made it needless for us to land; they have a bad reputation, so we persuaded some to come on board, and fired a few shot to give them an idea of the white man's power.

Cherry Island, 500 miles south-west of St. Augustine, was our next aim. Whilst on our way, on July

25th, a sad accident took place; one of our best petty officers was struck senseless by a blow on the head from a falling block during "sail drill," and died in a few hours. We were comparatively so few in number, and so mixed up together, that this death was almost as sad as a death in a family, and much feeling was manifested the day we buried him, as the poor body plunged sullenly into its "vast and wandering grave." Constantly as we had drilled aloft, we had never met with an accident till this, our first and last; and it was a double one, for another poor fellow had dislocated his thigh. On July 28th we made Cherry Island, a perfect little gem, which nowhere exceeds one and a-half miles in extent, and rises to a height of nearly 400 feet, in a hill, which produces the most abundant supply of vegetables for the inhabitants, who live in the wooded valley below. On nearing the island in our boats numbers of natives swam off to us through the surf, holding presents of cocoa-nuts and bananas high in one hand. I cannot describe the ease and grace with which they swam; it was a pleasure to watch them, the more so as they were altogether agreeable to look at, being fine specimens of the light-coloured Polynesian race. After a time they brought a canoe to us, and we landed safely; and, their first timidity over, were permitted to enter their huts, which are oval-shaped, and thatched close down to the ground. I saw no weapons amongst them, indeed they do not need them, as their nearest neighbours live on an island 120 miles distant.

G

Neither kidnappers nor missionaries have yet made any change for evil or good in the primitive habits of these lonely islanders. We left loaded by them with roots and fruits, and they crowded on the beach to see us off.

After much wild weather through the 29th and 30th July, we closed in next day on Duff's Islands, of the Santa Cruz group, where the people are of the same dark, treacherous, Milanesian type as their near neighbours at Nukupu, who martyred Bishop Pattison. As we came near we could distinctly see the natives hurrying their women and valuables into the bush. I went in with two boats, prepared for defence, but having the arms concealed, to speak a few canoes which kept at the edge of the reef. With some trouble we induced one young man to come alongside, and then our presents proved such a bait that all the canoes of the island were soon swarming about us—but my desire was to land. The natives were armed with powerful bows and arrows, which, they made signs, were poisoned, and their appearance was fierce and forbidding. They are ugly, tall thin men, and their nose-rings and the shell ornaments which they wear in their ears, dragging down the lobes nearly to the shoulder, make them quite hideous. After some bartering, in which their honesty was remarkable, I began to cross the reef towards their village, half expecting them to object, instead of doing which they broke out into a tumult of delight, and tracked the galley for us across the reef with willing hands (Mr.

Hayter remaining outside in the cutter), so that Dr. Goodman and I soon reached the village. It stands on a flat coral islet, about 200 yards in diameter, separated by a narrow lagoon from a lofty island, which rises behind to the height of 1000 feet. The larger island is densely wooded, but so precipitous as to afford no foothold, except in a few spots near the beach. The islet was surrounded by a wall or breastwork of coral rock pieces, thrown up for defence, through which they led us by an opening in the rear, and we found ourselves in the village, which differed from anything we had yet seen, in that the low thatched huts were not scattered about, but built in rows, with wide beaten footpaths between, in which cocoa-nut trees sprang up. At the rear of the village the great war canoes were drawn up, powerful-looking boats, from sixty to seventy feet long, with high ornamented prows, and a fighting platform in the centre. The islanders showed us everything they possessed, and then gave us some cooked bread-fruit and taro as a present—indeed the kindness of these poor savages was extreme. On our return they would not allow us to do any work, but insisted on tracking our boat and taking it outside the surf themselves. They may possibly have considered us supernatural beings, for they frequently took my hand and kissed it; they had certainly never seen a man-of-war before, if our interpretation of their signs was correct. I think they cannot have been visited by kidnappers, or our reception would have been different; these men could have made themselves very ugly customers. Their island is situated only some fifty miles from Nukupu; and, as I have said, the inhabitants are similar in appearance, and arms, and manner of living; how comes it then that such a kindly reception was accorded us here? I fear the answer must imply a condemnation of the general conduct of white men towards natives. This particular island has never (to my knowledge) been landed on before by Europeans, and the natives, being thus unprejudiced, took us, as they found us, and acted accordingly; whereas, at Nukupu, the deeds of kidnappers had distinctly led up to the good Bishop's death. This was one of the very few occasions on which I disregarded my general rule of never landing amongst savages unless the women and children were present, and I landed here, feeling considerable apprehensions of evil. We went apparently unarmed, but had our revolvers ready, and the men had their rifles concealed.

We had anchored the ship on a coral bank, in ten fathom water, but on going on board I found that the anchor had slipped off into 100 fathoms, and found no bottom. Such are the coral walls in these seas, or such, perhaps, the coral walls based on volcanic rock.

August 1st.—On our way to Santa Cruz we passed near the Island of Nukupu as the sun was setting. Used as I am to the glowing Devonshire sunsets that Francis Danby loved to paint, I had never seen sky and sea steeped in such colour and gold as here.

To the south, Santa Cruz reared its wooded heights through 2000 feet of soft, grey air—its bold headland

and coral water line, and the cocoa-nut groves that mark the site of the villages, just taking on their evening shades; to the west, from a glassy sea of crimson, soft purples and gold, the mighty volcanic cone of Tinakula rose abruptly into a sky as glorious, rolling out from its top volumes of smoke dyed into flame by the setting sun, whilst the base slept in its own cumbrous shadow; to the north-west lay the little island of Nukupu, low and wooded, the scene of Bishop Pattison's death; we felt that his last sunset might have been like this, and then thought went further than one cares to speak.

CHAPTER VII.

HONESTY OF A NATIVE AT SANTA CRUZ—SHIP CHANNEL FOUND THROUGH THE REEF AT EDGECOMBE ISLAND, AND BASILISK HARBOUR DISCOVERED—CONCILIATE NATIVES AT TEVAI BAY—BLUE CORAL—NATIVES DIFFICULT OF APPROACH IN TORRES GROUP—THEIR PECULIAR ORNAMENTS—HAYTER BAY—UGLY WOMEN OF ESPIRITU SANTO—VERY RICH COUNTRY—VOLCANIC CONE OF LOPEVI—MALLICOLO, AND ITS HUGE IDOLS—EXORCISM—HAVANNAH HARBOUR—INCIDENT OF "VAN TROMP" SCHOONER—COTTON PLANTING—RAPIDITY OF VEGETATION—CANDLE-NUT TREE.

On August 2d we anchored at Santa Cruz Island, in Byron's Bay, when we had scarce room to swing clear of the rocks at either side; and the natives, who have an evil reputation, not belied by their looks, came on board the ship in numbers, eager to barter their bows and poisoned arrows, shell ornaments, and mats, for our bottles and beads. Precautions were taken in case of any trouble with the savages, but as women and children mixed amongst the men I felt pretty easy.

The village is fortified by low coral walls, breast high, the openings in which are overlapped by other walls, calculated to throw an attacking party into some confusion. We were received there in a friendly manner, and, our diplomatic work over, a watering-party was landed, protected by a marine guard under arms, and we went to enjoy ourselves by bathing in the beautiful clear mountain stream that runs into the bay. This river, from which we watered easily, flows through tropical forests, over a clear sandy bottom. A track through the bush led to a favourable shady spot, and our men were soon to be seen gathered in groups on the river banks, bathing, washing their clothes, or lounging in idle enjoyment—all making the most of the few quiet hours we were able to spend there. Sailors well know how much pleasure was sure to be taken out of a little paradise like this, after long cooping up on shipboard.

Carlisle Bay, only a mile to the east of Byron Bay, appearing a good anchorage, I explored it in my galley, and, from a cursory examination, concluded it was so. Some of the officers came overland, and joined me in the bay, where the natives were as friendly as those of Byron Bay. An instance of honesty was shown here which surprised us. My coxswain had traded a fowl from a native, and, locking its wings, had laid it under the boat's thwart, but the bird freed itself, and flew like a partridge to the bush before we were 100 yards from the beach. The natives saw what had happened, and on our returning to the village shortly after, the owner of the fowl brought the trade back, and pressed it upon us. We highly commended his honesty, but of course refused to benefit by it.

The friendliness of these natives to us was remarkable; and I have deeply regretted to learn that some difficulty has since arisen between them and H.M. schooner "Sandfly," during her late visit to this place, resulting in the loss of numerous native lives. An event of this kind is to be regretted, not so much for the present effect, as for the misunderstanding, the want of confidence, and the revengeful feeling it produces in the future.

Santa Cruz is only inhabited on a narrow strip round the shore, the inner part being to all appearances given up to jungle and forest. This fact contains in itself an answer to one weak excuse which has been advanced in favour of the forced deportation of South Sea Islanders, to the effect that they will otherwise suffer privation of food as their numbers increase, for it proves that these islands are in most cases able to support enormously increased populations; and many of them have others in close vicinity, which are still absolutely uninhabited.

Leaving Byron's Bay on the 5th, we reached the volcanic mountainous island of Mount Edgecombe, which had never been surveyed nor landed upon, as far as we knew, and spent the day in surveying its surrounding reef, to find a channel through if possible. We had no success that day in finding a ship channel, although for some miles the reef was submerged to a depth of six or eight feet, so stood off and on during the night, which was an anxious one, blinding thick, with tremendous rain squalls. In the morning we turned to work with the first light, and were well paid for our trouble, for we found a passage of four fathoms over the reef, leading into a lagoon big enough to hold a navy, with a fine harbour at the head. This important harbour Lieutenant Hayter, Nav.-Lieutenant Mourilyan, and I roughly, but carefully surveyed,

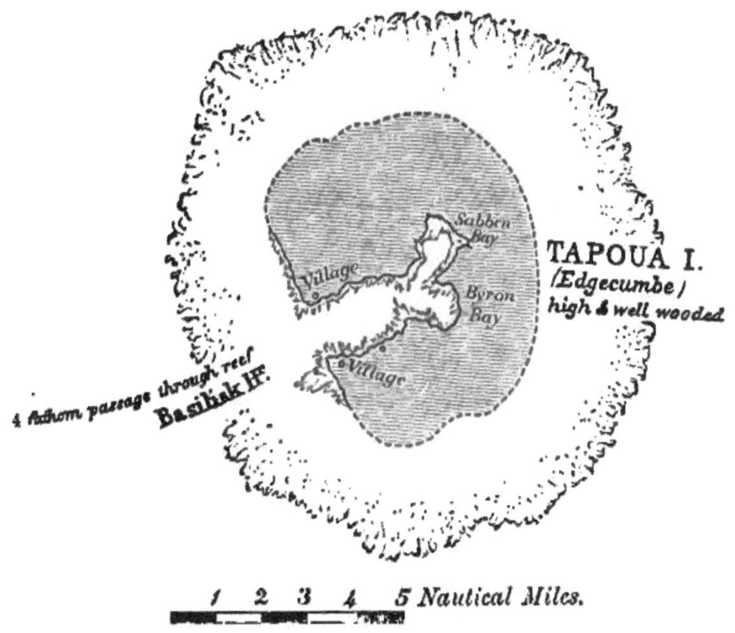

BASILISK HARBOUR, EDGECOMBE ISLAND.

and were satisfied with its capabilities. We called it Basilisk Harbour, in honour of the ship, and felt rather proud of our discovery; for previous visitors had pronounced the island wholly inaccessible on account of its surrounding reef. This fine harbour is shaped like a boot, the leg being about one and a-half miles long, and the foot, from heel to toe, about two miles, and contains anchorage-ground sufficient for the British navy. High, well-wooded land surrounds the harbour, and there are several native villages on the beach.

The natives, who were woolly-headed and black, were quiet and friendly, but a degraded, wretched-looking race. They had no mats nor articles worth bartering for, which we regretted, as this sort of little commerce often opens the way quickly towards a good understanding.

At Tévai Bay, Vanikoro Island, the scene of the disaster of "La Perouse," we anchored on the 9th. Lieutenant Smith landed to conciliate the timid and suspicious people we saw awaiting us, with arrows on the string ready for instant use; and going boldly amongst them, succeeded in winning half their confidence. They thawed, but still kept the arrows ready. They permitted us to go to their village on Direction Islet, and I took two armed boats there, as the distance from the ship was considerable, and very few women were visible. We found the village nearly deserted, and remained there an hour, successfully trading with the people that remained, followed all the time, however, by a number of men who watched our movements suspiciously.

We certainly left a good impression on their minds, which was of course the object in view; but I would gladly have spent a week with them and confirmed it. An interpreter would have been invaluable. They are precisely similar in appearance to the Edgecombe Islanders. The coral here is of extraordinary beauty; we saw some through a shallow depth of water on the reef, of an exquisite blue colour, the very tint that may be seen down the crevasse of a glacier, but it faded on being taken out of the water.

We sighted the Torres group on the 9th. It consists of four principal coral-volcanic islands, and a few small ones, from four to six miles in length, running north and south, and separated from each other by narrow channels. It was blowing hard; but directly we came under their lee we rode at shelter in blue water, with scarce a ripple, the coral beach, with its still dark green background, looking very peaceful after the stormy sea we had just crossed. I went with two boats to make friends with some natives on the beach, but when we landed they drew off to about half a bowshot from us, and stood ready with the bow. We advanced a few paces, and they retreated into the bush, where it would have been madness to follow them. At last, in despair of communicating, I sent every one back to the boats, except trusty Mr. Bentley, the gunner, and he and I advanced alone and apparently unarmed, but with pistols hidden, making friendly signs. On getting pretty near the bush I placed a bright coloured handkerchief on the ground, and retired a little. Two of the boldest soon came forward, and prodded it with their bow ends, evidently suspecting some trap, then they took it, went back into the bush, and came out again with cocoa-nuts, which they laid on the same spot for us to take them. This we did, making signs of acceptance and gratitude.

By degrees we got amongst them, and then our bright beads and fish-hooks completed their captivation. They are black Milanesians, perfectly unclothed, with hair frizzed out a foot from their heads, and rather repulsive looking. Before we left they surrounded our boats, eager to barter all they had. I mention our delay in establishing relations with them, to show that our successors need not be discouraged by a little difficulty at starting. Pleasant looks, a quiet confident manner, and a soft tone of voice, soon gain on them, and a judicious display of bright coloured articles easily catches their attention. It is also well to be patient, and not show any haste or anxiety. They are very children these South Sea people, and should be persuaded as such. The ornaments worn here are peculiar. No tortoise-shell nor pearl shell ornaments were to be seen; but instead, cylinders of polished ebony, neatly tipped with mother of pearl at the ends, were worn, thrust through the cartilage of the nose and ear. These cylinders are about an inch and a half long, and three-quarters of an inch in diameter. They also wore ivory armlets—the tusks of a peculiar kind of boar, which they always keep tied up, so as to prevent any injury to the tusk. Leaving these people, we ran down to the next island, and picking out a lovely bay, anchored for the night. The natives here were more easily approached than their neighbours, but did not become so confiding. They bartered, but only at arm's length, and with a few of us at a time. We could not discover their villages, and it would have been imprudent to venture into the bush to look for them. Indeed, I had a sort of escape here. Mr. Bentley saw a native on the point of striking at my head with his club, who refrained when he saw himself perceived; but Mr. Bentley's quick eye and ready pistol would doubtless have stopped the savage's blow had he attempted it.

Mr. Mourilyan and I were early astir next morning, and made a running survey of the anchorage, to which we gave the name of the senior lieutenant, and called it Hayter Bay. It is a roomy anchorage, and well sheltered from the prevailing wind. The two remaining islands of the Torres group were visited by us on August 10th, and we found the people very difficult of access at first. Eventually, however, we made friends with them, but not having interpreters could not find out if they had been visited by kidnappers. Our work as pioneers of Christianity and civilisation at many of these islands was very anxious, and to some extent dangerous, and kept our faculties in a state of tension. On the last island we found a native who spoke a little English. He said that kidnapping vessels had never been seen here; but he might have been a kidnapping agent himself, for what we could tell.

The north end of Espiritu Santo is indented by a large gulf, up which we steered on making the island, and found an anchorage at the head of the gulf, off the mouth of the river Jordan, so named by the old Spaniards, according to their delight in Scripture names. Lieutenant Hayter and I examined the river for some distance on Monday 12th, and found it navigable for boats for about a mile above the sea. It is simply a fine rapid torrent, coming from a lofty range of hills, and running, at the lower part of its course, through rich, open country, and forms a boundary between two powerful tribes, who appear to live in a state of warfare. The inhabitants of Espiritu Santo are black, fine athletic men, woolly-headed, many of them with really pleasing faces. They are well armed with clubs, and three-pronged spears barbed with human bones, which they throw to a great distance. They placed great value on their weapons, making signs of their urgent need of them to guard against the attacks of their enemies at the other side of the river, and would not sell me a club. They showed no jealousy of their women, which was a new feature since our leaving the Christianised islands; so we went freely about amongst the unsightly Eves, who regarded us with much amazement. They were all but unclad, and hideously ugly by nature and fashion, for the upper front teeth had been extracted, the hair cropped short, and in most cases the poor black face daubed over with charcoal. The material for civilisation to work on here is certainly very rough and raw. We made up a party for shooting wild duck, and ascending the river a short way, landed and went up the country, on its banks, of which we much admired the richness. Wild sugar-cane, wild pine-apples, and other tropical fruits, grew in abundance; and the land seemed easy of cultivation. Doubtless, in time, Australia will throw off settlers to this glorious island, which is capable of bearing all the spices of the East. The natives were delighted with us, and eagerly showed us the best spots for duck, which were there in any quantities, but very wild—probably from being constantly made targets for the native arrows.

There was a sort of natural lock across the river, from which it ran furiously down a steep descent for eighty yards, forming a fine slide for our many bathers, who allowed themselves to be swept away like corks the whole distance, and had good sport.

We visited, on Tuesday 13th, one of the curious volcanic cone-shaped islands, not uncommon in these seas. This one—Star Island—rises in a perfect cone to the height of 2900 feet, and is densely wooded and thickly populated, though it has no water and no natural soil. It is, however, highly fertile, for the pulverised scoria has been mixed with such a quantity of decayed vegetable matter as to create a rich deposit. The natives are well accustomed to white men, and many of them had gone in labour vessels to Queensland and worked in the plantations. Some told us that they meant to go again—an evident proof of kind treatment, and explained that they understood the nature of the agreement made by them with the Queensland labour vessels. One of the mission boys, with whom I talked at Norfolk Island, was a native of this isle. We climbed up the precipitous side of the cone for eight or nine hundred feet, through a thick forest, meeting with native huts perched about on every holding-ledge, halting often to refresh ourselves with cocoa-nut milk, for the ascent was almost perpendicular, and we were obliged to use hands and feet to surmount the gnarled roots which spread like bars across the rough native track, and to climb some overhanging ledges. The crater at the summit is now extinct. In many places the ground was artificially terraced, to make room for houses to stand. The natives lead a sort of fly-like existence, having to cling on with hands and feet whenever they stir outside their doors. They were innocent of clothing, and worshipped idols of the most hideous kind. It is to be hoped that the lads from this island, now being educated at the Milanesian college, will be able to cope with this idolatry on their return.

On August 15th we reached Mota, the principal island station of the late Bishop Pattison. This island, called Sugar Loaf by the English, from its shape, rises to a height of 1350 feet. Its people, about 2000 in number, are much attached to the mission.

I was met on landing by the Rev. —— Palmer, who led us by a steep slippery path to the mission-house, where every sign of real good work was to be seen. The system pursued appeared to be quiet and methodic. The educated deacons from Norfolk Island are evidently well-approved and instructed men. Having talked matters over with Mr. Palmer, I secured the pleasure and advantage of his company for a few days to the neighbouring islands,—Valua or Saddle Island, Bligh Island (where an extinct crater has formed a large bay), and St. Maria. At this latter place we received a hearty welcome on landing from several hundreds of savages, who wore no clothes, and were armed with deadly arrows. Amongst them we saw one who was the happy owner of a red shirt and double-barrelled gun, and he spoke English well, and told us that he had spent five years in Australia. We talked about kidnapping, and he observed, "All black men savey, no kidnapping now; if black man like to go he go, if he like to stop he stop," a valuable piece of testimony from this group of islands, long the principal scene of kidnapping.

On standing down the south side of the island we fell in with a ketch of twenty tons, with twenty-one natives on board, and no licence to carry them. The owner, as well as the master, was on board, and told us that he had a cotton plantation at Sandwich Island,

and was willing to provide himself with legal papers, but as yet had not had an opportunity. After much consideration, the natives being evidently free agents, and the new Act not as yet come into force, I decided on sending Lieutenant Smith to Sandwich Island in the ketch, and he parted company accordingly.

On Sunday, August 18th, we sheltered from a southerly gale under the lee of Aurora Island, where the paymaster of the "Rosario" had been cruelly clubbed, and all but killed on the beach. Knowing that here, and at all the islands south of this, the natives are very treacherous, I landed with great caution, taking some spare hands with loaded rifles in the galley, but walked apparently unarmed towards the natives. A lad of thirteen or fourteen allowed me to approach him, so I gave him some beads, after which the savages came closer, but kept a reserve body behind the rocks, ready to let their deadly arrows fly at a moment's notice. The women, who were repulsively ugly, were unclothed, and the men nearly so. They traded with us a little, but did not take to us at all heartily, and remained shy and distrustful to the last.

On Monday, the gale having moderated, we ran down to Aoba, or Leper's Island, only twenty miles distant, and here the natives flocked down quite unarmed to trade with us, which fact confirmed me in the idea I had formed that there is often very little inter-communication between the islands of some of the groups. These islanders were perfectly confiding, and eagerly surrounded us on the beach, seeming to take interest in our looks and gestures. One little occurrence cemented our friendship. Mr. Hayter turned up his sleeve to please them, and catching sight of some tattoo marks he had acquired in Japan, they compared them with their own tattooing, and went off into fits of delight. We stayed bartering with them for a long time, and they brought us down quite a collection of the boar's tusk armlets, which are really handsome ornaments, and if mounted with a golden snake-head and tail, and a pair of emerald eyes, would not be unworthy to be worn on fair wrists at home. They would not, however, dispose of the best armlets for anything we could offer. They were clothed in a small degree, both men and women.

We landed next day on Pentecost—a fine island, 38 miles in length; and using every caution, found the people friendly. On the night of August 21st we anchored under the lee of Ambrym Island, and I went on shore to open an intercourse, but in vain. The natives of all these isles are afraid of darkness, and never venture out after sunset. In the morning Mr. Hayter and I went again, and we became good friends. They sold us some of their common clubs, on which a certain two of us gave vent to our spirits, and celebrated the *entente cordiale* by dancing an English war-dance, whooping, and flourishing the clubs in true savage style. At this the savages shouted with delight and laughter, and called to all their friends to come and see. It will readily be believed that our friendship progressed rapidly after the exhibition of such kindred customs; and I was well pleased to have it so, the more so as a native had threatened to strike me with his tomahawk on landing. The act was perhaps only the result of timidity on his part, and I was prepared to intercept the blow; but it showed that these people might have been dangerous. Leaving this island, and steering south, we had a fine view of its volcanic mountain, 3000 feet high, from which volumes of smoke issued, and sometimes jets of flame. The sides of the mountain are cut into deep gullies, where rivers of lava have flowed down. Grand as this object was, it was eclipsed by the glorious cone-shaped island of Lopevi, which was here in sight, springing in perfect symmetry to a height of 5000 feet above the sea. Its summit is divided into two huge lips, from which belch continual smoke and fire. These two volcanoes are not twenty miles apart. We landed at the latter, and found the people friendly; but very few live here, and these only at the base of the volcano. It must need some courage to live in such proximity; we were surprised to find any inhabitants.

Off Mallicolo, a splendid island, 56 miles in length, we anchored in a fine harbour, about which the land was well wooded, and diversified by hill and plain. The natives received us well on our landing, and took us to the top of the hill on which their village was built, when we were met by a perfect picture of savage life. The thatched huts were scattered about under the trees, so low that we had to creep serpent fashion to get in, and when inside could scarce sit upright. The Devil-ground presented a unique picture of savage superstition. It was a large cleared space, and contained a collection of frightful-looking idols, some twenty feet in height, and broad in proportion, hollowed out to serve the purpose of drums. Soft-wood drum-sticks lay beside them, and on being struck they emitted a hollow monotonous sound. The shape of these idols was very rude; they were all head and body, with very small arms stuck on, of which the hands rested on the stomach, and the legs were smaller than the arms—the whole being devoid of action or expression. Near one, a gigantic idol surrounded by a bamboo fence, a poor girl suffering from an ulcerated leg was placed for cure, and lay looking dejected enough, as if she knew the hopelessness of the charm; nor was the behaviour of her elders at all calculated to increase the girl's reverence, for they showed no respect themselves, and only laughed when we struck the huge idols and made them emit a dull resonance. Most of the women wore waist-cloths, but the men were naked. The manners of both were most kind and friendly to us. Several of the men told us that they had gone to Queensland in the labour vessels, and having been well-treated by the planters, and given plenty of trade, were anxious to go again. Our views as to the evils of the labour traffic began to be much modified by the nature of the natives' testimony. In cases where the labour-compact is perfectly understood and agreed to by the natives, and where the conditions are afterwards faithfully adhered to, a positive good may result, and an impetus be given to the improvement of these races by the contact with civilisation. Stringent laws securing justice, paternal treatment, and religious instruction, are highly necessary; and will doubtless be hailed by the mass of employers, as assisting them to discharge their duties on a well-considered and systematic system; they will rejoice to see crime and cruelty made impossible, and to be relieved from the disgrace of any supposed partnership with wretches who have disgraced the English name.

Auxiliary labour is a necessity in Queensland, from the nature of the soil, which produces crops that require minute attention; and from the unfitness of the European for labour in its hot latitudes, it will always remain so. The fact of such a necessity existing, is, to a believer in Providence, a proof that it is capable of being dealt with in a satisfactory manner. Neither the philanthropy nor the power to alchemise this social difficulty into good are lacking in Queensland, and the experience of years has furnished a sufficient fund of fact to be drawn on in the construction of a perfect system—one beneficial to employer and employed. I say "perfect" advisedly, because we, in this generation, have attained to clear moral perceptions of duty towards aboriginal races, and an increased power of putting such into practice. It should be as perfect as possible, and made so speedily, because any neglect in treating so vital a question must be prolific of future evil in an incalculable ratio; and issues that can now be grasped in the hand, and dealt with, will soon by natural increase become too vast for control; witness the issues of the slave question in the United States of America. Our position makes us guardians of the nonage of these undeveloped races: and our responsibility should, in my opinion, be accepted, even to the limit of taking all the unclaimed islands in the Australian neighbourhood under our protection. The terrible atrocities which have occurred in connection with the labour trade, and which can never be forgotten—never remembered but with sorrow and shame, have drawn public attention to this subject, as perhaps nothing else would, and emphasised the demand for exhaustive legislation.

It presents itself to my mind, that the demand for labour will become increasingly disproportionate to its supply from these islands, as they are rather under than over populated. New Guinea, if annexed, will perhaps assist in the solution of this difficulty.

Lieutenant Hayter, Drs. Goodman and Haines, and I, visited a small island, named Shepherd Isle, near Api, on the 24th, when I was compelled to submit to a singular process of exorcism before we were permitted to land. A devil-man, fantastically painted, and adorned with leaves and flowers, waded out to meet our boat, waving a bunch of palm-leaves rapidly round his head, and as I jumped on shore he rushed at me, and grasping my right hand, waved the leaves round my head in the same manner. I saw that he meant no harm, so let him have his way, and he placed the leaves in my left hand, putting a small green twig into his mouth, still holding me fast, and then, as if with great effort, drew the twig from his mouth—this was extracting the evil spirit—after which he blew violently as if to speed it away. I now held a twig between my teeth, and he went through the same process, all the time showing signs of strong excitement.

He led me then to the edge of the bush, and I began to feel rather reluctant, and doubtful as to how all was going to end, but thought I had better see it out. Here two sticks, ornamented with leaves, were fixed in the ground, and bent to an angle at the top, with leaves tied to the point, and round these sticks the devil-man and I raced in breathless circles till I was perfectly dizzy. He, however, did not seem to mind it at all, and presently flew off with me up a steep path into the bush, when, at a short distance, we came to two smaller sticks crossed; here he dropped my hand, and taking the bunch of palm-leaves from me, waved them, and sprang over the sticks and back again. Then placing both his hands on my shoulders, he leaped with extraordinary agility, bringing his knees to the level of my face at each bound, as if to show that he had conquered the devil, and was now trampling him into the earth. When he had leaped for a while, he made signs that all was over, and we walked back together to the officers who had been rather anxiously watching these singular proceedings. The natives who had kept quietly aloof, now came freely about us, and showed by their manner that they considered us free of the island. Had I not submitted, we certainly should not have had any communication. They took us up to their fortified village by a walk of a mile and a half, through forest and cultivated fields of yam, taro, and sugar-cane; and there a roast pig was set before us, over which the devil-man and I were forced to go through no end of ceremonies, which he ended by stamping the devil into two large holes which he had worn in the earth by constant efforts. He then tore the pig into pieces, and gave me the first. I handed it to the chief, and he gave me a large piece for myself, which I had to hold with a great war-club in the same hand, till a given signal was made, when I was supposed to eat it. After the feast we were free to roam about as we pleased. Many of the natives here had been kidnapped, and had since returned home, and were consequently well able to make themselves understood. They also agreed in saying "white men no steal black men now." The idols in the village were similar to those I have just described. The same day we steered for a similar island only a few miles distant, named Three Hill Island, and here also were invited to visit the village. We reached it by a delightful walk of two miles through forest, and about one through well-kept plantations of yam and taro, the ground steadily ascending till it reached a height of 800 or 900 feet above the sea, where the village stood. Its natives have the credit of being bloodthirsty and treacherous. On this small island, which is only about four by three miles in extent, there are three tribes, each speaking a different dialect, and each at fierce war with the others. The tribe visited by us appeared highly prosperous and contented, and we were pleased to see that the women seemed to do the light work and the men the heavy.

We remained at the village for an hour, the cynosure of all eyes, and did a brisk trade at easy rates, giving a knife for a pig; two or three strings of beads for a fowl, and lesser prices for fruit and vegetables.

On our first visit to Montague Island, or Niguna, no natives were to be seen. I landed there and strolled along the beach, shouting for some to appear, for I had little doubt but that we were observed, but as they had recently been fired upon, and had their villages burned by one of our ships, they were timid. After a time five or six men, armed with muskets and tomahawks, appeared; and, backed by three followers, I went up and presented them with a couple of trade handkerchiefs, on which they became fairly friendly, and told me that the missionary, Mr. Milne, lived on the other side of the island. I was anxious to get to Havannah harbour, Sandwich Island, that night, and meet Lieutenant Smith in the ketch, so I resolved to defer my visit to Mr. Milne, and we sailed for Sandwich at once. On Sunday, 25th, we anchored in this really noble Havannah harbour, and were filled with admiration of its capacity and sheltering power. The island, which is the most fertile of the New Hebrides group, extends about 20 miles each way, and is almost English in appearance; partial clearings have been made, and wooden buildings spring up round the anchorage at the head of the harbour, and attest the presence of the pushing Anglo-Saxon race. All the settlers are cotton-planters, and seem to have a good chance for making money, as the natives sell land greedily, and the cotton grown is of good quality. It was a relief to my mind to find Mr. Smith and the ketch safe and sound, as we had experienced some heavy weather since our parting. This little vessel I restored with much pleasure to the master and owner, on their addressing a formal request, and stating the exceptional circumstances of their case. This settled, a deputation of planters came forward with a memorial, stating that a necessity existed for extra labour on their thriving cotton plantations, and praying for a license to import it. Then the land sales of the natives, and other magisterial affairs, came on for settlement, and just as we drew to a conclusion word came that a schooner, the "Van Tromp," had been wrecked on Three Hill Island, and her captain and part of her crew murdered by a tribe adjoining the one we had visited a few days before. This called for prompt action, and we left immediately for the scene of the wreck, taking with us some of the crew who had escaped, and brought the report. The evidence was very complete, and I woke on the morning of the 27th with the feeling that some of our number would be no more in all probability before the sun set, for the tribe accused was armed with muskets, and we should be at disadvantage if we had to follow up the offenders. At 8 A.M. we were abreast of the schooner lying on the reef, and saw that she was crowded with pilfering natives, who, on seeing us, cleared out and fled into the bush, after which neither native nor white man was to be seen; a little dog belonging to the ship was straying about on the beach, and howling pitifully.

I had not the faintest hope of finding the men alive, but determined not to begin hostilities till I had exhausted every effort to persuade or force the native chiefs to an interview. We boarded the schooner first, and I was surprised to see no trace of bloodshed; then I pulled for the beach, taking with me Mr. Freeman, the master of a trading schooner, whom I had brought on account of his knowledge of native character. As we landed a crowd of natives came out of the bush armed with muskets, of which some men carried two. When within a hundred yards of shore our boat grounded on the reef, and we had to wade the rest of the distance. Accompanied by four armed men, and backed up by the crew which remained in the boat, and which would have poured in a deadly volley at a sign, Mr. Freeman and I advanced, and every step that I took assured me more and more that the people were only frightened, and meant us no harm. It proved so; and further, to our hearty pleasure, we learned that the captain and men were alive. They were at a long distance from the wreck; but after some little delay they joined us safe and sound, and highly praised the humanity of the natives, who had actually helped them through the surf to land, and then treated them with kindness. After a little talk the natives brought back everything they had taken from the vessel; and next day, on clearing out the schooner to see if there was any chance of getting her off, I gave them two bags of biscuit and some tobacco and powder in return for the kind treatment which the shipwrecked captain and crew had received at their hands. They were delighted, and fully appreciated this and our praise. There was no hope of getting the schooner off, her bottom being staved in, so we dismantled her, took her stores on board to be landed at Havannah harbour, and then went on that evening to Montague Island, which we reached in the dark. The natives being as usual too superstitious to stir out at night, we could not find any when we landed, but by continued shouting we got some of the missionary people to hear, and they brought Mr. Milne the missionary to us, who kindly gave me all the information I required as to the state of the island.

On the 29th we returned to Havannah harbour, and at the request of the planters I visited some of the cotton plantations. Doubtless in a few years a flourishing town will have arisen where the rude open houses of the settlers now stand. Many acres of land are already cleared and producing the finest cotton.

Steam machinery for cleaning and ginning the cotton is already at work. The forerunners of civilisation in these splendid islands deserve all the support the Imperial Government can give them, and will doubtless have it as their wants become known. We came on many parties of natives grubbing away at the ground to prepare it for cotton, and they seemed to work cheerily and well. They had plenty of food and to spare, for the fertility and rapidity of nature here is unbounded. For example, I was shown sweet potatoes but nine days planted, and the stems were already from twelve to fourteen inches long. Castor-oil plants and sugar-cane, the growth of six months, were from fourteen to fifteen feet high. The trees here are very rich, some of them of large size, bearing lovely blossoms and rich oil-nuts. One, called the candle-nut tree, shoots up to the height of 150 feet, and its great branches, covered with small silvery-green leaves, bear millions of nuts. These nuts, which have a shell as hard as stone, contain a sort of oil as thick as the substance of a composite candle, and burn with a brilliant light.

I will not weary the reader with an account of our visits to all the small islands, for they presented features of much sameness. We often felt our duties monotonous, but had the comfort of knowing that we were collecting a mass of information which will all prove useful in time, and in some sort preparing the native mind for a good reception of our countrymen to come.

CHAPTER VIII.

DILLON'S BAY, ERROMANGA, AND MURDER OF MR. GORDON—OUR ACTION—A SUNKEN WHALE—WASTE OF SANDAL WOOD—TANNA—ITS VOLCANO—A LONELY COTTON PLANTER—ARRIVE AT FRENCH SETTLEMENT AT NUMEA, WHICH CONCLUDES CRUISE.

ON our arrival at Dillon's Bay, Erromanga, September 1st, I found that a missionary named Gordon had been murdered in the February before, a brother of the former Mr. Gordon, missionary, who, with his wife, had been murdered on this island. It appears that Mr. Gordon had worked nobly for five years amongst the worst heathen natives, in the east of the island, and drawn together a congregation of forty-five people, including children. His death was caused by the credulity of a father, to whose sick children he had given medicine. The children dying, he conceived the idea that the missionary had killed them, and murdered him in revenge. It is remarkable that Mr. Gordon, who was translating the Bible into the Erromanga tongue, should just have made a version of the last verse of Acts, 12th chapter, which relates the death of Stephen, before he went out to the grass in front of his house to rest, and was struck down. Had matters remained in this state, my course of action would have been plain; but a complication had arisen; the native Christians from Dillon's Bay had flown to "the wild justice of revenge," treacherously fallen on some isolated members of the guilty tribe, and killed four. Two of these retaliators were communicants.

On arriving at Dillon's Bay I consulted with the three white residents—a missionary, and two white men who have established a whale-fishery here; and having obtained from them an exact account of all that had taken place, decided to bring the Christian east and heathen west chiefs together if possible, and tell them that, as the Christians had improperly taken the law into their own hands, I should not inflict further punishment if they would give me an assurance of living peaceably for the future. I despatched messengers to secure the attendance of the Christian chiefs, and by 11 o'clock P.M. had nine of them on board the "Basilisk;" one old chief had an arrow-head in his back, which native skill had failed to extract, and was all but disabled, but we made him as comfortable as we could.

A beautiful stream runs between precipitous hills into the head of Dillon's Bay, on one bank of which lies the missionary settlement, and on the other a whaling establishment. Here the good John Williams was killed; and the graves of the martyred Gordons, and of a missionary who died of fever and ague, gleamed white in the setting sunshine before us that evening, and filled the heart with many thoughts of those who had not counted their lives dear unto them. Next morning we steamed round to the scene of the murder, on the east side of the island, taking the nine chiefs; and when arrived, Lieutenant Sydney Smith landed with them to meet the eastern chiefs, and invite them on board, with power, in case of their being too frightened to come, to cause them to "make a paper," *i.e.* to affix their mark to a satisfactory paper to be drawn up by him, after being made to understand our reasons for not punishing them. This done, he was to direct them to shake hands all round. Finding them terribly alarmed, he took the latter course with perfect success, and finished by informing them that the tribes must assemble and meet me on the following day, when I should bring plenty of white men to meet them, and show them that we had not lacked power to punish them.

Next morning, being joined by several friendly chiefs, we marched 100 seamen and marines four miles to the place where poor Gordon was murdered, and reaching a considerable stream, which forms the boundary of the offending tribe, found the people so terror-stricken that the only chance of getting at them was for me to cross, with two or three others alone. This I did, wading across, and having drawn the natives together on a grassy hillock, overlooking the opposite bank, I directed their attention to the movements of our men there, who were then put through skirmishing movements and volley firing by Lieutenant Hayter. The natives were ready to sink into the earth with fear and amazement. I then addressed them, one of the Christian chiefs interpreting, and told them that we forgave them this time, but that a ship would come and punish them if they ever harmed one hair of a white man's head again ; on which they made earnest promises, which, I trust, will be kept.

Close to the spot stood the remains of poor Gordon's house, with the floors torn up, and nothing but the roof and framework left—a picture of ruin. His tasteful garden was fast becoming a wilderness, and his books were all scattered about in an adjoining hut that he had fitted up as his little library. We collected as many as filled four large chests, and brought them down for auction. In the indignant feeling that such a sight provoked, we were for a moment ready to regret that the right to punish had been taken out of our hands. Reflection showed, however, that not only would our line of action have been approved by Mr. Gordon himself, but that it was wise, in view of the safety of present and future white inhabitants; as also in producing the settlement of a question that would otherwise have led to a *vendetta* between the two tribes, that would probably have gone on to the extinction of one.

Standing in for Dillon's Bay on the morning of the 4th, we saw the whaling boats belonging to Messrs. Smith and Guy, the enterprising whalers settled here, fast to a large whale; the lines fouled, however, and they had to cut adrift.

The whales are frequently lost after being killed, through the boats lacking power to tow them on shore. We passed a spot where a whale had sunk in forty fathoms water, some weeks before, and observed that the surface was covered with oil, and that a powerful stench prevailed. Messrs. Smith and Guy have now got engines from Sydney, and built a small steamer with their own hands, which will doubtless prevent such losses for the future. Erromanga was once famous for its sandal wood, which is worth £25 a ton on the spot, but most of the trees have been ruthlessly destroyed.

Such instances of a waste of natural riches, from want of knowledge, are to my mind an argument in favour of the annexation of these islands to Australia.

On September 6th we anchored off "Black Beach," Tanna Island, the scene of the engagement between H.M.S. "Iris" and the natives, some fifteen years ago, and since then of many a lawless kidnapping affray. Two labour vessels lay close to us, engaged in procuring natives, one of which, by a strange coincidence, was commanded by a man who twenty years before had served as a seaman on board the "Basilisk." The papers of both vessels were all right. Near the anchorage was the cotton plantation of one of the most notorious of those lawless men who have been charged with the commission of frightful crimes in procuring labour from the islands, and who, with reckless hardihood, have planted themselves in solitary independence on these islands, prepared to defend their possessions, purchased for a few old Tower muskets, by the terror they inspire. The owner of the plantation came on board to pay his respects, and I looked with curiosity on this specimen of a class of men who, with all their great faults, possess many of the rough strong virtues of Englishmen. He was a big, burly, middle-aged man, with a large red beard and moustache, a small nose, surmounted by light, restless, blue eyes, and a low square forehead, which betokened the power to will and do without regard to consequences. He walked with difficulty, from more than one gunshot wound received from the natives. Landing with him, and climbing the steep cliffs that bounded the beach, we found ourselves on an open rising table-land, about thirty acres of which was in full bearing of the best kind of cotton, and fifty or sixty acres more were lying ready to be added within the next three months. This land, with some thousand acres of grass land adjoining, all nominally belonged to my companion. Gangs of natives from other islands—(for natives will not labour on their own islands)—were at work, and appeared to be well fed, and happy enough in the prospect of becoming the possessors of a musket or two when their term of servitude should expire. There can be no doubt of this man's ultimate wealth, if he can secure his life, but *that* is the question. As we passed a small neat inclosure, I asked "What is that?" and he said "My partner's grave, sir. He was shot there, where he is buried, nine months ago, by some of the hill natives who had laid an ambush for him, and shot him as he walked along the path where we now stand." I asked why they shot him; and the reply was, "They owed him a grudge for something or other," and I did not care to press the question, as it was evidently not an agreeable one, and the matter had been settled before my arrival. When we reached his small wooden house, principally built of planks obtained from the labour vessels, and guarded by an outside fence to stop a rush, he stepped in before and gave me a hearty welcome; and I sat and talked awhile with this strange solitary man. Loaded guns hung round the room, and the pistols in his belt showed that he was ready for any emergency. He told me that he could obtain as many native labourers as he pleased, without recourse to kidnapping, and that he always returned them to their homes at the expiration of a year's service. His chief difficulty was from the hill natives of the island, who, he said, would attack him without any provocation, but he was doing his best to conciliate them. He was reticent as to his former life; but if report spoke truth, it had been a wild and wicked one. However there was no special charge against him, and I left him, feeling admiration for his indomitable pluck, although of a vagabond kind. On the following day we anchored in Port Resolution, when, accompanied by thirty seamen, we made an excursion to Tanna Volcano, led by guides provided by the missionaries. For the first five or six miles our road led through thick forest, where the interlacing branches of the trees formed a screen, that the tiniest sun ray could not filter through. Now and then we came to openings where the sky and a blaze of sunshine broke in at once, that seemed to blind us, and were glad to plunge into shade and dusk again. The ground soon began to grow warm under our feet in these openings; it was spongy and grassy, and steam was breaking out in many small jets. In bare places it was too hot to touch with the hand. We emerged quite suddenly on a broad barren space, covered with ashes and scoriæ, from which a bare cone-shaped hill rose abruptly for five or six hundred feet, with a crater at its summit, which seemed to be about two miles in circumference. We had heard the roar of the volcano miles away; but the sight was sudden, and we stood awe-struck for some moments, contemplating this great power of nature at work. The crater belched incessant smoke and flame; and at short intervals great masses of stone were shot high into the tormented air, and came down with heavy thuds. We resolved to climb to the edge of the crater, and with a fresh trade-wind blowing an ascent of the weather side is tolerably safe; but the wind happened now to be light and variable, and our guides were doubtful. A native chief told us not to run when we saw stones falling, but to stand and watch them, and jump aside as needful; and this we did, and spread ourselves out in skirmishing order to face the cannonade of white-hot stones, some of them large enough to crush an elephant, that fell amongst us. The men lit pipes, or cooked a biscuit on some of these stones. Finding it too exciting to be pleasant, we went streaming round the rim of the crater to what seemed the safer side. On one edge the descent of the cone lay below us, blasted and bare, and covered with scoriæ; at the other the crater went down, and we, marching on the narrow rim between, with our figures relieved by the leaden sky, looked not unlike what Dante might have conceived of a company of lost souls being marshalled to hell. At this side we stood with some safety to watch the ways of the volcano. For a moment we could look down into the vast pit, and see the vent-holes two hundred feet below—three of the largest full of a red-hot seething mass, mixed with flame, and streaked with black, till the smoke gushed out and obscured all, rolling up in volumes of tender grey colour, that seemed almost to woo us to throw ourselves on their soft convolutions and float upwards. Then a roar would come widening up from the abyss, filling the ears with stupendous sound, the flame burst out afresh, and the volley of stones shoot high into the air, fall with a rattle and thud, and all be clear again.

There is a small lake at the north-east side of the mountain, which communicates by an underground fissure with the volcano. It is a shallow dead sea, with arid banks at one side and rich vegetation on the other. Here we rested, and a number of Tanna women having found out our retreat, we prevailed on them, by promises of tobacco and beads, to give us one of their monotonous song dances.

We returned to the ship through a valley, richly cultivated by the natives, and found work awaiting us in the settlement of some disputes between a white man and some natives, which prevented our sailing that evening, as we had intended.

On Monday 9th we arrived at Aneiteum, the southernmost of the New Hebrides Isles; and on the 12th at Númea, the French settlement in New Caledonia, having, by the goodness of Providence, safely visited fifty-three islands in the course of our cruise, amidst many anxieties; much of the navigation having been unknown, and our constant intercourse with the natives having demanded unceasing effort. We met our orders from the commodore here, and, in accordance with them, sailed after three days' stay, for Sydney, which we reached on the early morning of September 24th, and dropped anchor in the friendly waters of the harbour.

On arriving, we found ourselves under orders from the Admiralty to proceed again to Torres Straits and the coast of New Guinea, for a period of four, afterwards changed to six months. We had gone through nine months of tropical service and ceaseless work; but the health of the ship's company was good, and the ship (some refitting being done) was available, so we turned ourselves from thoughts of rest, and set to work to make preparations for the cruise.

Our stay at Sydney was longer eventually than we expected, for a strike amongst the operatives delayed the caulking of the "Basilisk."

In the meantime the kidnapping Act of 1872 had come into force, and we were thus prepared to deal effectively with the kidnapping and South Sea Island labour questions, which were to occupy an important place in the forthcoming cruise.

CHAPTER IX.

LEAVE SYDNEY, DECEMBER 8TH, FOR SECOND TORRES STRAITS CRUISE — NAVIGATING LIEUTENANT CONNOR—MAKE PRIZES OF THE SCHOONERS "MELANIE" AND "CHALLENGE"—NOVEL MODE OF CLEANING SHIP'S BOTTOM—SEIZE THE BARQUE "WOODBINE"—THE "CRISHNA"—FIND THAT NO RIVER EXISTS IN LLOYD'S BAY—VENTILATION AND HEALTH IN THE "BASILISK"—RAINY SEASON—RING BIRD OF PARADISE—SURVEY BETWEEN SADDLE AND JARVIS ISLANDS—NAME PHILIP HARBOUR—SINGULAR PRACTICE WITH BONES OF THE DUGONG.

ON Sunday, December 8, we left Sydney bound on our second Torres Straits cruise, with permission to visit the coast of New Guinea, and went slowly north with a tumbling sea and a fresh breeze.

On the 17th we had a cheering meeting with Lord and Lady Normanby at Brisbane, who both took a deep interest in our labours, past and future. I informed the governor and Mr. Palmer that the principal object of the cruise was to put down illegal practices in connection with the pearl-shelling in Torres Straits, and that I was directed to make inquiries as to the fate or condition of Mr. Miklucko Macklay, the eminent Russian traveller in New Guinea, who has explored so much of its northern shores,—as he had been for some time lost to sight, and it was feared he had perished. I also fully explained to them that during the performance of these and the routine duties of the cruise, opportunities might occur for our rendering special services to the colony, and that I was prepared to take advantage of such to the best of my ability.

Much of the navigation of Torres Straits was still unknown, and not only were they now becoming a frequent resort of merchant ships, but it was actually in contemplation to run the line of mail steamers between Brisbane and Singapore through them. It was therefore of the last importance to throw as much light as possible on their many dangers, and to indicate a safe navigation, and the position of suitable anchorages where such might exist. This I was ready to do by surveying, whenever time and means lay at my disposal.

Lord Normanby and the Queensland Government cordially accepted my offer of rendering such service, if possible, in the course of duty, and at my request allowed Navigating Lieutenant Connor, R.N., a good surveyor, to accompany us in the "Basilisk." I had made attempts to get a surveyor at Sydney, and failed; so it was with much satisfaction that I received Mr. Connor in the capacity of "passenger," and stowed him away in my side cabin.

We reached Cardwell on January 2d, in a heavy gale, accompanied by thick weather, and anchored under the lee of Gould Island, whilst I ran in, in the galley, to gain information from Mr. Sheridan, the Police Magistrate. I found from him that the pearl-shellers had received warning that the new kidnapping act, which rendered the employment of natives illegal, without license, had come into force, and that they knew of the "Basilisk's" coming, and were clearing out of the Straits as fast as possible, on which I determined to make all haste north. On the 5th we chased and overhauled two schooners, the "Melanie," with fifty-five, and the "Challenge," with thirty-three South Sea Islanders on board, who had been employed as divers in Torres Straits. These schooners had been warned of the passing of the new Act by the Marquis of Normanby himself, who had visited the Straits some months previously, but they had stayed on to the last moment, and attempting to escape on hearing of our approach, had fallen into our clutches.

Each individual case of the islanders on board needed investigation, so we anchored with our prizes off Fitzroy Island, where the good anchorage was very welcome. The result of our examination was to bring out the facts that in the "Melanie" fourteen natives had been from four to six years, fourteen from three to four years, and one for one year, working without any wages beyond their necessary clothing and tobacco, and that no agreement had been made with them. Seventeen stated that they had shipped from their island on board another vessel from three to four years ago, and had since been transferred, against the wish of the majority, to the "Melanie," and kept at work without any agreement; the rest were on the ship's books as having been legally shipped at Sydney. The stories of these men were various; most of them had shipped voluntarily—seven had been kidnapped. "Captain gammon me—say I go back—I never go back," said one poor fellow; and two others had the same tale, "Captain gammon me." Another had been seized from a reef; two had been run down in their canoe by a schooner named the "Maria Renny," and taken on board.

To secure themselves from the penalties of the new Act, the pearl-shellers had induced these natives to sign an agreement to serve them for five months from August, and had fixed wages for them.

This analysis is a fair sample, and will give an idea of the then average state of affairs. We sent the vessels as prizes to Sydney, where they were condemned; but on a subsequent appeal to the Privy Council, the highest appeal court for the colonies, the vessels were restored, on paying all costs connected with the case, on the grounds that retrospective evidence could not be entertained, and that an intention to procure a license had been proved.

Whilst here investigating, our men had a good opportunity of enjoying themselves on shore, bathing, washing clothes, and hauling the seine; and the natives of both our prizes did us a good turn by cleaning the ship's bottom right up from the keel. It was quite a sight to see them, some eighty in number, swimming round the ship armed with scrubbing brushes, laughing and gesticulating, some disappearing every moment from the surface, to re-appear far below as shadowy undulating forms along the sheathing, where they were busy scrubbing off the grass and barnacles from the copper in the most systematic manner. As they reappeared they always gave vent to a clear, soft, whistle, which seemed to come from an involuntary effort of the lungs. They stayed a very short time—two or three minutes—on the surface, when they come up for air, and dived again as fresh as ever; and in about an hour and a half made the ship's bottom as clean as if she had been in dock.

On January 8th we continued our passage to Cape York, and next day boarded the barque "Woodbine." Her men were suffering dreadfully from scurvy, and our officers contributed with much liberality from their stores to help them. Finding that this ship had no articles, that she had twenty tons of pearl-shell on board, the result of coloured labour, and three South Sea Islanders without a license, and that the master could give no explanation, I sent this vessel to Brisbane in charge of Lieutenant S. G. Smith, where she was eventually released for want of sufficient evidence.

Our first penny reading on board H.M.S. "Basilisk"—a forerunner of many pleasant gatherings—came off on the evening of Tuesday 14th, and was a perfect success, owing to the organising talent of Lieutenants Hayter and Sydney Smith; and I was truly glad at the outset of this cruise to find that such a fund of amusement lay ready to be drawn on to beguile the tedium of the work before us. All experience goes to prove that every effort to vary the monotony of ship life is rewarded by increased efficiency; it is in the nature of things that it should be so.

On the 14th we boarded the barque "Crishna"

of Sydney, and found that she had thirty-five South Sea Islanders on board, whose history was so similar to that of the "Melanie" natives that I need not relate it. We sent her to Brisbane, where she was condemned, and sold for £3900, with her cargo, intelligence of which was very cheering to the ship's company. This amount has since been heavily cut down by law expenses, and the Imperial Government has claimed half the remainder.

Wishing to clear up doubt as to the existence or non-existence of a river reported at the bottom of Lloyd's Bay, we stood in and anchored near Low Island on the evening of the 15th. The chart at this point is marked, "apparent opening of large river;" and it will be seen, by a glance at the map of North Queensland, that a river would be a rich gift of nature here, as affording an opening into the country, and a highway for the transit of agricultural produce. Navigating Lieutenant Connor and I, in the galley, and Mr. Mourilyan in the gig, came to an anchor accordingly, off the supposed entrance of the river, at 11 P.M., and spreading our awnings and making ourselves as comfortable as we could for the night, we drank off a dose of quinine every man, and turned over to sleep. It was a hot calm moonlight night, and my companions were soon breathing measuredly. I had a lantern in the stern gratings, and enjoyed to the full the rare pleasure of a little quiet reading and thought. At daybreak we began our search for the river, and explored one salt-water creek after another; but each was a failure, and led only to entanglement in the swamp, where clouds of mosquitoes resented our invasion of their holds. There was no river. The drainage of a hill-range, six or seven miles inland, had created a swamp of many miles extent, covered with mangroves and intersected by these salt-water creeks; and this was all. Finding a piece of sandy beach, we breakfasted there with all willingness, for river-hunting is very hungry work, and returning to the ship, got under weigh directly.

The heat now began to be very trying, 90° on deck, under the awnings. We knew that the "Basilisk" had earned a bad reputation for herself as a sickly ship during former commissions in the West Indies, and a letter from a former commander had warned me of this. It struck me that the cause might be in the isolation of the engine-room, which was shut in by strong bulk-heads, right across the ship, at both ends, thus preventing a free circulation of air. To remedy this we cut a large scuttle about four feet square between the lower deck and the foremost stoke-hole, and the result was a success, particularly under steam, when the rush of cold air to the furnaces was such as to make the lower, or troop-deck, one of the coolest places in the ship. To this simple measure, and the allowance of a free tank for all purposes, I principally attribute the marvellous healthiness of the ship during the years of tropical work we went through. During the period of our service we did not lose a man from sickness, our total of deaths being two from accident, and one at Sydney from rapid consumption. On the whole, I am of opinion that the health of a ship's company can be kept up to the normal standard during exposure to intense heat and a rainy season, if incessant precaution is taken; clothing lightened to a bearable degree; cleanliness and ventilation attended to; food made as nourishing and various as may be; extra allowances of non-stimulating drinks issued to repair the waste caused by continual perspirations; leave given on shore whenever possible, and as much wholesome amusement provided on board as circumstances will allow.

On January 18th we took up our old anchorage off Somerset, and saw the anchor go down with different feelings from those of last year. Then, its plunge marked our work as complete, now Cape York was but a starting-point for arduous work. Mr. Jardine welcomed us, and gave us the benefit of all his information; and the next day, Sunday, was spent as a day of rest—Mr. Murray, the missionary, conducting our service on board. This gentleman had been absent from England on mission work for thirty-five years, without once returning, and had been instrumental in sowing the seeds of Christianity in very many islands.

The rainy season had now commenced, and we suffered the inconvenience of a constant downpour—a serious one in a flush-decked vessel. Our rain awnings, too, were insufficient, lacing inside the bulwarks to the deck, instead of outside. Whilst here we fell in with a lonely waif of society, named Cockerill, who has betaken himself to live in a tiny vessel of about eight tons, and accompanied only by his son and two natives, cruises about these seas as a naturalist, and seems to be happy enough in his own way. His boat was laden with specimens of beautiful birds ; and from the Aru Islands, 500 miles west of Somerset, which he had just left, he had brought some boxes full of the Great Bird of Paradise, and the still more exquisite King Bird of Paradise, of which he kindly gave me a specimen. This bird, only lately becoming known at home, is as large as a small thrush, the back glossy crimson, the head feathers being soft, and deep in tone like velvet, the throat crimson, and separated from the pure white breast by a wide band of green. It has the long wire tail of all Birds of Paradise, terminating, however, in two circular feathers, about the size of a sixpenny piece, of a burnished green. But its peerless ornaments are two small feather fans of intense emerald colour, set in the upper joint of the wing, and capable of being spread or folded at pleasure.

We had now a period of six weeks before us, to be spent in Torres Straits and on the coast of New Guinea, at the end of which time we were to return to Somerset and take in the coal and stores which would then await us there. The duty assigned us had been to put down all illegal practices against Polynesians in these waters, and having succeeded in doing this, I desired to make the most of the time at our disposal by rendering what hydrographical service should be possible. By a late Act of government, all islands, lying within sixty miles of the shores of Queensland, had been declared British possessions, and this Act had brought the Australian boundary to within twenty miles of New Guinea. It was thus important that something should be known of the navigation between.

On Friday, 24th, we left Somerset, after four hours' difficulty in weighing the anchor and getting clear, for the ship was whirled round and round in cross currents at such a rate that the chains kept continually fouling, and we lost both flukes of our best bower anchor before we could extricate ourselves. We anchored that night near Saddle Island, and next morning proceeded through an unsurveyed portion of the Straits to Brothers Island, surveying as we went; whilst Navigating-Lieutenant Connor laid down a line of soundings in a different course between these two islands. On our return to the Brothers, we saw seven large boats belonging to the vessels we had captured in Torres Straits, hauled up under orders not to work till their owners had obtained license to fish.

On Sunday we found a clear deep water channel on our way west to Jarvis Island, thirty miles from the Brothers, till on coming close to the island, and reaching a supposed clear patch of surveyed water, we struck, and remained fast on a sandy knoll. All were at their posts; so, vexatious as it was, we had the consolation of feeling that we had gone ashore, strictly according to Act of Parliament. It was ebb tide, and we ran out an anchor and cable astern, got the guns aft, and

K

waited the flow, when the old ship floated off much to our joy, unharmed. A ship is never safe in Torres Straits when out of the beaten track, the lurking dangers are so many. The changes made during heavy gales in the shape of rapid shifts and accumulations of sand, defy calculation; added to which the sea is so discoloured by the New Guinea rivers flowing down, that such dangers are made imperceptible. Jarvis is a lofty volcanic island, 525 feet high, and about fifty-five miles from Cape York, and is within the line of British possessions, and the headquarters of three pearl shelling stations. We were anxious to make a survey of the anchorage, so next morning Lieutenant Connor and some of our officers began to survey it, and after three days' arduous labour, proved it to be a valuable harbour, protected by the island and surrounding coral reefs, having sufficient water for large vessels, but tides of great strength. This harbour we named Philip Harbour, and were glad to find it so available, as it will always be a main resort of the pearl shelling industry. The space of thirty-six miles which lies between Jarvis Island and the low mangrove-covered coast of New Guinea is a mass of coral reefs, and contains no passage for ships, and scarcely any for boats. Thus all the passages by which ships can enter Torres Straits lie between Jarvis Island and Cape York, and are now British waters. These passages are very narrow, under two miles in width; whilst the one most generally taken—the Prince of Wales's Channel, between Hammond Island and the north-west reef—is barely a mile and a half wide. We hold this great highway of the ocean therefore on the best strategic terms. The average depth of water in these channels is only seven or eight fathoms, and a few torpedoes judiciously placed would effectually block up this route to an enemy.

The natives of Jarvis Island are black Papuans, quite uncivilised and unclothed. At their village I saw signs of a custom which will perhaps one day puzzle the naturalist. The huts were pitched under the shelter of some enormous banyan trees, in the massive trunks of which the bones of the dugong were so deeply imbedded as to seem one with the wood. Looking farther, I saw that many tender shoots, just drooping to root themselves, were twined round the bones of freshly killed dugong. They are placed thus as a propitiatory offering, and are never removed. The large teeth and ribs of the dugong are ivory of an inferior sort, and doubtless give the unfortunate animal a market value that will lead to its speedy extinction.

CHAPTER X.

PICK OUR WAY TO CORNWALLIS ISLAND—SAIBAI, AND ITS TWO STORIED HOUSES—MR. CONNOR AND MR. PITT LEFT BEHIND FOR DETACHED SURVEY—SAIL FOR NEW GUINEA—DARNLEY ISLAND, AND BÊCHE DE MER FISHERIES—SINGULAR MODE OF BURIAL—REDSCAR BAY, NEW GUINEA—EXPLORE THE RIVERS FALLING INTO THE TOWTON-OPENING—USBORNE RIVER.

WE sailed for Cornwallis Island on the 30th, but were soon obliged to anchor under the lee of a coral reef, the weather became so thick and dirty. On the 31st we crossed an unknown part of the Straits, supposed to be closed by coral, to reach an anchorage between two large islands. One—Mount Cornwallis, once believed to be an integral part of New Guinea, is high and healthy land; the other, which we placed on the chart last year by its native name of Saibai, is low ground, and probably malarious. Cautiously we picked our way through these dangerous waters, often with only a few feet of water to spare under our keel, and reached our desired anchorage off Cornwallis, late in the afternoon. This island, which lies about five miles from the New Guinea coast, is lofty, rising to a height of 790 feet, rugged, covered with huge granite boulders, and in part with dark green trees. On its north-eastern side lie some fine patches of grassy land, well supplied with fresh water, and a richly cultivated valley, producing taro and melons; and here the village and native mission station are placed, but the native houses are only occasionally occupied, as the natives live on Saibai, three miles to the eastward. I visited Saibai with Lieutenant Hayter, Dr. Goodman, and other officers, and found it a low island, about twelve miles long by three broad, having a large brackish lagoon within, which abounds with curlew, wild duck, and other wild fowl. The northern shores are cultivated, and produce abundance of yams and other roots, cocoa-nuts and fruits—the rest of the island is swampy, and covered with mangroves. Saibai is well populated, and the principal village contains about 600 inhabitants. The houses are well sized, and two stories high—the latter a peculiarity not elsewhere seen by us. These houses are built on poles in the ordinary way; the upper room is used as the better chamber and sleeping place, and the lower, which is formed by thatching in the poles, as a store-room for weapons and fishing-gear. The sleeping place contains some rude mats on which to lie at night, and is reached by the simplest of ladders—a piece of notched wood. Human skulls are suspended round the houses, but the people are not cannibals; they have plenty of vegetables and fish, of pigs, in which the island abounds, and a supply of turtle and the flesh of the dugong, which is very good eating, and tastes rather like veal. The canoes are large, and made of a single tree dug out, to which wash-boards are lashed on with cocoa-nut fibre, and head and stern pieces of wood, that are fitted to meet them. They have very long outriggers, and on either side a platform, on which wicker cages are fixed to hold weapons. They carry two mat sails on shifting poles, and are frequently ornamented by a short pole at the stem, with a bunch of grass floating from it, and picked out prettily with ochres, and devices burnt out. The weapons used here are iron tomahawks, bows, and arrows barbed with wallaby bones, and poisoned, which are said to cause convulsions and rapid death. The people, who are tall and muscular, are jet black; their eyes are brown, and very lustrous, and they have good noses and mouths, the former sometimes inclining to the aquiline, and a facial angle of about sixty-five degrees. The head, which is well shaped, is covered with crisp woolly hair.

The women wear their hair cut close, except a narrow ridge from ear to ear, which is left under an inch long. Many of the men cut theirs quite close, and wear wigs made of matting, with narrow ringlets fastened in so closely, that for some time we thought them the natural hair. They go nearly quite unclothed. Polygamy is general amongst the natives of the Torres Straits Islands, and the crime of infanticide prevails. The principal diseases are fever and ague, for which they bleed the sufferer freely from the forehead, back, and limbs, with flints. Ulcerated mosquito bites are frequent, and some few cases of hydrocele and elephantiasis have been seen. These last remarks I make on the authority of Navigating-Lieutenant Connor, who spent many weeks in surveying amongst these islands.

Having finished our inquiries at Saibai, we left this zealous volunteer behind, with Mr. Pitt, midshipman, and four men, in the pinnace, and a fine whaleboat, lent us by Mr. Jardine, manned by five of our best seamen, to survey these newly known islands, and the opposite coast of New Guinea, and sailed ourselves for the eastern islands of Torres Straits, and the New Guinea coast 300 miles east of this point. As we passed out of sight of Mr. Connor's boats, an anxious feeling filled my breast—there were so many chances possible against his safety and success—quarrels with the natives, sickness, sudden gales, and dangerous navigation; but I had full confidence in his prudence and seamanship.

On February 4th we called at Warrior Island, where we found that Mr. Bedford had been succeeded at his post by a worn-out sailor, who seemed very incapable. Pearl-shelling had ceased, and thirty-two South Sea islanders were waiting in idleness till their masters could procure licenses to fish. It came on to blow hard, with a confused, dangerous sea, and we had some difficulty in communicating. Next day we steered through Basilisk Pass, and anchored off the low coral shore of Cocoa Nut Island, where a Scotchman has recently established a pearl-shell fishery. The fishers in his employment have more decent dwelling-places than those at other pearl-shelling stations. They close in a small square of white coral sand with a light fence, trample it hard, and build two oblong huts with sticks, and thatching, in opposite corners, about four feet high, and ten long by eight feet wide, leaving a small hole for a door in each, large enough to admit a man's body. The natives in these parts are not able to supply visitors with any refreshments, neither is there any water on this island, which has a population consisting of nearly 150 souls, and all the water used has to be brought from Sue Island, about fifteen miles distant, in large hollow bamboos.

Friday, 8th, found us at the mountainous Darnley Isle, situated at the eastern entrance of Torres Straits, past the region of pearl-shell, but the headquarters of the bêche-de-mer fisheries. It is now generally known that bêche-de-mer is a large sea slug, and is found left in large quantities on the coral-reefs by the receding tide, falling an easy prey to the fishers. The slugs are cut open, cleaned, and placed on thin iron plates in a smoke-drying room, where, after being thoroughly dried, they are packed and sorted for the Chinese market. The bêche-de-mer is divided into three qualities. The best, called the Red Fish, is worth £140 per ton at Sydney; the second, or Black Fish, £120; and the worst, or Teat Fish, about £80; and as slugs are plentiful on the reefs the trade is a lucrative one.

The natives here are tall, well-built men, quick in understanding, able to drive a bargain with Europeans, and good cultivators of the soil. This is the only island in Torres Straits on which sago palms grow. They are to be found here in a well-watered glen, where their emerald-plated trunks, furnished far down with great feathery branches, form a pleasing contrast to the tall bare-stemmed cocoa-nut trees with their top-heavy crowns. The inhabitants treat their dead precisely in the manner of the Capuchin Friars of Sicily, save that they dry the body in the sun instead of in an oven. When fully hardened, the ghastly object is placed recumbent in a deserted dwelling-house. I shall not easily forget our disgust, when, seeing one of the pretty well-thatched oval houses standing in a thick grove of palm and fruit trees, we went to it, expecting to be met by the usual group of dark, plump, bright-eyed children, and found instead silence and rank vegetation round the door, and inside two shrivelled corpses. This is the only island where I have seen this custom practised in all these seas.

Having transacted our fishing business, and given the native teachers some biscuit and beef, we sailed for a solitary sand-cay, about thirty miles distant—a noted resort of turtle—as we were anxious to give the men some fresh meals. When half-way there our paddle-wheel sustained a shock, and we perceived that it had struck an enormous basking turtle. The creature was wide awake now, and lay on its back, flapping violently till we had secured it. The weight was 472 lbs., and it proved to be the Luth, or Leathery Turtle, so called from the soft leathery plates, similar in appearance to the armour of an ironclad, with which it is covered. This specimen was a small one, for they are known to attain a length of nine feet and a weight of 1600 lbs. Naturalists say that its flesh is hurtful, and causes many symptoms of poisoning in those who eat it, but this one afforded all hands nearly two good meals, and no harm resulted, the only fault found being that its flavour was somewhat fishy.

On the 11th, after visiting the Murray Islands, we left Torres Straits and stood across the Gulf of Papua for Redscar Bay, about 200 miles distant, on the east New Guinea coast, to visit the mission station established there, where the missionaries were said to be sick and half-starving, and to gain kidnapping information. Some large rivers were reported to exist in this neighbourhood, and we determined to explore sufficiently to make sure.

We had quite an alarm at daybreak on the 13th, for the officer of the watch reported "reefs right ahead, and close to!" and sure enough there appeared to be long lines of reef stretching away in patches as far as the eye could see, the nearest within 100 yards of the ship. Fuller light, however, showed that they were not reefs, but collections of huge trees which some flood in the New Guinea rivers had torn from their banks and swept thirty miles out to sea; and showed us also the magnificent Owen Stanley range purple against the sky.

This part of the coast was partially surveyed by Captain Owen Stanley in 1849, but landing was but once attempted by his party, as the natives were believed to be dangerous.

Anchoring in Redscar Bay, we pulled for four miles over a dangerous shallow flat, formed by the alluvial deposit of the rivers which empty themselves through the Towtón-Opening at the head of this bay; and passing through the opening entered a splendid expanse of inland water which appeared to be about three miles wide, and showed no limit as to its length, except where a wooded islet intercepted our view to the north-east. It seemed to offer a promising water way to the interior of the island, and we resolved to explore it, but our first object was to visit the starving native teachers at Redscar village. We pulled in for the village, where crowds of natives were anxiously watching and waiting for us, beached our boats amongst a crowd of canoes hauled up on the black sandy beach, and stepped on shore amongst our new friends, who, wholly unarmed, and without a sign of distrust, gave us a hearty welcome. We were surprised to see that these people differed totally from the tall, muscular, fierce-looking, naked black Papuans we had left in Torres Straits. These men were more of the Malay type—small, lithe, copper-coloured people, with clean well-cut features, and a pleasing expression of countenance. They wore their own hair, frizzled out mop-fashion, and were slightly tattooed with stars and small figures, on the breast and shoulders, as I have never seen the black Papuans. They had nothing in the way of clothes but a sort of leaf girdle. The young men were ornamented with white cowrie shells, bound round their foreheads, arms, and legs, and bird of Paradise and Cassowary plumes, on their heads and shoulders; the older appeared to dispense with these adornments. The septum of the nose and lobes of the ear were pierced, and tortoise-shell rings, pieces of bamboo or shell put through. The women were ill-made and slovenly-looking as compared with the men; their dress was the "Ti-ti" or grass petticoat; but the otherwise nude body was adorned by the most extensive tattooing, so well executed as to excite the admiration of all amongst us who had not seen the exquisite tattooing of the Japanese. The village is built on low swampy ground, from which the mangroves have been cleared, and numbers about one hundred houses, raised on poles of the unusual height of fifteen and twenty feet, probably for safety in case the river should overflow its low banks, and also to lift them somewhat above the range of the vicious mosquitoes that blacken the air in these swampy places. Some of the houses are thirty or forty feet in length, and not more than ten feet broad, and look like long narrow passages inside. The entrance is at the gable end, where there is a large bamboo platform before the door, which forms a pleasant chatting place, or cool seat for the family at meals. At the other extremity a small space is divided off by bamboo poles into one or two small compartments, which we supposed to be intended as sleeping places for the girls. The little children were all dressed like their elders of either sex, and did not fear us in the least as we walked about, but played round us, shooting with small bows and arrows.

Our visit was short, for on reaching the mission

hut we found three teachers so near death's door that Dr. Haines requested me to send them on board the "Basilisk" immediately, as the only chance of saving their lives. They had little or no food, and it needed but a look round on the low malarious country to make sure that any but aboriginal natives must be visited more or less by disease here. These three poor creatures, who were without any necessary medicines, were carried by our men to my boat, and placed under a canvas screen on deck, to be treated by the skilful hands of Drs. Goodman and Haines, and their wives were brought on board and made comfortable in my side cabin.

On Friday, 14th, the gunner and I in the galley, and Mr. Hayter and Dr. Haines in the gig, left the ship to ascend, if possible, one of the rivers debouching here, to its home in the mountains of Stanley Range, the nearest peak of which is not more than twenty miles from the flat belt of low country bordering here on the sea. We called first at the Towton village and induced one of the native teachers to go with us as pilot, and then, with a fair breeze aiding us against the strong downward current, we passed up the wide estuary, named by us Galley Reach, which is formed here by the confluence of many streams which fall into it, and escape to the sea by the Towton-Opening.

We regretted as we crossed it that no navigable passage connects it with the sea, for such a passage would make it one of the finest harbours in the world.

Instead of proceeding to the head of Galley Reach we made for the mouth of a fine stream which lay to the right, about three miles above the Towton or Redscar village, afterwards named by us Usborne River. Our pilot told us that it led to the home of a warlike tribe about fifteen miles distant, and added that the coast villagers were much afraid of this tribe. I determined to meet and gain the friendship of these people if possible, and obtain their concurrence in an attempt to reach the interior; but my time was short, as my orders obliged me to be at Cape York in three weeks' time, and I was anxious, after exploring these rivers falling into Galley Reach, to examine the almost unknown coast of New Guinea farther to the eastward, the outline of which had been traced from a distance by Captain Owen Stanley, R.N., twenty-five years before, and had never since been visited by white men.

The river now entered by us had a rapid current, and was from 100 to 120 yards broad, with an average depth of twelve feet. The banks were composed of black fetid mud, from which sprang tall, melancholy, mangrove trees, ranking their bare thin trunks so closely together that it was difficult to pass between them, whilst their dank foliage mingled seventy or eighty feet overhead in a mass of darkness. We frequently landed, and strove to penetrate this slimy mangrove forest, in the hope of reaching some clear ground; but after many efforts, much slipping off the mangrove roots deep into the slime, and much startling of little red and brown crabs, lizards, snakes, and other ugly creatures in their happy homes, we had to return to the boats without success. On one of these occasions, seeing a serpent of the boa tribe twined round the trunk of a tree, gorged, and fast asleep, we shot it, and it quickened at once, and glared savagely at us, till killed by repeated blows. The edge of these mangrove banks was lined with a gigantic shrub, which, for want of better knowledge, I call a Bastard Palm; it has no trunk, but sends up great leaf-branches of a palm shape, each thirty or forty feet long, that arch over the stream at a height of five or six feet. A small species of the same kind was armed on the edge of its leaves with sharp strong hooks, and these bending low over the water, often cruelly lacerated our flesh, as we were obliged to keep close under the banks to avoid the strong current. By four o'clock in the afternoon, we had reached a distance of ten miles above the Towton village, without having come to any break in the mangrove swamp. At last, when we had almost ceased to expect a change, we were cheered by seeing the banks rise a little, after which a grassy glade soon showed itself, and we were speedily on shore, with triangles rigged, and our dinners cooking over fine wood fires, the smoke of which somewhat daunted the mosquitoes. After dinner heavy tropical rain began to fall, but we struggled manfully on under it, and against a fierce current, till nightfall, and then anchoring in midstream prepared to pass the night. We covered the boats in with rain awnings, changed our clothes, and had an impromptu penny reading, with plenty of songs. When ready for sleep we drank a dose of quinine, and settled down for what we hoped would prove a quiet night. A "quiet night"! if ever poor mortals suffered the torments of the lost in a small way, we did. The air was thick with mosquitoes, armed with stings that pierced us as easily as though we had only been arrayed in the woad of our ancestors. They nearly drove us into the water, and I had to caution the men continually to keep their arms and legs on board for fear of the alligators.

We were glad to be at work again before daylight broke, and slowly forcing our way up-stream, through a country which soon revealed itself to sight, for the banks were now open, and broken into undulations, so that we could see all kinds of huge palm, and great bread-fruit trees, the lovely tree-fern, and trees which we were not botanists enough to name, stretching away on every side into seemingly interminable forest. Here and there we observed a creeper of a rich, dark, green colour, climbing to the top of the loftiest tree, and crushing the life out of its support. This beautiful destroyer had quite killed some mighty trees, and clung now to the dead branches, assuming all their stark shapes. In other places it ran down and formed impenetrable hedges seventy or eighty feet high, between which the river ran like a deep ditch. The silence, but for our oars, was unbroken—land and water seemed asleep—not a breeze stirred, not a creature, man nor beast, appeared to peep at us, or question our passage; but after a time the birds began to awake with discordant screams. Parrots and cockatoos abounded, so also did the great crowned pigeon, a specimen of which we shot, but it fell into the jungle and was lost. Large white storks were numerous, and other birds of kinds unknown to us, all unusually wary, keeping to the highest branches of the lofty trees, out of gunshot; but no animal was to be heard, and the birds soon quieted down again. We breakfasted, and pushed on again against a still increasing current, through which we made headway only by continually shooting the stream from side to side, and gaining the shelter of the projecting points; but it was difficult to make progress, for huge snags and fallen trees impeded the stream, and we had many narrow escapes from upset. The hills now began to rise, and rocky knolls showed themselves occasionally, and this cheered us to fresh exertions. We came to a place where the river divides itself, and keeping to the main stream, found ourselves in a grand, rapid river, twenty-five feet deep. I now felt sure that such a volume of water must have a clear course for many miles; but in one short mile we were brought to a stand-still by a vast accumulation of fallen and uprooted trees, swept down during ages from the mountains, which had completely bridged the river, which is here about sixty feet wide. Rank vegetation grew out of the decaying trunks, and several small islets, formed of debris and alluvial matter, bound the mass together. The river rushed furiously under, but could not sweep away this barrier of its own creation. We made long and fruitless efforts to find a way through, but as we had not time nor means at our disposal to haul the boats overland and relaunch them, and the current above appeared too strong for oars to contend with, we had to give up, and unwillingly turn back. I would have given much to have explored to the head of this river, and reached the mountain range, and I hope that others will follow me here and succeed, as river communication will be of the last importance in opening up New Guinea.

We went down swiftly with the current, and reached Towton, where I slept at the Mission-house, and the good Samoian teachers made me most comfortable. There was but one apartment in the hut, with separate spaces, screened off by tappa, and it rocked gently on its long poles in the breeze, with the motion of a ship at sea.

Disappointed in reaching the interior of New Guinea by this stream, and in finding any trace of inland inhabitants, I resolved to make another effort at the head of Galley Reach to find a stream which should form an inland highway, but as the examination of the coast to the east was more important, and it was necessary for the "Basilisk" to call at Redscar again on her way back to Cape York, I deferred this attempt till our return from the eastward.

CHAPTER XI.

EXAMINE THE COAST FOR FIFTY MILES EAST OF REDSCAR BAY—FRIENDLY UNARMED NATIVES—FIND "BASILISK" PASSAGE THROUGH THE BARRIER REEF—AGE OF STONE IN NEW GUINEA—DISCOVER PORT MORESBY AND FAIRFAX HARBOUR—EXPLORE INSIDE BARRIER REEF TO HOOD'S POINT—A HILL VILLAGE—DESCRIPTION OF COUNTRY, TREES, SOIL, AND GRASS-PLAINS—EDITH RIVER—BACK TO CAPE YORK—EPISODE OF THE BARQUE "SPRINGBOK"—NAVIGATING-LIEUTENANT CONNOR REJOIN FROM SURVEY ON NORTH SHORE OF TORRES STRAITS—REPORT TO REV. W. A. MURRAY.

On Monday, 17th, Navigating-Lieutenant Mourilyan and I started in the cutter and galley, well armed, and taking a week's provisions, to examine the coast for fifty miles to the eastward of Redscar Head. This coast had been surveyed by the "Rattlesnake," outside the Barrier Reef, which was correctly laid down, as also the general outline of the coast. But no attempt had been made to survey inside the reef, and this deficiency we desired to remedy.

Immediately to the east of Redscar Head, the out-lying Barrier Reef lifts itself to the surface, at a distance varying from three to eight miles off shore, and guards the coast from the surf. Simultaneously with its appearance the coast rises, and precipitous round-topped grassy hills, openly timbered, and backed up by higher ranges inside, spring from the white coral and sandy beach. Between these hills fertile valleys lie, and villages nestle, with groves of cocoa-nut trees surrounding them. The houses are built in the Malay fashion, on poles, some standing far out on the shore reefs, in quiet waters, others clustering amongst plantations on the hill side. This change from low mangrove swamp to fine hilly land is as refreshing to the eye, weary with that dead sameness, as it is sudden. From Redscar Head to Hood Point, a distance of seventy miles, not a stream was to be seen falling into the sea. We found some trickling rivulets and some water holes, but no clear running stream. The soil in the valleys is of a black, peaty, spongy nature, which probably absorbs the rain as it falls.

After examining a vast extent of unknown reefs, we landed the first day to dine on Cliff Island, a flat coral rock covered with grass, and a few bushes and trees, and Mr. Mourilyan shot the two solitary inhabitants, a pigeon and a jungle fowl. From this spot as far as eye could see, the water inside the Barrier Reef appeared to be blocked up by coral, eastward, but on continuing our soundings, we found a fine deep water passage leading east between these reefs and the mainland. Reaching an island, since named by us Lily Island, Mr. Mourilyan in the cutter kept to the deep water passage outside it, and I attempted to take the galley between it and the island, and found that there is no inner passage, as the island is joined to the mainland by long sandy spits. We grounded opposite a large village, standing on poles, far out in the clear blue water, and stretching back into the verdure that climbed the undulating hills. The natives came off at once, some in canoes, some wading, all unarmed, to the number of about 100, and closed round us, with amazement in their faces, but not a shade of fear. This was a new experience to us, for at all the unchristianised islands we had visited, the natives had been armed and on their guard. We were probably the first white men seen by them, and their curiosity was so eager that our men mistook it at first, and seized their arms; but I had noticed not only that the natives were unarmed, but that their women and children had all turned out on the beach to see us. I therefore bid our men lay down their arms and welcome the New Guinea men as friends—and friends the kindly creatures proved.

After they had handled us to their heart's content, we induced them to track our boat through a narrow channel, and thus rejoined the cutter. We then took a series of soundings from Lily Island to Fisherman's Islets, which are of low sandy formation and covered with scrub, which is the home of innumerable Torres Straits pigeons. Here we supped on a delicious stew of these birds, and then the boats, converted by their rain-awnings into floating tents, were hauled off and anchored. The men lit their pipes, and readings and songs followed, each boat trying to outvie the other, till nine o'clock, when all lay down to sleep. There were no mosquitoes, and it was a calm moonlight night, so we slept like princes till half-past 5 A.M. Then we landed, cooked breakfast, cleaned our arms, and had the usual morning prayers, after which Mr. Mourilyan took the cutter to examine a large bay in the mainland, to the north of Fisherman's Islets, whilst I attempted to find a passage by which a ship might pass through the Barrier Reef. From the boat I could see nothing but a mass of reefs, so climbing the steep rugged sides of Pyramid Point on the mainland, about eight miles from Fisherman's Islets, I stood at the height of 643 feet above the sea. From thence I could see, for miles on either side, every coral patch that lay relieved by its clear pale green from the blue of the deep water. The Barrier Reef stretched away like a green ribbon floating on the sea, till lost to sight; its edge fringed all along by a line of snow-white surf, that looked as soft as down. At one point the ribbon was broken into two—a piece of blue untroubled water lay between—and this I felt would prove the entrance I sought. A group of small islets, unmarked on the chart, lay just below us; so, turning to the fine young seaman beside me, I asked him if he would wish them to bear his name, and shall not easily forget his look of pleasure as he assented. The islets accordingly appear in the chart as "Head Islets." The whole scene was lovely; the sea was studded with green islets, beautiful bays ran into the land, villages came clustering down to the brink of the calm water, and running out into the shallows, and the rich high land behind, closed in all with its wooded hills, steeped in the glow of a vertical sun. I made my notes, and descending, found my men on the best of terms with a crowd of natives, who were bartering their feathers and cocoa-nuts for beads. These people were perfectly harmless and friendly, but we found out, after their leaving us, that they had pilfered some small articles that were lying loose in the boat. It was now too late to make use of the knowledge I had gained from Pyramid Point, and I was tired out besides, so we supped on our frequent fare of pigeons, and anchoring under the lee of a newly found islet, were asleep as soon as our heads were laid down.

Next morning saw us early astir, making for the hoped-for entrance; and on reaching the spot we soon assured ourselves that a passage did exist there, about three-quarters of a mile wide, and bottomless as far as our lines went. With our boat's bows resting on one horn of the reef, her stern was in deep water, so perpendicularly does this coral wall rise from its ocean depths. The cutter had gone to the bay to complete her survey, so we joined her there, and Mr. Mourilyan met me with the news that an opening existed at the head of the bay, which might lead to a landlocked harbour. The bay itself was a reward for our labour, as it formed a fine sheltered anchorage, but we earnestly desired that our hope of finding a harbour here might be realised, as up to this time the wild exposed anchorage of Redscar Bay had been the only known shelter for ships on the entire south coast of New Guinea, east of Torres Straits. We went at once to examine the opening at the head of the bay, and to our delight found that it was a deep water passage, leading into a broad sheet of calm water, two miles by one and a-half in extent, deep enough nearly everywhere to float the largest ship; and we resolved that the "Basilisk" should be the first ship to honour the new harbour with her presence. We landed on a wooded island, about 600 feet high, at the head of the outer bay—since named by us Jane Island—and found a fine well there, from which the natives aided us to fill our water barricoes. They were as friendly as possible; even the women and children thronged round us for strings of red beads. We had come upon them in their "age of stone," and they had no knowledge of the use of iron, which we offered them; but they were willing to exchange their axes and adzes, made of a kind of green stone, and set into curved wooden handles, for our beads. By sunset we had regained our first camping place on Fisherman's Islets, and there, after supper, and reading and songs as usual, we betook ourselves to rest. Next morning early we started for the ship, and were dismayed on coming within five miles of her, to see her steaming out to sea. After an hour's anxiety she saw us, and when we got on board we found that Lieutenant Hayter had grown anxious, and was coming down the coast to look for us.

The ship, where we met her, was surrounded by coral reefs, in an open bay, and had barely water enough to float her, and this so discoloured as to hide the reefs, we therefore gave it the name of Caution Bay, as a warning to future navigators. We had an anxious time in getting out of the bay, but Providence was good to us, and we extricated ourselves at last, and proceeded for the new harbour which all hands were anxious to see.

At ten o'clock on Friday morning, the "Basilisk" was off the opening we had found in the reef, henceforth to be known as Basilisk Passage, and from the foretop, whence every reef could be seen, I conned her through the passage into the still waters of Port Moresby to Jane Island, and past it into landlocked many-bayed Fairfax Harbour, where we anchored in five fathoms water. As we broke into these unknown waters I determined that the outer and inner harbours should bear these names of my father, the venerable admiral of the fleet.

Port Moresby, situated where coral and white sand has succeeded the low mangrove-covered coast, lies in latitude 9° 30′ south, and longitude 147° 10′ east. The entrance is good, and the land, which is covered with many trees, rises gently on either side, to a considerable height. The inner, Fairfax Harbour, is an irregular basin surrounded by round-topped grassy hills, having the Australian gum-tree scattered over them, with rich valleys between. The depth of water is from between seven and four fathoms to within a few yards of the beach. The sides of the hills are well cultivated, and yield abundance of yams and taro.

We must have been a surprising sight to the natives, for they flocked on board in hundreds, eager and curious, chattering like monkeys, as they pointed out to each other the marvels that took their fancy.

Mr. Mourilyan and I now began to make a survey of the harbour, and Lieutenant Hayter went away with the galley and a fresh crew to continue our exploration inside the Barrier Reef, for forty miles east of Port Moresby to Hood's Point, where the barrier reef curves in and joins the mainland, forming a *cul-de-sac.*

A singular feature in this hilly country, intersected by deep valleys, is the almost total absence of running water. The soil is very porous, and the streams probably take an underground course till they reach the mangrove swamps, in which the valleys abutting on Fairfax Harbour terminate.

We went to visit one of the hill villages in the afternoon, going quite unarmed, such was our confidence in the people, and climbing a steep hillside sprinkled with gum trees, and covered with granite boulders and quartz, found ourselves overlooking a rich tropical valley, and saw the village on the opposite hillside amongst abundant trees. The thin rocky soil gave place as we began to descend the slope, to rich dark mould, from which grass sprang nearly shoulder high, varied with occasional clumps of splendid hard wood, tropical trees, and groups of the sago palm. Here and there spaces, some three acres in extent, were enclosed by stiff bamboo fences, and produced bananas, yams, and taro in profusion, although no effort seemed to be made to keep the weeds under. The bananas, which were nearly ripe, were tied up in leaves to save them from the flying foxes.

The village consisted of about six houses, built on poles, and looking as if they were marching out from amongst the trees on stilts. The houses, which consisted of one room as usual, were tenanted below, in the space between the poles, by pigs and wretched looking dogs, that kept up an eager fight for the pieces of broken cocoa-nut that had fallen from above to their share. The villagers gave us a few stone clubs and wooden spears in exchange for our bottles and beads, but would not look at our iron-hoop and axes. They were not nearly so much adorned with feathers and shells as their neighbours on the seashore, and I fancied their complexion to be of a slightly darker shade. Their only tools for turning up the soil were stone adzes, capable of penetrating for about four inches. We showed the women a looking-glass, and they started back and would not look a second time. I offered my watch to be examined, but no one would touch the possessed-looking thing.

All the valleys we travelled over were covered with rich grass, shoulder high, and had we possessed an army of Irish scythes, and an English market, we might have cut down our fortune. The hills on the north of the harbour are separated from a loftier range behind by extensive grass plains, abounding in water holes, well dotted over with timber, and having a rich black soil.

Nothing could exceed the kindness of the natives, in proof of which I will mention but one fact. Mr. Watts, one of our engineers, lost his way the evening before our visit to this village, and when beginning to grow anxious, fell in with a party of natives; far from attempting to take any advantage of his helplessness, they fed him, and took him to their village, making signs that they wished him to sleep there. Finding that he wanted to return to his companions, they offered to guide him, stipulating, however, that he should show himself off in the village first, and permit all the inhabitants to admire his white skin. This he did with a great deal of pleasure, placing himself on a verandah, to be handled and gazed at by scores of beholders.

The large village at the entrance to Port Moresby, which consists of two rows of well-built houses, separated by groves of cocoa-nut trees, was often visited by us. Its inhabitants, numbering perhaps 800 of all ages, were well fed, contented-looking people. The women seemed to busy themselves much in pottery, and moulded clay into large globe-shaped jars, which they baked slowly amongst the embers of wood fires. They use these jars much in their cookery, and I have partaken of a vegetable porridge cooked in them, consisting of mangrove fruit, taro, and yams, with cocoa-nut finely shred over all, and found it excellent. They are skilful in netting bags and fishing-nets, which they do so precisely in our mode that our men often took up their shuttles and went on with the net. These nets are made of the fibre of a small nettle-like plant, and are shaped like our English seine.

On one occasion an incident happened here which

bringing with them a bundle of rushes, and knotting them together carefully measured the length and breadth of the ship. They evidently wished to preserve a record of the size, for they stowed the rush line away in their canoe with many signs of wonderment.

At most of the villages on this coast we observed that the men liked to hold our hands as we walked through, and that they did not wish us to enter their houses; but if we pressed the point they yielded in this, and awaited us patiently outside. We used sometimes to sit and rest on the verandah or landing-place outside the door of the upper storey, and they would bring us fresh cocoa-nut milk, or some of the sago they had boiled for their meal. These people, and all the light-coloured Malay race of eastern New Guinea, are without bows and arrows. As far as Redscar Bay we saw toy bows amongst the children, but beyond that point the bow ceases altogether, till it reappears on the northern shores, west of Astrolobe Gulf. The houses visited by us all contained spears and stone weapons, some of the latter very well shaped and finished.

On Wednesday, 26th, Lieutenant Hayter returned, having made some soundings and diligently examined over fifty miles of coast, in which neither harbour nor river were to be seen. He confirmed our good opinion of the natives, saying that he had found them friendly on all occasions. Walking over the hills that evening, Dr. Goodman and I were much struck with the surprised us. A number of natives came on board, beauty of some parrots flying from tree to tree. The bodies were black, wings green, and heads and tails scarlet.

Next day was an anxious but successful one. I had set my heart on finding a passage for the ship by an inshore route between the mainland and Barrier Reef back to the anchorage in Redscar Bay, so as to prove that Port Moresby might be reached thus, as well as through the opposite opening in the Barrier Reef which we had named Basilisk Passage. With Mr. Bentley by my side, therefore, I conned the ship from the foretop for twenty miles through the winding channel which we had previously discovered running between reefs, and giving us several times but three feet of water to spare under our keel. It was an anxious time, but we never touched, and dropped anchor safe and sound in Redscar Bay, having established the fact of the existence of a passage. What a miserable spot the bay seemed after lake-like, mountain-girt Port Moresby!—so dreary-looking, so exposed too to the full strength of the S.E. monsoon. And this anchorage, lying four miles out at sea, was the only one known on the S.E. coast of New Guinea till the discovery of Port Moresby. Was it any wonder if we were all inclined to exult a little?

At daylight, on the 28th, Mr. Mudge and I started with the galley to explore the remaining or northern branch of Redscar River, and calling at the Towton village, shipped one of the native teachers as pilot, and made sail over the broad sheet of Galley Reach in a north-easterly direction to its head. Arrived there, we could find no principal river. A mangrove swamp lay before us, subject to frequent inundations, and cut up into innumerable channels, some of which were broad enough to raise our hopes. We explored several of these, but invariably the mangroves and bastard palms closed in on us till we could no longer move our oars; and farther on, the canoe paddles, to which we betook ourselves, were stopped by the narrowness of the ditch and the rank vegetation that overhung it. More than once we lost our way, though every precaution was taken, and each change noted on a tracing; and a dread came over me that we might have to pass a night in this dismal swamp, the home of reptiles and fever. The thick vegetation caused a gloom that amounted in places to darkness, and at times we had to stand up in the boat and cut our way through the tangled creepers. As our paddles struck the muddy banks, little slimy creatures slid away from us, and myriads of spider-crabs crawled out, tiny things, with burnished shells, white, brown, and red, not larger than a shilling, and escaped with great swiftness. This was the only animal life we saw here.

After much effort we succeeded in extricating ourselves from this foul choking labyrinth, and anchored in the head waters of Galley Reach, where we refreshed ourselves with dinner. Here myriads of flying-foxes came about us, and I shot one, but it hung on by the hooks of its wings on a high tree, and when dislodged by another shot, fell into the water and sank like a stone. Dinner over, we once more took to our oars, and pulled for the mouth of a considerable river which we had observed emptying itself into Galley Reach, about two miles from its head. The heat was most oppressive, but we pulled up this new river till dark. We had divided ourselves into two sets, each of which took a half-hour's spell at the oars in turn. Mr. Mudge, two seamen, and I, made one party, and the four remaining seamen the other. As evening closed in we looked out anxiously for a spot on which to land and boil some water for our tea, but could see none. At last, on a knot of dryer mud than the rest, we contrived to make a fire and refresh ourselves with that greatest of all comforts after such a day's work—a basin of tea; after which we prepared ourselves as if for an Arctic night to defy the mosquitoes—pulling on two pairs of trousers and two coats apiece, boots, thick stockings, and gloves; wrapping the head, neck, and ears in bunting, and smearing our faces with oil; and this done we hauled off into the stream for the night. Some of us had three hours of broken sleep, but those who had left any part of the body unprotected did not even doze. In the morning our clothes were as wet with perspiration as if they had been dipped over the side, but anything was better than being covered with mosquito bites. We began our work with the first streak of day, and groped along through the dense malarious fog that filled the channel, till the sun arose and drank it up, when we pulled on cheerily, looking for a spot to land on and cook breakfast; but all was dank swamp, covered with rank vegetation, through which trees shot up to a height of 200 feet, whilst bastard palms trailed their leaves, thirty and forty feet long, in the muddy tide of what had now become a rapid fresh-water river.

We landed at last, and tried hard to light a fire, but could not succeed, though we used carbolic acid, so had to content ourselves with a cold breakfast.

The swiftness of the current now increased rapidly, and uprooted trees and logs came shooting with the stream round its abrupt corners, and made progress dangerous. These trees at last made such a barrier that we were obliged to yield to circumstances and turn the boat's head backwards, leaving to those who shall follow us the honour of reaching the Highlands of New Guinea by this water-way. The depth at our turning-point, about ten miles from the mouth of this branch, was close on twelve feet, the breadth some thirty yards.

It is impossible for me to express an opinion as to how far the swiftness of these two rivers, named by us the Usborne and the Edith, may be due to the obstructions which have fallen across their course, but I think they must considerably influence it. Explorers coming to the two points where we left off, with light portable boats, could easily settle this question. Both rivers could be ascended without difficulty by steam-launches, and used for rafting down timber and other produce to the sea. Leaving an ample supply

M

of provisions with the Samoen teachers, we weighed at sunset for Cape York. Sunday, 2d, was a day of rest, hailed by many, for those of us who had been most away from the ship were tormented with boils and prickly heat, the result of continual exposure, and fatigued with constant rowing, and effort of all kinds. We anchored for the night off Bramble Cay, where Mr. Hayter and party were fortunate in capturing a fine hawk's-bill turtle before morning. It rained and blew hard next day, but we ran on from island to island, and anchored at Albany Pass, Somerset, at 8 o'clock P.M., on Wednesday 5th, in a heavy squall of wind and rain, where we found our store-ship, the "Restless," awaiting us. Monday came with water-spouts of rain, but we got the "Restless" alongside, and began to take in our stores.

At Somerset we found eighty-five disappointed diggers returning from the gold-fields at Port Darwin, in the barque "Springbok." They were suffering dreadfully from want of provisions and stores; and the master had proved so incompetent that a Naval Court, which I appointed to examine into the charges, removed him from his command. I placed Sub-Lieutenant Alan Waters in command of the "Springbok," thus entrusting him with as difficult and responsible a task as could well fall to the lot of so young an officer; not only had he to keep in subjection these eighty-five unruly men, rendered doubly difficult to manage by the privations they were enduring, but also to navigate a heavy ship against a strong monsoon, through most intricate navigation, inside the great Barrier Reef. It speaks well for the professional ability of young officers of the present day that Mr. Waters was able to maintain his authority over these rough diggers, under exceedingly trying circumstances, and thrashing his ship through all dangers, to bring his half-famished crew in safety to Newcastle, N.S.W.

On March 7th, Navigating-Lieutenant Connor, and Mr. Pitt, midshipman, rejoined us from their survey on the northern shore of Torres Straits. These two officers, and their nine men, had been detached for six weeks in open boats, exposed to a tropical sun, and to severe weather on a lee shore, and now returned, having made a highly valuable trigonometrical survey of Saibai and Cornwallis Islands, and of a part of the New Guinea Coast. It is impossible to describe the relief and pleasure it gave us to welcome our shipmates amongst us again, all safe and in rude health; burnt nearly as dark as Papuans with exposure, but willing to start away again if more work should call them.

We handed over the three native teachers and two wives, brought by us from Redscar Bay, to Mr. Murray, with their health all but re-established, which was satisfactory, the poor creatures being very grateful for the kindness shown them on board. I addressed a report to Mr. Murray on the state in which we had found the mission stations visited by us, and gave him a full and true account of the unprovided and actually starving state of the Polynesian teachers placed on these Torres Straits Islands by the London Missionary Society, and left alone to fight a losing battle against famine, sickness, want of knowledge of the languages required, and the contempt and hostility of fierce Papuan heathen. The Rev. A. W. Murray, with his wife, had arrived from Sydney, and taken up his quarters at Cape York, in a bungalow, kindly placed at their service by Mr. Jardine, and from this central point he hoped to control and sustain the various mission parties scattered not only on the islands of Torres Straits, but even as far as Redscar Bay, on the New Guinea coast, more than 300 miles from Cape York. He laboured, however, under the difficulty of having no vessel, nor other means of communication with these widely separated stations; and reports of death and disaster attacking these unfortunate native teachers were arriving up to the time of our leaving Cape York to make this late cruise. Under these circumstances I had been glad to make myself useful, and take such supplies for them as Mr. Murray could provide. I had now to inform him that I had found the real state of these poor creatures far worse than anticipated. At Jarvis Island their only store of food, when visited by us, consisted of ten or twelve pounds of salt meat for four adults and two infants, but this island being a pearl-shelling station, they were kept from actual starvation by the humanity of the pearl-shellers; and were living in a poor and very uncleanly native hut, wholly without influence of any kind over the natives of the island. At Cornwallis they were better off, having a roomy house, and good sweet potato and melon gardens; but of the four teachers, their wives and children, one child and three adults were down with fever, and Dr. Goodman, on examining their medicine, had reported that they possessed no proper medicines, nor any understanding to guide them in using such medicines as they had. At Murray Island the two teachers and their wives were well off, having good native houses, and plenty of yams, but they complained much of having no trade to purchase other food from the natives. The circumstances of the teachers at Redscar may have already been described, but it may be added that but for our visit, and the abundant supplies we gave them, it seemed most probable that all would have perished.

At Bampton Island the two native teachers and their wives, who had been posted there some months previously, and had not since been visited nor supplied, had been murdered by the natives.

I am glad to know that matters have now been put on a better footing. The Society has sent out a small steamer, which is to have her headquarters at Cape York, and by means of this vessel regular communication will be maintained with the various stations. Several younger labourers have also taken the place of the venerable Mr. Murray, who has well earned rest after a lifetime of faithful labour and much success. It pained me to make the above reports to this worthy gentleman, but I felt that he would generously understand that an onus lay on me to see to the welfare of all natives claiming the protection of the English flag, whether pearl-shellers or Christian teachers; and in this belief I was not mistaken.

CHAPTER XII.

DETACH MR. CONNOR AND PARTY AGAIN—SAIL FROM CAPE YORK—FIND WATER ON HAMMOND ISLAND—RE-VISIT PEARL-SHELLING STATIONS—SAIL FOR EAST COAST OF NEW GUINEA—ANCHOR OFF YULE ISLAND—FIND AN ENTRANCE TO ROBERT HALL SOUND, SURVEY AND NAME IT—EXPLORE HILDA AND ETHEL RIVERS—SAIL FOR EAST NEW GUINEA—STATE OF KNOWLEDGE THEN EXISTING AS TO THIS COAST—TESTE ISLAND—BELL ROCK—TRACES OF DEVIL-WORSHIP—FIND THE SO-CALLED "SOUTH-EAST EXTREMITY OF NEW GUINEA" TO BE AN ERROR—OUR INTERCOURSE WITH THE NATIVES.

WE expected to receive fresh orders from the commodore by the "Restless," but none having come I had to remain in this part of the station till relieved by another ship, about the 1st of June. Two months, therefore, lay at our disposal, to be employed in cruising in Torres Straits and on the south coast of New Guinea.

From Lord Normanby I had received a request to co-operate with Mr. Jardine in selecting another site for the establishment at Somerset,—one better suited to increasing requirements. I also determined to revisit the principal pearl-shelling stations, and see that all was right there; but these two duties would barely occupy a week. Before our leaving Sydney the question of the exploration of the unknown south-east coast of New Guinea had been publicly discussed, attention having been particularly called to that great island by the sad fate of the "Maria" expedition.

Notes of alarm were sounded, to the effect that

Russian, French, and Italian travellers were now exploring this island, the possession of which must in the future be a necessity to Australia because of its near vicinity and its strategic and relative geographical position, and it was feared that these efforts might lead to a foreign occupation in time.

Amongst other rumours it was reported that Americans were about to send an expedition from San Francisco to examine the eastern shores of the island. I deeply felt the importance of forestalling any attempts of alien nations to establish a claim to this great island, knowing that foreign possession might lead to complications, and feeling that the development of the great Australian Empire would be cramped in the future should its progress be arrested in the north. I desired also to secure for England the honour due to a country which had sent Cook, and Dampier, and Owen Stanley to these seas, by filling in the last great blank remaining in their work, and laying down the unknown outlines of East New Guinea on the map of the world.

My means to accomplish these desires were very small; I had but two months' time at my disposal, and was confined by my orders to the eastern limit of 148° E. longitude, just the longitude of Port Moresby, a paragraph in which, however, gave me power to go beyond this degree should circumstances warrant it.

I had received directions from the commodore to make all possible inquiries and search for Mr. Macklay, the eminent Russian traveller, who had been wandering in New Guinea, and this search, combined with duties to be performed under the kidnapping Act, might, I hoped, give us opportunity to render good service.

Before leaving Cape York I again entrusted Navigating-Lieutenant Connor with the charge of a survey on the northern shores of Torres Straits. This energetic officer had not been idle during our stay at Somerset, but instead of enjoying the rest he had so well earned, had busied himself in making a trigonometrical survey of the harbour at Somerset, which I had pleasure in forwarding to the Admiralty.

Mr. Pitt, midshipman, was succeeded by Mr. Grant, midshipman, as second to Navigating-Lieutenant Connor. Every possible precaution was taken to secure the comfort and safety of the small company to be left behind; and our shipmates left us for two months' work with that light-hearted energy which young officers and seamen always feel when going away on detached service.

The gun-room mess was now reduced to the number of two midshipmen and an assistant-paymaster, Mr. Byron, a zealous young officer, ready to make himself useful on all occasions. Our senior lieutenant, boatswain, and gunner, were now our only executive officers; but no ship ever had better petty-officers than the "Basilisk," and during the frequent absences of these remaining officers on surveying work during our coming cruise, they performed the ordinary duties of lieutenants in a satisfactory manner.

On March 20th we sailed from Cape York for our anxious cruise, which seemed to hold out possibilities of useful issues. Our first object was to examine Hammond Island, which is situated at the western entrance, by which all ships are advised to enter Torres Straits, and to leave them when coming from the eastward, and is thus on the direct track of all passing vessels, besides being in a position that commands the pearl-shell fisheries. These advantages seem to mark it out as the proper site for the English settlement in these waters. The island is about three miles and a half by one and a half in extent, high and rocky on the western side, which commands the entrance to Torres Straits, and sprinkled over with boulders. The hills on the island are precipitous, and rise to a height of 600 feet. Mr. Mudge and Mr. Bentley went on shore with two parties to explore in different directions. I took a third party; and Mr. Mourilyan went to take soundings off shore. One object was to find water, and this we all succeeded in doing. My party fortunately landed at a bay into which a stream of fresh water, almost large enough to be called a river, was discharged, and this was the more welcome as the Torres Straits Islands are almost wholly destitute of water. We followed the stream up through a deep rocky gorge, amongst scenes as picturesque as can be imagined. Sometimes it was lost to sight in a gloomy depth, overhung by tropic growth, then it rose again, racing and foaming over huge boulders, forming here waterfalls ten or fifteen feet deep, and there deep stilly pools, from which it slipped softly down. On reaching the summit we found that the hills spread themselves out into a large concave plain, forming a great natural reservoir, from which many streams descended, a very cheering discovery. The island is well wooded, and also possesses extensive clear grass plots, but except on the heights the soil is poor. Mr. Mourilyan's soundings soon showed that safe and commodious anchorage can be obtained here in perfectly smooth water, and out of the strong currents which sweep through Prince of Wales's Channel, on either the north-east or north-west of the island, according as the north-west or south-east monsoons prevail. The shore-reefs here also afford facilities for running out piers, whilst the loftiness of the island would doubtless render it a healthy station. Having thus enabled ourselves to report favourably of Hammond Island, we proceeded to take up the second part of our work, and revisited the principal pearl-shelling establishments on the various islands, which we found still idle and awaiting government licenses.

We visited Cornwallis, and sailed for Warrior Island on the 26th, when we had a narrow escape, for, set out of our way by a strong flood-tide, we ran right over an unknown shoal, and for some time had only three fathoms of water—nine inches above our draft—under the keel. Every moment we expected to hear the horrible grating noise, and feel the life-like motion of the ship reduced to stillness. We anchored, and when the tide slackened got clear without having touched a grain of sand. The anxieties of years seemed to have crowded into that short time—all our hopes of good service; the very safety of the ship, were jeopardised.

Leaving Torres Straits on the 28th of March, we sailed on our way to the east coast of New Guinea, glad indeed to be clear of the intricacies of Torres Straits, with a new and unentered field of work stretching away before us. At Bramble Cay we tried for türtle as before, with no success; but the men brought off buckets full of sea-bird's eggs, which were sweet and well-tasted. Many of the stupid birds allowed themselves to be knocked down with sticks, and the men appeared to enjoy eating them, in spite of a rank fishy taste.

Our first point was Yule Island, off which we had seen the large quantity of driftwood, that had led me to hope we should find some great river issuing from the New Guinea mainland here.

On Sunday, at 7 P.M., we anchored off Yule Island, and spent a quiet day; lying just opposite to what seemed the mouth of a large river, but we had learned by this time not to trust to appearances, and did not hope too much. Yule Island had been laid down on the chart by the "Rattlesnake," when she passed along the coast in 1849, but no white man had ever penetrated to the noble-looking sheet of water which lay inside between it and the mainland. We began on Monday 1st to sound for an entrance into it, attempting this simultaneously by the north and south channels, Mr. Mourilyan and I working at the north, which we believed to be the most hopeful, as the Stanley survey marked it as "probably a clear passage," whilst Mr. Pitt sounded out the south. The result of our work was exactly contrary to our expectations, for we found the north entrance blocked by reefs, and the north side of the harbour a great mud flat; whilst the south entrance, supposed to be blocked by reefs, proved to be a good safe channel. The former surveyors had doubtless been deceived by the discoloured state of the water, caused by the amount of fresh water escaping here. Through this channel we now took the "Basilisk" in, and she soon lay at anchor in the broad waters of *Robert Hall Sound*, as we decided to name this, our second found harbour on the south New Guinea coast, after the secretary of the Admiralty. Robert Hall Sound lies in lat. 9° N., and long. 146° 3′ E., and is well marked by Yule Island at its entrance. It is perfectly protected and land-locked, and has deep water, where hundreds of ships may lie in safety. The land surrounding it, excepting for some comparatively bold headlands, is low and swampy ground, backed up six or eight miles inland by low hills, behind which range rises after range, till the magnificent Owen Stanley range is reached as a culminating point.

Yule Island, near which ships would anchor, is high and healthy ground. At the head of the harbour two rivers issue, combined, forming the river mouth which had raised our expectations on Sunday. Of these, Hilda River, a rapid powerful stream, with too swift a current to be ascended by row boats, but navigable for steam launches, falls into Ethel River, a mile and a half from its embouchement, and is doubtless destined in time to bear the rich produce of the interior downwards on its rapid bosom. Ethel River upwards, from the point of junction, assumes the character of a sluggish stream, from 80 to 100 yards in width, and twelve feet deep, and leads eastward through an immense mangrove swamp. We ascended it for about ten miles, when, much to our disappointment, it divided itself into a number of small channels without a current, some of which were examined by us, but proved not to lead to the hills. The scenery on the river banks was monotonous in the extreme—a dense growth of mangrove and other moisture-loving trees prevailing, with no animal life to enliven it, for, with the exception of flying foxes and some screaming gaudy-coloured birds, nothing living was to be seen or heard.

Occasionally ill-made native huts were to be seen on the banks, from which a track through the swamp led to some acres of raised ground, like an oases in a desert. These were carefully cleared and cultivated. Here also were some permanent houses, built as usual on poles some eight feet from the ground, with one room common to the whole family. The natives hid themselves in the swamp when we came into sight; indeed it must have appeared to them as if we had dropped from the clouds. It seemed marvellous that human life could exist in such a malarious vile place. Even in the glare of a noonday sun the air was thick with mosquitoes.

I longed for a steam pinnace to ascend Hilda River, for it maintained its depth, and evidently ran up into the heart of the country, and it was bitterly disappointing to have to leave the fact unverified. Our men pulled their hardest, but the current was too powerful, and the banks were a mass of intertwined jungle. I started, after our return to the ship, with an armed party, to try and find out the villages on Yule Island, and on landing we met with some natives, who seemed very adverse to our going to their village. After a while I made them signs that we wanted rest, and they took us by a long winding path through the bush, to a large cleared space where their village stood, each house being the usual large oval-shaped room raised on poles. At a little distance in the rear were large vegetable and fruit plantations, neatly fenced in, and well kept. Taking us to a large house, some forty feet in length, and entirely unoccupied, they made signs that we might rest in it, which we did, whilst refreshing ourselves with cocoa-nut milk. The villagers continued very timid, and all their young women and children were kept out of sight in the bush, where we could hear them chattering and laughing. Any movement of ours in their direction met with energetic remonstrance from the men. However, the older women were about amongst us, so I was satisfied that we should not be attacked. The houses, except the one devoted to our use, were all shut up, and the entrance-doors barred.

Our attempts to trade met with small success, for, having no conception of the use of iron, they would not barter their handsome stone implements for our axes. The more we endeavoured to show their superior value by cutting and chopping branches, the more incredulously they smiled, and preferred their own rude instruments.

Before long their curiosity at our white skins, clothes, and watches, etc., having become exhausted, they made signs that they wished us to go. Before going I thought to try the effect of firearms on their minds, so, placing a mark against a tree, and preparing the natives to expect something wonderful, I had a shot fired. The first effect was blank amazement, and the second, when they saw the hole made by the ball, an increased anxiety to be rid of us. They would not touch our rifles, but pushed them away with terror. Returning to the ship we met natives in their canoes diving for cray-fish on the coral reef in one and two fathom water. Standing in their canoes, they waited till they saw the big unsuspicious cray-fish crawl leisurely over the coral beneath, and then flashed overboard, and rarely missed their prey.

A quantity of fine steel sand was found in Robert Hall Sound.

The people here are of the Malay type, but differ from the pure Malay in being less in stature, coarser in feature, thicker lipped, and having less hair on the face—being, indeed, almost beardless. They have high cheek-bones, like the pure Malay, but their noses are inclined to be aquiline, and are sometimes well formed; their eyes are dark and beautiful, with good eyebrows. The men have their hair frizzed out in a mop, but the women cut theirs short, and tatoo their bodies in graceful lace-like patterns, which the men never do. They, however, are not without adornment, for they paint with black, red, and white pigments; and wear flowers, and the plumes of the Bird of Paradise, fastened to their heads and shoulders, and occasionally two great beaks of the hornbill, as horns on the head. They were much disfigured by constant use of the betel-nut. Unlike the Port Moresby natives, they are possessed of bows and arrows, of spears, and clubs of wood and stone, and they seemed to us to be less kindly disposed than the Port Moresby people. They are equally ignorant of the use of iron, and no sign of cannibalism was visible at either place. This race abuts on the black Papuan, somewhere in the vicinity of Cape Possession; but I do not believe that a fixed line of demarcation exists, for here both types of race were present, and the natives varied in colour, stature, and cast of feature. A mixture of habits also obtained here, which confirmed the idea of a fusion of races, for some chewed the betel-nut Malay-wise, whilst others rejected it; some wore the specially Papuan adornment of the great bill of the hornbeak on the head, and all were entirely destitute of the ornaments of human bone that we afterwards

N

found to be generally worn to the eastward. It must, however, be taken into account that natives from different parts of the coast, perhaps attracted by the news of our presence, kept arriving during our stay, as this would perhaps account in part for the different habits and shades of colour we observed.

On the morning of April 6th we weighed at eight o'clock, and stood for East New Guinea, having anxious work before us, and very few hands to do it with just then,—Mr. Hayter being laid up with a throat affection, and Mr. Shortland ill; so that Mr. Mourilyan, Mr. Pitt, and the two warrant officers, were the only ones left at this time to do duty. Our work lay where no navigator had ever laid down a line for us to follow.

Bongainville, D'Entrecasteaux, D'Urville, and Captain Owen Stanley, had all seen what they took to be the eastern extremity of New Guinea, but did not approach near enough to define the outline of the land seen by them. H.M.S. "Blanche" had the previous year approached the eastern shores of New Guinea from E.N.E., but, meeting dangerous shoals, had anchored thirty-four miles from the nearest point of the mainland (East Cape), at which distance it is not visible, and twenty-one miles E.N.E. of Moresby Island, the easternmost of the large islands off the south-east extremity of New Guinea, which was thought by the "Blanche" to be the mainland (see Admiralty Chart, Papua, sheet 7, A.D. 1875, and hydrographic notices, Pacific Ocean, A.D. 1873, page 105, paragraphs

2 and 3). The "Blanche" remained in this position one night, and the following day retraced her way without having made any nearer approach, leaving the configuration of the eastern shores of New Guinea still unknown; but arriving at the same intelligent conclusion as D'Urville, that the south-east extremity of New Guinea was formed of a number of high islands.

The state of knowledge previous to the visit of the "Basilisk" as to the supposed shape of South-East New Guinea will be evident on referring to the map attached to this book.

Captain Owen Stanley, deceived, doubtless, by the configuration of the land, laid down the great range of mountains which bears his name for thirty miles farther to the eastward than it actually extends, and marked a point of land, indistinctly seen by him, as the south-eastern extremity of Papua—a point afterwards found by us to be no part of the mainland, but existing as a small island some thirty miles from the mainland of New Guinea.

Of the north-east shores of New Guinea from East Cape, as since laid down by us, and shown by the accompanying map, no knowledge existed, nor is there any record of their ever having been seen by a white man, till a point is reached, 190 miles as the crow flies, to the west. There land was indistinctly seen from a distance by D'Entrecasteaux, and named by him Cape Sud Est, by a mistake, as this position falls in reality twelve miles inland on the mountain range which rises there, and was doubtless believed by D'Entrecasteaux to be the coast-line. Beyond this a blank succeeded, which was unbroken for forty miles, till another high point of land, seen indistinctly by D'Entrecasteaux, and named by him Richie Island, was marked on the chart—a misnomer, for no island exists there, and he had in reality caught a glimpse of the mainland. This was followed by another blank of some sixty miles to the west, when Huon Gulf was marked down, after which the mainland had been traced with tolerable accuracy. The D'Entrecasteaux Islands, so named by their discoverer, who had never visited them, lying off the north-east extreme of New Guinea, were so unknown, that the sailing directions supplied to us said that they would probably be found to be not islands but an integral part of New Guinea.

The principal cause which appears to have prevented navigators from nearing these unknown shores, has been the enormous coral barrier of the Louisiade Reef, which extends from Teste Island to the east for 200 miles, and is beaten on by an everlasting surf, blown on by the S.E. monsoon for eight months of the year, and set on by strong currents which make approach dangerous. These dangers, and the supposed ferocity of the natives, have caused the mariner to give this locality a wide berth, and prevented all attempts to explore the eastern end of New Guinea. Bongainville, even in his distressed condition, preferred to beat to windward round the entire Louisiade group, rather than seek for passage here, on his way to the Dutch settlements; but my conviction was strong that a passage might be found, through the Louisiade Reef, which would open up a navigation between Australia and North-East New Guinea, and shorten the route between Australia and China.

On April 9th we finally passed out of surveyed waters, and steered for Teste Island, there to anchor for the night.

Immediately to the west of Teste Island the great Louisiade Reef sinks from the surface to a depth of ten or twelve fathoms, and remains submerged for more than 100 miles to the west. Over this, aptly named by Captain Stanley "The sunken Barrier Reef of New Guinea," I intended to pass at a point near Teste Island, and take up the survey from the Heath Point of Captain Stanley's survey. Teste Island, twenty-two miles south of the then supposed south-eastern extremity of New Guinea, had been seen from a distance of six miles by surveying ships, and put on the chart by Captain Stanley, but not visited. It is a narrow island, about two miles and a half long, and is traversed by a line of hills which rises into a peak at each end, and dips in the centre—the western peak being about 500, and the eastern 470, feet above the sea. The sides of the hills are wooded, and the tops bare and grassy. On the ridge, near the western summit, standing alone, are two remarkable trees of great size and beauty. I am unable to name their species, but we were several times struck with the prominence of similar trees towering on lofty positions.

In Teste Island, and Bell Rock—a noble mass of rock about two miles west of it, which is not more than 100 yards in circumference, and rises steep from the sea to a height of 420 feet, wooded wherever a crevice offers room for a tree to grow—nature has placed striking landmarks. Passing close to this splendid rock we saw many of the natives, whose canoes were rocking on the calm waters at its base, perched like monkeys far up on its rocky ledges, waving green branches, and making all possible signs of friendship. We returned these signs, and steered for Teste Island, from which we must have been early seen, for numerous canoes and catamarans came to us miles from the island, whose rowers did not manifest any fear of us, although an accident happened to one poor fellow which might have caused suspicion. He had seized a fishing-line which our indefatigable fisherman, Dr. Goodman, was using, to save himself the trouble of paddling, by being towed; the hook caught him, and his hands were a good deal torn. Steering for a grove of cocoa-nut trees on the north side of Teste Island we found a precarious anchorage within a cable's length of the shore.

The natives here were similar in appearance to those at Redscar and Port Moresby. They were shy of coming on board at first, but we tempted one by stripes of red cloth, and I went down into a catamaran to assure his friends, after which they crowded on board — copper-coloured intelligent-looking people, who number about 300 souls. We made up a party to visit their village, and they received us in a friendly manner, taking us by the hands as we stepped on shore, and so leading us the distance of two miles to their villages on the opposite side of the island.

Teste Island is rich in soil, and well cultivated in parts, and its backbone, of high grassy hills, slopes away at either side into fine cocoa-nut groves, and fenced-in plantations of fruits and vegetables, sufficient to feed three times the number of inhabitants. The houses, which are large, and are kept clean and neat, are simply wooden frames thatched over. I cannot better describe their appearance than by asking you to think of a large clothes-basket as inverted and placed upon poles six feet high, the basket to be forty feet long by twelve wide, with a floor laid four feet below its rim, neatly covered with mats. We found distinct traces of devil-worship here—a thing unknown in our after experience of New Guinea. The people possessed small ugly figures, carved on sticks and bowls, of hard wood, which by signs they made us understand had great power. These things were all in the keeping of the women, with whom we found it impossible to trade, whilst the men were ready to give us all they possessed for our red cloth and knives; that is, with one exception, for it was hard to induce them to part with their ornaments made from the bones of slain enemies. These consisted of bracelets of human jaw-bones and spiral rings, and as we examined these they made us understand, in a boastful way, that they had eaten their first owners.

The skulls of these unfortunates were also hung up in numbers in the villages. We made a collection of wooden swords and clubs, and then returned to the ship by a course which took us nearly all round the island, and kept us scrambling over volcanic rocks all the way, so that we were heartily ready for a plunge into the cool water when we reached the coral beach where our boats lay at anchor.

From our anchorage at Teste Island, the blue outline of the supposed New Guinea coast showed to the north at twenty miles' distance. Anxiously I scanned it for some indication of its character, and drew comfort from its lofty appearance, for it was a bold honest outline, not a mass of swamp and reef.

Hoping for the best, we left Teste Island, and steered for what was marked on the chart as the "south-east extremity of Papua, indistinctly seen," and distant from Teste Island about twenty-two miles, laying down a line of soundings as we went, and having occasional false alarms of shoal water, which proved only to be tide-rips. As we neared our destination, we found to our surprise that the so-called "south-east extremity" was nothing but a point on an island, which evidently made one of a group of small lofty islands lying about a mile off what we were now led to suppose was the true east extremity of Papua.

The weather now came on thick and squally, so we sought for an anchorage in a large bay some twelve miles to the westward of the island, which fortunately answered our expectations, and took up a sheltered berth under what we now believed to be the mainland of New Guinea. The southward land of the bay having somewhat the appearance of an island, our boats were sent to explore, and found it was such, the officer reporting it to be a small island about two miles in length, separated from the mainland by a channel only a quarter of a mile broad.

Our anchor was scarcely let go before, from the villages on the sandy shore of the bay, and from the newly-found islets, canoes of all sizes issued and hovered about us at a distance. We turned all our attention to gain the good-will of our visitors, knowing how much our future success depended on it, but for more than an hour all our peaceable signs and baits of bright-coloured cloths were unavailing. The men, in some sixteen or twenty large canoes, armed with spears and stone tomahawks, sometimes made a few strokes with their paddles as if they would venture alongside, but their hearts always failed them, and they stopped and anxiously scanned our every movement, ready for instant flight. At last, when we despaired of success, four men in one of the small canoes were induced to come near enough to receive our presents on the extreme ends of the paddles. They came still closer, and at last one bold islander, enticed by many presents, and encouraged by much patting on the back, with, "Come along, old fellow!" slowly climbed the ladder, and stood on our quarter-deck, looking scared, and squeezing his nose spasmodically with one forefinger and thumb, and his navel with the other. Guessing it might mean some form of salutation, we all responded in the same fashion. The sight was most ludicrous, but the effect was instantaneous; the scared look gave place to one of delight as he looked round, and his confidence was complete. Rejoicing in our discovery, we all stood on the gangways, and so displayed our knowledge that we made friends of the whole crowd. The only difficulty after this was to keep our new friends out of the ship. It was dark before they left us that evening to quiet and consideration of the friendly intercourse of the day, so unexpected by us after the reports we had heard of the ferocity of these people. Their surprise was always great on first coming on board at the size of the deck, and at all they saw, particularly at the brass rails and glass hatchway coverings, and they expressed it by a peculiar inarticulate sound. Our first visitors at a new place would come up the ladder by degrees, and peeping through the gangway, return to their canoes, telling the others what they had seen; then others would steal up, till at last one more bold than the rest would venture on deck. One of us would take him by the hand and lead him forward to look at the wonders of the ship, and he would then return to his companions, bring them up and (evidently proud of his position) lead them forward, and show them what he himself had seen. It was with great difficulty we could get them to approach the sheep we had on board —they appeared to think them ferocious. It appeared to afford them great amusement to watch us at meals; and they would sit in a circle round the wardroom skylight, pointing at us, and occasionally roaring with laughter, and afterwards they might be seen relating the details of the meal to their companions, and imitating our use of the knife and fork. They were willing to take anything that came from the ship in the way of barter; cocked-hats manufactured out of newspapers had a great run for a short time; pictures they seemed slow to comprehend, but would take them. Hoop-iron, however, was always in the greatest demand from the time we first offered it, and thus this anchorage came to be named "Hoop-iron Bay." The price of a pig varied here from one to three trade hatchets; and, as a proof of the honesty of the vendors, it should be told that a pig which had been bought in the daytime and had jumped overboard at night and was drowned, was brought to us by a canoe in the morning. From henceforth in New Guinea iron-hoop became the standard of value; for these natives, unlike those at Robert Hall Sound and Redscar Bay, were alive to the value of iron—some few carefully preserved specimens of which, in the shape of sharpened bolts and spike-nails, we found scattered in most of their villages. These relics were probably obtained from the eastern islands of the Louisiade Group, where ships are known to have been wrecked, and with whose inhabitants intercourse is probably held by means of the large trading canoes hailing from New Guinea, which were frequently met by us at sea.

The iron hoop and scrap iron had the most value in their eyes, for it was readily shaped into the form of their stone hatchets and fitted into the handles, so all Her Majesty's iron hoop on board was served out in equal proportions to the various messes, and our men were enabled to purchase an abundant supply of yams, fruits, and pigs. The natives here are a small, active, copper-coloured race, with frizzled hair standing out a foot from their heads, and similar in appearance to those at Port Moresby. They paint and adorn themselves in a hideous manner, principally with black and white pigments, shells, strips of bark, and palm leaves. Cassowary and Birds of Paradise head-dresses were commonly worn; and they, as well as the Teste Islanders, wear the bones of their devoured enemies as bracelets. Some of the men had the entire body blackened with a mixture of charcoal and cocoa-nut oil; and they made us understand that this was done as mourning for the death of a relation. They appeared to treat their women kindly, and permitted them to have their say in bartering, and to meet us freely. The good feeling shown towards us by these poor savages was an unspeakable comfort to me, for every reason; not the least being, that any hostility on their part would have hindered or even stopped our work.

CHAPTER XIII.

DISCOVER MORESBY ISLAND — VIEW OF D'ENTRECASTEAUX GROUP FROM CAPE LOOK-OUT—FRESH WATER FISH—TONS OF YAMS BOUGHT FOR IRON HOOP—TRADING CANOES COME FROM THE EAST—FIND A NEW STRAIT, AND CUT OFF "BASILISK" ISLAND FROM NEW GUINEA—DISCOVER CHINA STRAITS AND HAYTER ISLAND.

EARLY on Good Friday morning, Mr. Mourilyan and I started to climb to the top of the island under which we were anchored—to a height of 600 feet, for the purpose of taking angles. From the ship, O'Neill Island as we named it, appeared a precipitous ascent, crowned at the summit of the highest peak by one large and graceful tree, which forms a good landmark here, and covered with what seemed a soft velvety emerald grass. How deceitful was this latter appearance! This velvety sward proved to be coarse, sharp-edged, thickly interwoven grass, from ten to fourteen feet high. Our party—Mr. Mourilyan, the coxswain, two of the boat's crew, and I—landed at a spot clear of the village, so as to avoid delay from the natives, pushed our way through a belt of scrub, and found ourselves amongst this grass. We faced the perpetually rising grass wall boldly, thinking, at first, that every step would show us daylight beyond, but it was no short work that lay before us. Our plan was for the leading man of the party to throw himself bodily forward, and press the grass down with his dead-weight, pick himself up, and repeat the operation; and we relieved each other at this post at very short intervals. We were soon all bleeding from the sharpness of the grass; the want of circulation of air between our grassy walls, and the fierceness of the sun also, tried us sorely. The coxswain, a fine powerful man, became exhausted, and we left him behind in charge of one of the men, and struggled on, till after about two hours of effort we stood under the noble tree, with clothes cut into rags, and skin not much better, but still there, which was worth it all. After a little rest we climbed the stately trunk, and were able to look down on our grassy enemy from its branches. The glorious prospect before us took all our thoughts; but what was this? There lay the south-east end of New Guinea with its great mountain chain, cleft suddenly in twain by a bright blue thread that lay across it! We thought our eyes must be playing us false—that it could not be water, but was perhaps a blue mist lying in a deep valley, or a river. It was only visible in parts between the hills; but the valley through which it passed afforded an opening by which the sea was visible on the other side, running up in a bay to the end of this blue strait, if strait it was; and this made us exclaim "We have not yet found the true south-east extreme of New Guinea." Having taken a round of angles, we descended easily by our beaten track, found Jenkins all right, and went on board to discuss our hot-cross buns. Then came Divine service as befitted the day; and after the men had dined, Mr.

Mourilyan and I left the ship to make sure of the new discovery. There it was, plain to be seen, a noble strait, contracting in one part to a width of about a quarter of a mile, and expanding to that of three or four miles of deep navigable water, unmarked by reefs, sprinkled with islets, leading through from sea to sea. It was flanked on both sides by mountains covered with forest, that rose steep from the water's edge to a height of 1400 or 1500 feet, and were broken into picturesque valleys and gorges. A fierce tide ran through Fortescue Straits, as we named them, causing an overfall dangerous for boats in the narrow parts. These straits cut off nearly fourteen miles from New Guinea, and gave us Moresby Island. Our south-east cape of the day before was now proved to be a point not on the mainland but on Moresby Island. On Saturday 12th we began a running survey of our discoveries. My first object was to examine Fortescue Straits, with the hope that they would prove a navigable channel by which we could pass to the north side of New Guinea; and if found such, it occurred to me that I might be able to point out a new and shorter route between Australia and China, as well as open up the northern shores of New Guinea to trade. It was therefore with an exhilarated feeling that I satisfied myself that the "Basilisk" could be taken through Fortescue Straits.

Easter Sunday brought us some welcome rest, but not silence, for all day long the ship was surrounded by canoes filled with men, women, and children, who kept up a Babel of sound. On Easter Monday we made an early start, and left Hoop-iron Bay, to the great regret of our new friends, amongst whose villages our officers and men had gone freely. Taking the ship through the narrow waters lying between O'Neill and Moresby Islands, we turned sharp to the northward, and entered Fortescue Straits, through which the tide was rushing fast.

The broad waters of the great bay into which the straits opened, showed plain before us, studded over with islets that seemed asleep in a great calm. The variety of the tints seen in northern climes alone, was wanting to make the colouring of this landscape as perfect as its form. We could scarcely believe that such beauties had been hidden from European eyes till now. The "Basilisk" had to do her best to stem the tide, for we had chosen the time when it should be against us, to avoid the greater danger of being suddenly carried into unknown reefs. On clearing the straits, I congratulated myself on gaining the open sea safely, and had left the deck for a few minutes when the sound of "Three fathoms!" called from the chains, brought me quickly on deck, to find that we had passed into a labyrinth of reefs. On one of them we struck, but fortunately passed over. Reefs and broken water now appeared in all directions round; but we found our way to a snug anchorage off a good-sized inhabited island, named by us "Carrie Island," at the northern extreme of Fortescue Straits; and, as soon as the ship swung to her anchor, sent all our boats away to search for a channel through the reefs. Our disappointment at meeting these reefs was keen, as their presence threatened to make the Straits almost valueless from a practical point of view, and the more we laboured the more reefs we found; and of a particularly dangerous kind—small detached masses, from twenty to a hundred yards in circumference, with deep water channels between, scattered about everywhere, like flowers in a flower-bed. I was not without hopes of picking out a safe channel for the few miles needful, and of finding it lead speedily into a clear sea. I was possessed with a sense of the importance of finding a passage round the east end of New Guinea, and believing then in the general report of a vast extent of reefs barring the sea to the east of the land just found by us to be an island, I based all my hopes of finding a passage on this strait. All, however, was in vain. The most diligent search only proved that no safe outlet existed through the reefs that blocked the northern entrance of Fortescue Straits.

Almost despairing of taking the ship through to the northern shores of New Guinea in the limited time at my disposal, I resolved to make such surveys as were possible in the boats, which unfortunately were of the most useless description supplied to H.M. ships. A slow, heavy, eight-oared cutter, and my galley, which was a fast boat, but so lean at her ends as to be very dangerous in a sea-way.

Leaving the ship anchored at Carrie Island on April 15th, Mr. Mourilyan, Mr. Pitt, and I, made an early start in the galley and cutter, to survey the north and east shores of Moresby Island. We completed a running survey of the northern shores, which extend about twelve miles east and west, before evening, and found it strewn with villages built in the usual Malay fashion, and surrounded by plantations of sago-palm, cocoa-nut, and other fruit trees. The abrupt hills, of which the highest peak, 1326 feet high, was named by us, "Fairfax," were covered with forest trees, except on the extensive cultivated patches which ran up their sides. Towards the north-east end of the island several deep bays were passed which we had not time to examine; till, reaching the eastern extremity, I ascended a considerable hill, which I named "Cape Look-out," and anxiously scanned the sea to the east. Well it seemed to justify its supposed dangers, for reefs and broken water abounded. The view was very fine, and it was a stirring thing to be the first to gaze on the new groups of low wooded coral, and lofty volcanic islands, which thickly studded the eastern sea; and turning north to see the dark purple D'Entrecasteaux Islands, twenty miles away, separate their lofty heights from the mass of New Guinea, of which they had hitherto been often supposed an integral part. To the north-west ran a large extent of lofty land, which I supposed then to be a great unknown island, and resolved if possible to visit. I came down deeply impressed with the vast amount of work waiting to be done, and regretting the smallness of our time and means. As night closed in we ran into a capacious bay, which I named after the midshipman in charge of the cutter, "Pitt Bay;" and landing on the white coral beach of a luxuriant little island, we lighted our fires, and cooked, and ate, and talked of the events of the day, over our evening glass of grog, till the stars shone out. We were weary enough to keep early hours, and soon covering in the boats with their awnings, and paddling out into the bay beyond mosquito range, we resigned ourselves to rest. The softly lapping water was very lulling, but it was not easy to sleep at once. The half-pleasing feeling of loneliness, which the quiet and isolation of the spot was sure to produce, the sense of distance from home and friends, speculations as to what unknown thing the next day would give to our knowledge, and as to the effect our discoveries might have on the course of trade, and the future of New Guinea, refused to be dismissed. One beautiful object was of itself enough to make one wakeful—the reef over which we lay; it shone with such a clear pale effulgence, from the phosphoric creatures that floated over it.

The following morning all hands were turned up as usual, and paddling to shore we lit our fires and cooked breakfast. Then arms were cleaned and inspected, morning prayers read, and we were ready to work. During the night I had noticed that a considerable body of the tide escaped through a narrow opening into what seemed to be a part of Moresby Island, so we first explored this creek, which was scarcely wide enough to admit the passage of the boats, even when using native paddles instead of oars. and found that it cut off a considerable piece of land from Moresby Island, and led us out on the south-eastern shores. Here a multitude of islands, dotted with picturesque villages, of channels, creeks, and wooded bays, formed a fairy archipelago, which it was not easy to place on paper. It was a living picture, too, for many natives were fishing on the reefs, and paddling about in their graceful canoes. We spent as much time as we could here; but it was important that we should explore the strange land seen from Cape Look-out to the north-west, so having joined the outline of Moresby Island to the point where we had fixed it in the ship, we turned our faces towards the "Basilisk;" landing on the way, that these eastern natives might know something of us, at a large village, at the head of a fine deep bay. We were few in number, and its inhabitants might easily have attacked us had they been so disposed; but they received us with the greatest cordiality; making the usual absurd sign of welcome, and our men strolled about, feeling quite at home, taking care of course not to separate from each other, and to be pleasant with the natives. Mr. Mourilyan and I were taken by the villagers to a fine mountain stream, with deep pools, that contained fine fresh water fish, some of which were a pound in weight. They also let us have a large supply of yams, cocoa-nuts, and a pig for our trade. A strong favourable breeze brought us back to the ship at Carrie Island in the evening, where I found that all was well, and that so extensive a trade had been opened up with the natives that several tons of yams had been bought for hoop-iron—a grand supply of farinaceous food. During our absence the ship had been visited by some trading canoes of large size which came from the east—we supposed from some of the Louisiade group. The natives appeared to fear these new-comers, and hid away till they were gone, making signs to us on their return, that they were bad men.

The two following days were devoted to attempts to find a safe passage by which the ship might pass to the north end of Fortescue Straits, but the discovery of reefs after reefs, with no anchorage near them, compelled me at last to give up this hope, and to fall back on our boats for the proposed expedition to the land seen to the north-west. This was rather a serious undertaking, but officers and men were willing workers; the weather appeared settled, and I resolved to attempt it. My chief anxiety was with respect to the conduct of the natives we might meet; they were, however, certain to be unacquainted with firearms, and the mere report of a gun would probably be sufficient to ensure our safety. Having provisioned and stored our boats for a week's cruise, a supply which was as much as we could conveniently carry, we made an early start on April 19th leaving the ship still at anchor off Carrie Island; Mr. Mourilyan being with me in the galley, and Mr. Mudge, boatswain, in charge of the cutter, and made sail to the north-west, for the lofty unknown land seen in that direction. Towards noon it fell a dead calm, with no signs of a coming breeze, and by this time we had opened an extensive bay about ten miles west of Fortescue Straits, which, it was evident from its depth, must nearly unite with the sea on the south side of New Guinea. I should have passed on had there been any wind, but the importance of giving the men a good night's rest decided me to pull in south and examine this bay, which seemed to extend about twelve miles from east to west, by five or six miles in breadth, and was studded over with wooded islets. Nearing its southern shores we looked sharply for an opening in the neck of land, a southern entrance to the bay, and every moment our impression strengthened that we were cutting off another island from the supposed length of New Guinea; there certainly could not be half-a-mile of land lying between us and the Southern Sea now, as we stood towards a sharp range of wooded hills. These hills were five or six hundred feet high, covered with thick forest, and sank in one or two places to the height of about 150 feet; I resolved to try and reach the summit of the highest of them. Presently two overlapping points seemed to separate, and through an opening, at first not bigger than a window, we saw the distant horizon. Expressions of wonder passed freely round—there lay a narrow strait before us, uniting the waters of the bay to the broad blue Southern Sea, and cutting off ten or twelve miles more from the supposed length of New Guinea. It looked as though a giant had bitten a morsel out of the narrow ridge of mountains that ran along the neck of land, and let the sea sweep through. Being anxious to explore this discovery before dark, which was just approaching, the men gave way with a will, forgetting their fatigue, and we entered these fairy-like straits, about a hundred yards wide, to which dark steep hills came down on each side. Numerous canoes were fishing in quiet coves off the straits. The crews of which paddled wildly for shore, and disappeared in the bush at our approach. We had no time to land and conciliate them, but pushed on through this remarkably beautiful opening into the great Southern Sea.

We had separated another island from New Guinea, and found ourselves now in an open bay, near a large village, on the shores of the newly discovered island, the inhabitants of which were watching us with intense interest. We were anxious to find if this narrow opening would afford a passage for the ship, and spent the remainder of daylight in examining it; but a rocky ledge, which ran across, barred it to ships, and made it dangerous even for boats at the strength of the tide, the overfall of pent-up water was so great. The island, now added to the map, formed three sides of a hollow square open to the west, its length being about nine miles east and west, and its greatest breadth about eight miles on the east, where it formed the western boundary of Fortescue Straits. We named it after our good ship "Basilisk;" and its highest peak, 900 feet high, Mount Goodman, after our worthy Doctor. The soil is generally poor, and it contained only three villages, but Mount Goodman is extensively cultivated.

I named the bay after my coxswain, Jenkins; and the islands scattered on its broad bosom after the boat's crew—fine cheerful young English seamen as ever pulled an oar. We found rest for the night on a little luxuriant button of an islet in Jenkins Bay, a high mound of rock and earth, about thirty yards in diameter, and set to work to cook; it was a good spot, and our fire soon burned cheerily. The place swarmed with pigeons, of which Mr. Mourilyan shot a goodly bag, that vastly assisted our supper; and here I may remark that the quantity of fresh food procured by our guns had certainly an influence on the health of the boats' crews employed in detached work. We hauled our boats off after supper, and anchored just over the exquisite grottoes, and bright-painted gardens of a South Sea coral-bed. Every fragile branch and blossom shimmered up through the still water in intense moonlight, and little fishes glided between, azure-blue, purple, crimson, and golden—beautiful as rainbows. But there were creatures yet more lovely—small animalculæ, that shot about like flashes of living light. Literally like living light, and more beautiful than I can describe, are these little phosphoric things, which do not emit a steady ray but seem to palpitate light. When seen quiescent they look like tiny motes of silver, then they throb, and throb, swelling larger, and brighter, with every effort, and stream away at last in a train of splendour. We finished our evening with an impromptu penny-reading, followed by many songs, and as the last notes died away in silence, we stretched ourselves on the thwarts and oars to sleep.

Next morning was Sunday; and up to this time we had always, when possible, made a point of keeping Sunday as a day of rest, but as a ship prosecutes her voyage on Sunday so our boats had now to go on with their work. After reading the proper morning prayers, we continued to track Jenkins Bay round, and watch for what it would develop; and the farther we went the more the formation of the land led us to suppose that even now we had not found the real terminating point of New Guinea. After pulling six or seven miles to the west, we found our conjectures verified by the discovery of a clear broad blue channel, two miles wide, leading fair from sea to sea—fit for a fleet to pass through under sail. Our hearts filled with delight and wonder as we looked. There and then I named it China Straits; the wish being father to the thought, that I had found a new highway between Australia and China.

Before reaching China Straits our fresh water had all been used, and our efforts to find a supply on shore had failed; for there are no villages in Jenkins Bay. To get water was a necessity, so seeing one of the large trading canoes standing in for China Straits, we gave chase, to the great alarm of its crew, who numbered about fifteen, and had several women and children on board. There was no wind, so we soon came alongside, and when the astonished creatures found that we meant no harm, they gladly supplied us with water from cocoa-nuts, the orifices of which were stopped with grass, and pointing to a large village in China Straits, made signs that we could obtain plenty there. Accordingly, we pulled in for the western shore of this third new island, named by us after the senior lieutenant, "Hayter," by the discovery of which we had now cut off in all forty miles from the supposed length of New Guinea. As we approached the village, which was situated partly on a small islet, and partly on the mainland, to which it was joined by a reef, numbers of canoes came out to meet us; manifesting some doubtfulness, until they had communicated with their friends in the large trading canoe, after which they became assured, and crowded round us. One old bald-headed fellow jumped into the galley, and patting me in the most friendly manner on the back, sat himself down, and pointed the way over the fringing shore reef to the village, which was large, and straggled for more than a mile round the shores. High land rose immediately behind it; the highest point of which, Mount Haines, is about 800 feet high, and cultivated in terraces to its summit.

Two or three hundred natives waited our landing, all of the copper-coloured Malay type, carrying stone tomahawks over their shoulders, but not showing any spears, or clubs. Women and children were amongst the crowd, so I did not hesitate to land at once; and leaving half the men to guard the boats, took the rest up to a small stream shown us by the natives, where we got water—they carrying our barricoes, and helping us in every possible way. This done we began to barter with them for their fine stone hatchets, their yams, cocoa-nuts, and large crabs, with our iron hoop. We found the women, who were more ugly than can well be described, with their close-cropped hair, blackened skin, and mouths wholly disfigured by constant use of the betel-nut, much more difficult to trade with than the men; and they would not allow us to go near them as they sat on the verandahs in front of their houses.

The stone axes we found here were the most perfect specimens I have ever seen, and had been clipped into shape, and polished with a skill that must have been the result of practice for ages. The stone used was a kind of green-stone, hard, close-grained, and susceptible of high polish, but liable to chip off in irregular scales. The blades were some as large as seven inches round the edge, narrowed to three at the hilt, the length from edge to hilt was fifteen inches, and they tapered away in a beautiful curve to a sharp edge; they were set into a cleft in a handle, which described two sides of a triangle, and secured by stripes of rattan. The axe was carried over the shoulder. The southern entrance to China Straits is full of wooded islets, and to one of these, named by us "Dinner Islet," about a mile in length, and 200 feet high, we went to dine, apart from our savage friends; but we were followed there by the fighting men to the number of about 100. As they seemed in nowise alarmed themselves, we only kept a little more together, and went on cooking our dinner.

We sat at the edge of the bush, under the shelter of gigantic banyan trees, that dropped their hundred roots into the soil beneath the white coral sand; and this was a strategic position, for it kept the natives in our front, and prevented a surprise—a point I was always particular in guarding, as savages are never wholly to be trusted. They squatted between us and the blue rippling water, watching all our proceedings with intense curiosity, and expressed utter disgust on tasting our dish, which was as delicious, according to our ideas, as ever explorers sat to—a stew made of preserved soup and potatoes, salt pork, curlew, and pigeons. As we grew more friendly, several of our men got into the native canoes to try their skill; and, after a few attempts at paddling, were ignominiously capsised, to the great amusement of the natives; and the rest of us were surrounded by inquiring groups, who opened the breasts of our shirts and stroked our white skin with much wonder and admiration. The rest of the day was devoted to a cursory examination of China Straits, which convinced me that the ship could be taken through, and I determined at once to return to her, hope again reviving that I might thus take her round to the unknown coast-land to the north-west, which was not more than twelve miles distant from China Straits. We were twenty miles from the "Basilisk," but by dint of hard pulling, and favoured occasionally by a little wind, we got back to the ship before midnight, well pleased with our discoveries.

CHAPTER XIV.

SCENERY IN CHINA STRAITS—TAKE THE SHIP THROUGH—REASONS FOR TAKING CONDITIONAL POSSESSION OF NEWLY DISCOVERED ISLANDS—TAKE POSSESSION—DISCOVER MILNE BAY—PANIC AT DISCOVERY BAY—REMARKABLE WAR CANOES—FIRST TOMB SEEN IN NEW GUINEA—KILLERTON GROUP—DOG SACRIFICE—SPLENDID TREES—NORTH SHORE OF MILNE BAY—FIND THE TRUE EAST CAPE OF NEW GUINEA.

On the morning of the 21st we got the ship under weigh, and took her through Fortescue Straits, now so completely thrown into the shade, and passing to the westward along the southern shores of Basilisk and Hayter Islands, found, as I expected, a fine clear passage leading into China Straits. We dropped anchor in a bay on the western shores of Hayter Island, and looked round on the beautiful scene revealed to us with a sanguine trust that our hopes of finding the desired passage were at last to be realised.

The southern entrance to China Straits is guarded by Heath Island—a bold lofty island, 1000 feet high at its highest point, and five miles in length, luxuriantly wooded, and having large villages on its northern slopes, surrounded by cultivated ground. Many islets and coral sandbanks offer the most lovely little boat harbours off the northern shores of Heath Island, and the sea that surrounds it on the south, east, and west, is enriched with many islands that vary in size, form, and colouring. Turning from these, and looking northward up China Straits, the eye rests first on two salient features at their entrance. On the left hand a great rounded, almost perpendicular mass, dips from a height of 2000 feet into the blue waters of the Strait. This great bluff is the real and majestic terminating point of the Owen Stanley Range, and of south-east New Guinea itself. It is covered with sombre monotonous forest, and contrasts strongly with Hayter Island, which fronts it on the right side of the entrance, and is much lower land; its culminating peak, Mount Haines, being but 800 feet high, whilst its surface is varied by being broken up into heights, wooded or bare, or cultivated in patches, and the whole is enlivened by picturesque villages.

Twenty miles to the north the view up the Straits is closed by the lofty purple peaks of a then unknown land. Between us and these peaks lay first the broad southern entrance to the Straits, then six miles of narrow river-like scenery, terminating in the northern entrance, which was sprinkled over with a fresh group of islets.

We had many doubts at first as to whether the great bluff which overlooks the western entrance of China Straits was indeed part of New Guinea, and not another island, we had been so often mistaken; but the work of the ensuing days convinced us, and proved also that China Straits offered a wide safe channel, by which ships, as I then thought, could gain the northern shores of New Guinea, and I trusted that we had indeed found the passage I desired, and that these Straits would form the highway of a new route.

The importance of our discoveries led me to consider their bearing on Imperial and Australian interests. There lay the vast island of New Guinea, dominating the shores of northern Australia, separated at one point by only twenty miles of coral reef from British possessions, commanding the Torres Straits route, the transit of the Queensland mails, and our newly-discovered route for Australian trade to China; commanding the rich and increasing pearl-shell fisheries, with the working of which we had obtained a complete and interesting acquaintance, and also the bêche-de-mer fishery, which furnishes an important article of export to China.

I felt that the occupation of this island by any foreign maritime power, more especially since the discovery of the "Basilisk's" harbours and anchorages, would be a standing menace to Queensland.

I was also impressed by the richness and beauty of the new islands, and the number of their vegetable products—fine timber, the cocoa-nut, the sago-palm, sugar-cane, maize, jute, and various vegetable fibres, fruits and rich grasses, and my conclusion, after weighing all the considerations involved was, that it was my duty to take formal possession of our discoveries in the name of Her Majesty. Such a course secured a postponement of occupation by any Power till our Government could consider its own interests, and whilst the acquisition of these islands might commend itself, and my act result in annexation on the one hand, it might be negatived on the other, with easy simplicity, by a neglect to confirm it.

On April 24th we made the best dispositions we could to give some little eclât to the ceremony of taking possession.

The trunk of a tall cocoa-nut tree, deprived of its crown, standing on the west beach of Hayter Island, was fitted with a block to be used as a flag-staff; officers, marines, and small-armed men landed under arms, and all standing uncovered, the following proclamation was read—

"I, JOHN MORESBY, captain in the royal navy, commanding Her Majesty's ship 'Basilisk,' having discovered three considerable islands, from henceforth to be known as Moresby, Hayter, and Basilisk islands, off the east coast of New Guinea, together with various groups of detached islets, and deeming that the possession of these islands may hereafter prove of considerable importance, do hereby, by right of discovery, take possession of all the aforesaid islands and islets, lying within the parallels of 10° 25′ and 10° 40′ south latitude, and between the meridians of 150° 35′ and 151° 20′ east longitude, in the name and on behalf of her most gracious Majesty Queen Victoria, her heirs and successors, in token whereof I have hoisted and saluted the British flag on the shores of these islands.

" *God save the Queen.*

"H.M.S. 'Basilisk,' Possession Bay,
"Hayter Island, April 24th, 1873."

The Jack was then run up and saluted, and three hearty cheers were given. All listened to the few sentences read with attention and with pleasure, for every man present had a right to identify himself with the work done. A *feu-de-joie* was then fired, and I said, "Lads, in honour of what the old 'Basilisk' has done, we will splice the main brace to-night," and so our little ceremony ended.

The few natives present had watched our proceedings with amazement, little guessing how much their own future was involved, but the firing and cheering sent them off frightened into the bush.

We named the bay in which we had anchored Possession Bay, in honour of the event. Here, at the foot of a mountain torrent, which formed a succession of deep pools, in running down its rocky channel on the side of Mount Haines, we dug a deep well for the convenience of future visitors.

Dr. Haines and I changed to our cool working clothes after the ceremony, and started to reach the summit of the hill which bears his name. Taking a native track which led at first beside the rocky channel of the stream, but soon deviated from it, and led through forest to enclosures of sugar-cane and banana, we came out quite unexpectedly on a small village of the usual kind, consisting of long tunnel-shaped houses, standing on poles, and surrounded by cocoa-nut trees. On a rocky ledge above the village stood a group of natives, armed with spears and wooden clubs, evidently waiting our approach. We were rather taken aback at this, for we were quite unarmed; but we put on a bold face, and walked towards them, making the usual grotesque sign of greeting. They were evidently dubious as to how to act, but consented presently to point out our way; they would not accompany us, however, but stood and watched us with doubtful faces till we were lost to sight. The village stood about two-thirds from the hill top, and the remaining height was roughly terraced, and planted with yam, sugar-cane, and taro, which were growing luxuriantly. The view from the top rewarded us for our climbing —groups of islands were in sight that had no existence on the chart, and away to the north-west stretched the unknown land that now drew all my desires. To the south the islands of the Louisiade group studded the blue expanse; to the east lay Jenkins' Bay, with its islets, bays, and coves, backed up by the bold wooded outlines of Moresby and Basilisk Islands, which lay asleep in sunshine; to the north the unvisited D'Entrecasteaux Islands reared lofty lengths of deep violet blue; to the west our noble China Straits streamed northward from beneath the mighty bluff that terminates the Owen Stanley Range, all clothed in solemn forest to the foot. The more I gazed on all this grandeur and beauty, the more persuaded was I that these islands will some day become English homes; for all the conditions were here, beauty of aspect, high land, unbounded fertility, position on an open sea, and at the entrance of the shortest route between Australia and China. I felt that the future might safely be trusted to time.

Having completed our surveys, we left China Straits by its northern entrance on April 25th, and rounding the great bluff end of New Guinea, which we named the North Foreland, we considered ourselves now fairly to the north of that vast island, and stood west, keeping close to the New Guinea shore, for it was evident that the channel would not be a broad one which separated the unknown land, so often observed by us, from the north coast of New Guinea. After much deliberation, we had come to the conclusion that this unknown land was a part of the D'Entrecasteaux group, not seen by D'Entrecasteaux, as he only passed by the eastern shores of the group.

We were anxious now to prove whether the D'Entrecasteaux Islands was an integral part of New Guinea, or could be resolved into separate islands. Our sailing directions inclined to the first belief, but the chart, copied from the French, showed islands there. The shore that we were coasting was wooded, precipitously steep, and falling sheer into the sea, which had a depth of ninety fathoms at a cable's length from the shore.

Ten miles to the west of China Straits, a powerful mountain torrent, dashing down through a gorge, formed a small lagoon at its mouth, which offered the chance of an anchorage being found in alluvial deposit at its entrance. The weather had turned out thick and squally, so I wished if possible to anchor here till it cleared, as well as to replenish our stock of water from so bountiful a source, and we stood in cautiously till our mast-heads seemed almost to mingle with the dense foliage of an overhanging hill, and dropped anchor in eighteen fathoms, off the entrance of the lagoon. The officer in charge of the two boats sent for water—not an Irishman—took them into the lagoon, and loaded them deeply, and this done found himself a prisoner, as they would not now float over the bar at the entrance. He had therefore to discharge his cargo and load again outside, and was chaffed most unmercifully for his exploit. We were weather-bound here for twenty-four hours, and some of us took occasion to climb up along the course of the torrent for two or three miles, till we were stopped by perpendicular cliffs some hundreds of feet in height, over which the torrent rolled from various channels, and broke into soft showers of spray. All about us stretched thick forest and jungle, full of an oppressive silence, only broken by the occasional scream of some parrot from a high tree top. There were no fish in the torrent, and we washed the sand in places for gold, but none was found. One of our exploring parties found a small village in a deep narrow valley. It was ill built, and its people were dirtier, and seemed more savage, and slightly darker in complexion than the Moresby Island natives. They were much alarmed on seeing our party, but were assured after a little, and brought crabs and oysters, and bird of paradise plumes, off to the ship in wretched little canoes. The weather cleared on the afternoon of April 27th, and we weighed and continued to run up what we supposed was a strait leading between New Guinea and the D'Entrecasteaux. The land was closing in on us, and was soon not more than eight miles apart; and as headland after headland opened out, all hands watched with interest for the secret to reveal itself; all the officers were on the bridge, and the men crowded the bulwarks. It was one of those exciting moments which rarely occur and are never forgotten. The scene was indeed beautiful; the New Guinea mountains had receded from the sea, and left behind them a strip of rich plain country, strewn with villages, and beautified with groves of palm, behind which the Owen Stanley mountains swelled again into noble height, and this made a sharp contrast with the northern shore, where the land was broken and rugged, and rose into lesser heights. Before us, to the north-west, lay a group of small islets in a stream of light from the setting sun. On the near shore the natives, excited beyond expression, raced along the black volcanic sand, brandishing club and spear as we passed. The mountain streams, swollen by the late rain, brought down floods of discoloured water, which we crossed with anxious hearts, not knowing what it might hide; but at last, passing another headland, we saw the blue distant hills to the westward meet the unknown land and touch, and knew that we had only sailed up a great unknown bay, and that the north side of New Guinea was yet to be reached.

My disappointment was extreme. I had set my heart on China Straits forming the noble passage which nature had seemed to intend to be the northern shores of New Guinea, but all was once more thrown into doubt and uncertainty. Pressing on in hope of getting to an anchorage before dark—so necessary in these narrow waters—we came in sight of the head of this great bay, which was closed to the west by a considerable extent of flat country, backed by a range of high mountains, which ran south till it joined the Owen Stanley range, and north to the high land which forms the northern shores of this bay, and was afterwards named Stirling Range. The waters at the head of the bay were dotted with ugly-looking reefs, and were far too deep for anchorage; but our good star prevailed, and we opened a lovely oval-shaped cove, on the shore of which was a large well-constructed village, standing as usual amid tropic surroundings. Mr. Mourilyan went at once to examine the tiny bay, which lies about twenty miles west of China Straits, and though half its space was blocked by a long reef, there remained a space in which the "Basilisk," accustomed as she now was to narrow waters, might make herself at home. Passing so close to a lovely green point fringed with black sand that the gesticulating natives might have thrown their spears on our decks, we entered the little bay and anchored in twelve fathoms, our stern just swinging clear of the beach in eight fathoms. Words fail to describe the feeling of rest and satisfaction we felt on reaching such a secure haven as this after our work amongst unknown waters, when the responsibility I had taken added to my anxieties.

The cove we had entered was semi-circular, and fringed all round by graceful cocoa-nut palms, the blue water rippling up to their roots. Pretty native houses were scattered amongst the trees, every one of which seemed to have sent forth its inmates to gaze at us. There was no unfriendliness; canoes of all sizes, and catamarans darted about us, bringing fine pigs and vegetables, which were gladly exchanged for our hoop-iron. The next day was Sunday; but except during divine service, when we sent the natives away, their jabbering over the bartering kept the noise of a fair about us all day. I disliked the turning of Sunday into a market-day, but the natives would have thought us offended with them and retained a bad impression had I stopped the trading; and our seamen, deprived of the only pleasure the incessant nature of their work permitted, would have hated the day. Half our men spent the afternoon on shore and thoroughly enjoyed themselves. Mr. Mourilyan took the galley and surveyed the head of Milne Bay (thus named by me after the Senior Naval Lord of the Admiralty) on Monday, and came back with a report that it was full of reefs, and that the natives had been troublesome in pressing on him. I was too ill to go with him from the effect of sundry bruises and strains received during the last fortnight in climbing and other work, added to which I had been attacked by one of our usual enemies, a tumour, which had fallen in the right ear; but the work was in safe hands.

We had quite a scene during his absence, caused by the manning and arming of our boats, which went outside the cove for target firing. The natives had crowded down to the point near the boats, curious as to what was to happen, and at the first report of the sharp ringing Armstrong guns, had shrieked in terror and scampered off. The panic seized the village, all valuables were hurriedly taken away, and every living thing cleared out and made for the bush, except a few women, who finding that no harm came to them, stayed on the point, and watched the firing to the end. I was well enough to land, and found several natives in the rear of the village in a state of alarm, but the presence of the brave women who had watched the firing and our signs, and a few presents given, soon brought them round, and they accompanied us back to the village, and were persuaded to venture alongside the ship as usual. In the evening we had the satisfaction of seeing the natives bring back their valuables, and before dark their confidence was quite restored. Tuesday was devoted to a survey of our anchorage, after which it received the name of Discovery Bay. The catamarans here are made of three or more cocoa-nut trees lashed together and sharpened at the ends. Some have a small platform about a foot high in the centre, on which to carry the goods dry, but most are without this, and the sea washes freely over them. They require careful handling, but were freely used by our men and officers.

The natives of Discovery Bay were friendly from the first. They were similar in appearance to those we had as yet met on this coast. Their numbers on board and alongside amounted at times to three and four hundred, who kept us plied with their merchan-

DISCOVERY BAY—NEW GUINEA.

dise,. ornaments, weapons, and their beautiful canoe paddles, which were shaped like the long narrow leaves of some water plants, with a spine running down the centre. As a rule they traded honestly. Our method was to drop a piece of iron hoop at the end of a cord into a canoe, on which the natives would touch one article after another till consent was nodded from the ship, and then joyfully detach the iron and tie on the pig, yams, or ornaments sold, to be hauled up. Our men, when on shore, used to sit down freely and partake with them of their evening meal—a mess of yams and vegetables, to which pork was sometimes added, seasoned with cocoa-nut finely shred over, and cooked in large earthen bowls. The mess was eaten with exquisite little spoons cut out of pearl shell, and made a meal not to be despised. The women generally presided at the feast, and the men looked well pleased to see the children receiving their shares in little cocoa-nut basins; indeed, their whole manner spoke well for their treatment of these weaker ones.

I never saw Indian corn used as food, nor did it appear to be cultivated in large quantities. The most palatable native dish was made of the mamy apple, stewed. Our friends were always anxious to be rid of us at dusk, and would make signs that they wanted to sleep, on which we always conformed to their wish. It was amusing to see our men come paddling off to the ship in catamarans and canoes, the natives screaming with delight as a clumsy stroke sent some frail craft rolling over. They always came to the rescue though—righted the canoe, and gave it some sharp jerks backward and forward, checking it abruptly, so that the water was projected over each way, and then a man got in and baled it out.

It must not be supposed that our men were allowed to be at the mercy of the natives, for savages, as I have said, are never to be trusted. Armed boat-keepers always kept the boats ready for instant embarkation; the liberty-men were told off into two companies, each under the command of an officer, who had orders to keep his men generally together, and to serve as a rallying-point in case of need. These parties were sub-divided into fours, which were ordered never to separate, and every second man carried fire-arms. The completeness of our precautions was happily never tested—a fact owing as much to the unexceptionable good behaviour and prudence of our men as to the friendliness of the natives. It is a gratifying reflection to me that, during the constant intercourse maintained by our men with the New Guinea people, they never offered the slightest insult, nor quarrelled with a native man or woman. The war canoes at Discovery Bay were very remarkable, and were carefully kept under sheds between the houses. They were from fifty to sixty feet long, dug out of a single tree, with topside planking laced on. The ends were ornamented with high movable prow and stern pieces, grotesquely carved and painted, from which cassowary feathers floated, and all round the sides of the boat strings of white cowrie shells were looped up.

We saw a tomb here, the first since our leaving Teste Island; evidently the grave of a great man. A small space inside the village, about ten feet by five, was enclosed, in which stood a miniature house, neatly made, and painted with ochres and lime, covering the remains. Two or three pretty shrubs were planted in the enclosure, and the whole was kept in good order. We afterwards saw similar graves in the Engineer group, adorned with strings of cocoa-nuts; otherwise no burial-places were seen, and we were unable to learn from the natives how they disposed of their dead. We never saw any sign of religious observance amongst these people, unless the cocoa-nuts hung on poles on the reefs or on their houses were intended as a propitiatory offering; and there was also a peculiar ceremony to which I shall presently allude. They had many pets, tame cassowaries, which ran about the village freely, several varieties of the (Wallis) custus, and some exquisitely plumaged birds, which they kept in wicker cages.

Having completed our survey of this part of Milne Bay, we left our pleasant anchorage on April 30th, to trace its northern shores to their eastern termination. The width of Milne Bay at Discovery Bay is about six miles; and we stood to the north-east, sufficiently near to take the bearings of the prominent headlands. Unfortunately it came on thick and rainy, and we were obliged to seek shelter amidst the group of islands we had seen from the entrance of China Straits, about twenty miles north-east of Discovery Bay. Passing over some dangerous coral patches, we found a good anchorage between the principal island and the mainland. The group consisted of three larger islands, about a mile in length, and several smaller ones, and was named Killerton group by us. Its inhabitants at first seemed inclined to be troublesome, and met our boats in canoes waving their stone weapons, and shouting defiantly. Two or three canoes full of fighting men came round Mr. Mourilyan's boat in a most threatening manner; but his resoluteness and good temper told after a while, and the natives began to consult with each other. Some paddled off to shore and presently returned, bringing one of the lean wolfish curs that infest their villages. They sprang up the side of the "Basilisk," the leader carrying the dog in his arms, and dashed out its brains on the quarter-deck, before any one could stop them. On this all the natives near us changed their manner, and showed a desire to be friendly, by making the usual uncouth greeting; but the ire of the officer of the watch and petty officers was so kindled at seeing Her Majesty's quarter-deck defiled, that the dog-sacrificers and their friends were bundled out of the ship at once, and their victim thrown after them. I had been below at the time, and was sorry to hear of this summary treatment, for I felt that the rite had, doubtless, either a religious and sacrificial meaning to its perpetrators, or was intended as a seal of amity between us. I therefore went on shore immediately, to show friendliness, at a spot where a large crowd had assembled round the body of the dead dog in noisy consultation, and received so friendly a welcome, that my companion and I did not hesitate to go on to the village with our new acquaintances, who, similar in physique to their neighbours, were painted in so extraordinary a manner as to look more like monkeys than men. They had black lines like spectacle rims drawn round their eyes, one cheek and half the chin was painted white, and the other half and the nose black. One old native led me by the hand, and the crowd followed us for about a mile through sugar-cane plantations, melon, taro, and yam gardens, interspersed with palms and fruit trees, to the village, which is beautifully placed at the foot of a high range of hills, and on the banks of a rapid stream. Many forest trees had been suffered to remain in the cleared ground about it, and had developed into more magnificent proportions than any trees I have ever seen, not excepting the giant pines of California. Their girth at a man's height from the ground is about thirty feet; twenty feet above which the foliage commenced, and threw a shadow on the ground about 100 feet in diameter. A large talking-house, about sixty feet long, stood in the centre of the village, and round it, on a hard trampled space, the saddle-roofed houses were grouped. The natives had brought us to their village, but would not let us enter their houses; and for this I could discover no reason, as their women were all about us. I looked into several of the houses, and could see nothing beyond the usual belongings, weapons, fishing-nets, stores of yams, and lumps of sago wrapped up in dried cocoa-nut leaves. As they would not admit us, we leaned against a huge tree trunk, and made signs that we were thirsty, when they brought us fresh cocoa-nut milk.

Returning on board, the remainder of the day was spent in examining the various channels between the islets, but their number obliged us to be cursory. The Torres Straits pigeon swarmed on these islets. On May 1st the weather had cleared sufficiently for us to make a fresh start, so keeping close along the northern shores of Milne Bay, we made for the unknown north-east point of New Guinea.

Immediately to the east of Killerton Islands the mountains dropped from a height of near 2000 feet, and became low wooded hills of 300 or 400 feet in height, with plains between; and we began to feel that we were coasting a narrow neck of land, though the water at the other side could not, of course, be seen. Coral reefs and broken water were visible ahead, but we pushed on and were soon rewarded. The land had now narrowed to about a mile in width, of low undulating forest-country, sprinkled with villages. Suddenly an abrupt double-topped hill sprang upward to a height of 300 feet, with a village at its foot, half hidden in a grove of bread-fruit and cocoa-nut trees, and two small flat coral islets off it; beyond them a broad strait rolled its waters for eight miles, till it washed the shores of the D'Entrecasteaux Group. My desire was answered; the true terminating point of New Guinea was found; the D'Entrecasteaux Group lay afar, distinctly separate, never more to be confounded with New Guinea, and ours were the first European eyes which had looked on these things. Continuing our course, I hoped to double East Cape, as the terminating point was now named by us, and take the ship round to the northern shores of New Guinea, but immediately to the eastward of the cape we fell amongst the reefs before seen, and being completely embayed by them were compelled to seek a precarious anchorage to windward of one of the small coral islets off East Cape, on which a strong monsoon was blowing.

CHAPTER XV.

EAST NEW GUINEA FOUND TO BE FORK-SHAPED—GO ROUND TO THE NORTH COAST IN A BOAT—SUP WITH THE NATIVES AT EAST CAPE—PETS AND CURIOSITIES ON BOARD—SAIL FOR SOMERSET—NAVIGATING-LIEUTENANT CONNOR AND MR. GRANT REJOIN FROM THEIR SURVEY—TAKE STEPS TO SET THE PEARL-SHELLING FISHERIES FREE TO WORK—BRISBANE—SYDNEY—NEW ZEALAND CRUISE—LIEUTENANT DAWSON SENT OUT BY ADMIRALTY—JOINS BASILISK—SAIL TO JOIN THE COMMODORE AT FIJI.

NEW GUINEA was now known by us to be fork-shaped to the east; the lower prong consisting of Moresby, Hayter, Basilisk, and other islands—the upper, of a long narrowing strip of land, ending in the double-topped point to which we now gave the name of East Cape; and between these prongs lay Milne Bay. Our next efforts were directed to find a channel through the reefs which had so unfortunately obstructed us, but the more we searched the clearer it became that no channel round East Cape existed here. I was confident that a way would be found, on search being made, farther to the southward and eastward, but having a distance of about 2000 miles to accomplish against the monsoon, before a further supply of coal and stores could be obtained; and it being necessary that I should be at Cape York in a few days, I had neither the time nor means to make it.

With great reluctance, therefore, I abandoned the idea of taking the ship farther, and thought that the elucidation of this part of the new route was reserved for some happier navigator, possessed of means and leisure. The importance of such a discovery, in shortening the route to China, and opening up the rich New Guinea coast to trade, impressed itself so much on my mind that I resolved to suggest to Admiral Sir Alexander Milne the advisability of allowing me to try if I could not find my way to England by the new route, when the ship's time was expiring, instead of taking the usual course from Australia round Cape Horn. This application was afterwards made by me, and permission given, of which the result will be told farther on. Before turning my back on Eastern New Guinea, I resolved on visiting its unknown northern shores in my boat. The ship was riding uneasily at her exposed anchorage, and a disagreeable sea was running, but it did not prevent the natives coming off in their frail canoes and catamarans to communicate.

Taking Mr. Bentley in the galley, I rounded East Cape, passing between it and the Island off which we were anchored by a narrow channel, where a hollow dangerous sea was running; passing this we shot under the lee of East Cape, and found ourselves in a moment sheltered, and floating on a deep, tranquil sea, ruffled but gently by the monsoon.

Full of pleasant excitement, we lay on our oars to take in the exquisite scene revealed. Behind us, on a breaking sea, the tall masts of the ship were rocking to and fro over the coral islet, whilst we lay motionless. To the eastward rose the lofty wooded D'Entrecasteaux Islands; within a hundred yards of us a large village lay peacefully amongst its palms and fruit trees—its canoes floating before it, full of anxious gazers; on and on the eye travelled to the westward, from the near thickly-populated shores to the blue shadowy outlines of the massive New Guinea mountains, seventy or eighty miles distant. The sight of a clear reefless sea, added to the exhilaration we felt, but it enhanced the disappointment of thinking that not to us would be given the honour of bringing a ship into these waters. Fate proved kinder to us afterwards than we then expected. We steered to the west for several miles along a shore more luxuriant and beautiful than words can describe, and then returned and landed at the village of East Cape, where the natives came down in numbers to meet us, and crowding round like a number of delighted children, led us to their village, where mats were spread for us under the shade of great cocoa-nut trees. Then they examined us from our hats to our shoes in the most minute manner, wondering over everything, especially at our white skins; the young women, who were agreeable enough looking, and had beautifully small hands and feet, being specially interested. We decorated some of the babes with strips of turkey red, on which our popularity became unbounded, and all the mothers came round us holding up their copper-coloured, dark-eyed, babes. We shared their evening meal, and returned to the ship, voting the East Cape people the pleasantest savages we had ever met. The ship lay uneasily at her anchor, but next day the strong monsoon which was blowing moderated, and Mr. Mourilyan and I were able to leave her, and explore to the west along the north shore of New Guinea. We passed between East Cape and the two outlying islets, and ran some fourteen miles to the west, along a thickly-populated, well cultivated coast, without meeting a single outlying reef—the narrow shore reef dropping down "steep-to," into a depth that gave us no bottom, with thirty fathoms of line. We made a running survey as we passed along the north coast of the narrow neck of land, which, as I have before said, encloses Milne Bay on the north, and terminates north-east New Guinea; and, disregarding many invitations of the natives to land at their villages, pushed on to a mountain, which, rising in the rear of Killerton Islands, throws a ridge into the northern sea. This mountain was intended by me to be the limit point of our work in this cruise, the boats having to return against the monsoon. We rested and dined under its shadow, in as perfect a little boat-harbour as ever mortal eyes beheld; shaded overhead by the foliage of overhanging trees, with two fathoms depth of water round the boat, through which a perfect forest of branching coral glimmered up. This point was the western limit actually reached by us, but we named a cape, seen by us some fifteen miles beyond, Cape Basilisk.

As soon as Mr. Mourilyan had sketched the D'Entrecasteaux group, as seen from this position, we turned our faces towards the ship, with many regrets at being forced to leave this unexplored coast behind us, and returned, landing at some of the villages on our way, where we found the people as gentle and friendly as possible. At times I found myself drawing a contrast between the squalid poverty, too often seen in humble life in England, and the plenty and cleanliness that met us here at every step, where the small cane houses lay in valleys rich as the garden of Eden, and no man had to go more than a stone's throw from his own door to find all the necessities of his simple life.

They possess cocoa-nuts, the bread-fruit, citron, oranges, and sago, by the bounty of nature, and they cultivate yams, taro, bananas, and various other roots which we found very good to eat, but were unable to name. They are great fishers and traders, passing from island to island in large canoes, forty or fifty feet long, made of a hollowed tree, with top sides secured by cane lacing and large wooden knees. They use a great oval-shaped mat sail, and handle it so skilfully, that when we met them at sea, and the "Basilisk" was going five knots, they easily sailed round us, and luffing under our lee were with difficulty prevented from boarding us whilst under weigh. What have these people to gain from civilisation? Pondering on the fate of other aboriginal races when brought into contact with the white, I was ready to wish that their happy homes had never been seen by us; but considerations of this kind cannot be entertained by those who see a simple duty before them, and have means to execute it; we were not responsible for the issues, and Providence may surely be trusted to work out its own ends.

The great Owen Stanley range may be said to terminate at the head of Milne Bay, but one of its spurs, named by me Sterling Range, runs at a diminished elevation through this new neck of land or narrow peninsula which terminates in East Cape. The double-topped hill which marks this henceforth important promontory on the map of the world, was crowned to the summits, when first we saw it, with tropical forest, but the noble trees afterwards fell to our axes, as we made it a theodolite station.

I left East Cape with the "Basilisk," May 3d, which was marked by an unlucky accident; for in trying to weigh our anchor we lost it, through its catching in a coral rock, and the chain carrying away. Running a fresh line of soundings across Milne Bay, we re-entered China Straits, and re-anchored in Possession Bay, where five days were spent in watering, and further examination of the surrounding coast.

We felt that we had much reason to be satisfied with the results obtained in our cruises, especially that, as Englishmen, we had secured to our country a right to take possession of a territory that will every day become more important to Australia; and had found safe commodious harbours, by means of which a healthy commerce might be carried on.

The ship was full of strange pets and curiosities. The most remarkable of the pets was a cassowary from

Cornwallis Island;* there were some New Guinea pigs, some varieties of cuscus, and any amount of birds. We had stone and wood weapons and instruments of all kinds; amongst which the large greenstone axes used by the natives in making canoes were the most conspicuous—the blades very sharp, and the stone resembling the prized greenstone of New Zealand. We had canoe paddles made of a fine dark wood, shaped like a long water leaf, and well carved, which were really graceful objects. There were gourds of all sizes and shapes, with patterns delicately burnt out, ornamenting the whole surface; cocoa-nuts, used to carry water, and carved all over; bowls of red fire-baked clay, such as the women may at any time be seen making in the villages; baskets also, made of sinnet, lined with the envelope of the young leaf of the palm, and fitting compactly one inside the other, to form a large set; netted bags, fish-hooks, and bait, carved out of pearl-shell; plumes of the cassowary and red bird of paradise; fillets for the head, and breastplates made of fibre, and beautifully embroidered with shells and berries.

The day before we finally sailed from Possession Bay, one of our stokers wandered away by himself when on shore, in disobedience of the general orders, and was relieved by a party of natives of all the iron hoop he had about him. I mention this as being the only instance in which they took advantage of their superior numbers.

Having paid our last visit to the villages, we

* Now in the Zoological Gardens, London.

weighed and stood south; but wishing to ascertain whether a passage into China Straits existed on the west side of Heath Island, took the ship out by this untried channel. We got out in safety, but had to pass over the tail of some dangerous reefs, which it required much conning from aloft to avoid. Fifteen miles south of Heath Island we crossed the line of the sunken barrier reef in seventeen fathoms water, and looking back could more easily understand from the configuration of the land, how it was that our predecessors in these seas, viewing it from a distance, had mistaken the facts.

It was a relief to feel our good ship once more rising and falling on the free ocean swell; but I left New Guinea with regrets for what we had left undone, thinking that I should never see it again.

A pleasant passage of ten days brought us once more to an anchor at Somerset, where our hearts were rejoiced by an accumulation of three months' home letters. Here Navigating-Lieutenant Connor and Mr. Grant rejoined, after laborious work on the northern shores of Torres Straits, where they had spent two months in open boats, exposed to unusual severity of weather on a lee-shore during the south-east monsoon; but in spite of difficulties they had accomplished a trigonometrical survey of 46 miles of the great Warrior Reef, and 148 miles of the south coast of New Guinea and islands, including those of Cornwallis and Saibai, which had been placed on the chart by the "Basilisk." They had not met with any trouble from the natives, who had been quite friendly all through; and the health of the men had been excellent. They would scarcely have been recognised by their nearest friends, so tanned were they by sun and wind; but they were happily none the worse for their work. Navigating-Lieutenant Connor's labours had added so largely to the amount of our geographical work, that I felt rewarded a hundred times over for the anxiety and responsibility I had accepted in detaching him in so unusual a manner.

Having made a tour of all the pearl-shelling and bêche-de-mer stations before sailing for New Guinea, on our return to Cape York I drew Mr. Jardine's attention to the fishery question. All fishing operations were now suspended till the receipt of government licences. The Polynesian islanders had been freed from their servitude and sent to their homes; and the law had now provided such enactments as would secure righteous treatment for them in case of their making a compact to serve their old masters again. The Torres Straits islanders entertained a perfectly-friendly feeling towards the white men stationed on their islands, and were willing and anxious to serve them for fair pay; whilst such service would be useful in civilising them, by adding to their comfort in the present, and affording opportunities for their gradual moral elevation. Under these circumstances I felt the importance of setting the fishing establishments free to work again without further delay, lest an industry so valuable in its results should be paralysed; and urged

Mr. Jardine to grant such temporary licences as his powers permitted, for the employment of Torres Straits natives: this after some difficulty he did.

On the 24th we bid what all hands hoped might be an eternal farewell to Somerset. Indeed, what with the bad anchorage, ruinous aspect of the buildings, and want of any kind of fruit or vegetable, there is little to make a stay cheerful or comfortable. Falling short of coal on our return, we anchored under the lee of Gloucester Island for four days, and cut a supply of wood. On June 21st we arrived at Brisbane, where we were received with the utmost kindness by the governor and Mr. Palmer, who took a most generous view of the importance of our services. On the 2d July our eventful six months' cruise came to an end, and we took up our old position in Farm Cove, Sydney. The ship was of course thronged by people coming to hear something about New Guinea, and to see the curiosities we had brought thence, and many of the seamen drove lucrative bargains with the Sydney people. One, in particular, received five pounds, as I was afterwards informed, for a New Guinea pig, which was immediately shaved by its purchaser, painted in stripes of different colours, and otherwise decorated. A small tent was then set up in one of the principal thoroughfares, and the proprietor informed the public that a wonderful striped New Guinea pig, brought by H. M. ship "Basilisk," was on view, and charged sixpence a-head for entrance, with a result that was said to have answered his most sanguine expectations.

At Sydney, in accordance with orders awaiting us, we refitted and proceeded to New Zealand, where we remained till December 1st, making a tour of the New Zealand ports. At Auckland, on the 1st, we received the English mail and were joined by Lieutenant Dawson, Admiralty Surveyor, who had been sent out to assist us, my desire having been assented to, that we should return to England by the route which I believed would be found to exist round the east end of New Guinea. We were ordered to spend six weeks in making additional surveys on the New Guinea coast, and Lieutenant Dawson came provided with a supply of the best surveying instruments for the purpose. I ought here to express my sense of gratitude to Admiral Richards, late Hydrographer of the navy, for kindly giving us some surveying instruments on our leaving England, which I asked for, on the chance of their proving useful, little thinking how much I should need them.

Lieutenant Dawson had only given me this news unofficially, and our orders had gone on to Commodore Goodenough, whom I knew to be at Fiji, so that two or three months must elapse before I could receive them from him, by waiting which time I should lose the fine weather season in New Guinea, which was all important to the success of the work entrusted to us.

I was loath to shorten by a day the pleasures of our stay in this colony, for officers and men deserved a little enjoyment and rest; besides, we were the only man-of-war in New Zealand, and the rule was stringent that New Zealand was never to be left without a man-of-war; but having weighed all considerations, I telegraphed to Sir James Fergusson, Governor of New Zealand, who was then at Christ Church, to ask if the colony could spare us, whilst I took the ship to Fiji to communicate with the Commodore. Sir James, who had taken a warm interest in our New Guinea work, answered, saying that we could be spared, and we started at once for Fiji, coaling at the Bay of Islands on our way thither.

On December 21st, at 1 A.M., we were standing for Levuku, with studding sails set in a light fair breeze, when we unexpectedly found ourselves close to a dangerous reef, having been swept twelve miles out of our reckoning by an unsuspected current. Before the ship could answer her helm she was on the reef, and lay there bumping for six hours before we could get her off. It was a terribly anxious time; for some hours I thought the good old vessel's hours were numbered, but fine weather continuing, the efforts we made were successful.

We arrived at Levuku next day, and I was gratified by finding that the commodore approved of my proceeding in leaving New Zealand, and was prepared by every means in his power to assist in promoting the success of the expedition, by helping me to carry out my views, and aiding me with his own valuable advice.

CHAPTER XVI.

PROVIDED WITH A STEAM PINNACE—LAST FAREWELL TO SYDNEY—TESTE ISLAND—MAKE A THEODOLITE STATION ON GLENTON ISLAND—VIEW FROM THE SUMMIT—ENGINEER GROUP—NATIVES SUSPICIOUS—FIND A PASSAGE BETWEEN GRANT AND SHORTLAND ISLANDS—FIRST LANDING ON D'ENTRECASTEAUX ISLANDS—HUMAN FIGURES PAINTED ON GABLE-ENDS OF HOUSES—RUNNING SURVEY OF D'ENTRECASTEAUX—NAME TWO OF THE ISLANDS RESPECTIVELY NORMANBY AND FERGUSSON—DISCOVER DAWSON STRAITS—ARMED NATIVES COME DOWN—WE CONCILIATE THEM—DISCOVER MORESBY STRAITS SEPARATING THESE ISLANDS FROM A THIRD, WHICH WE NAME GOODENOUGH ISLAND—MUSHROOM CORAL—MOUNT GOODENOUGH—FERGUSSON ISLAND—ITS FRIENDLY WOMEN—INLAND PLANTATIONS—THE SAGO-PALM—BOILING MINERAL SPRINGS—SMALL RUBIES AND AMETHYSTS—SEARCH FOR A BETTER PASSAGE ROUND THE EAST CAPE OF NEW GUINEA—HOME OF THE MEGAPODES—A LAND SNAKE—FIND THE DESIRED PASSAGE FROM TESTE ISLAND TO THE NORTH OF NEW GUINEA—H.M.S. "SANDFLY" AND THE NATIVES.

ONE of H.M. schooners, the "Sandfly," commanded by Lieutenant Nowell, was ordered to accompany the "Basilisk" to New Guinea, and the Commodore kindly offered to give us the assistance of H.M.S. "Rosario," an intention, of which after circumstances prevented the fulfilment. Encouraged thus by the good wishes of my old friend and esteemed chief, we sailed, December 26th, to refit and prepare for the expedition. On our passage a singular alarm happened. A heavy sea struck the ship and shook her violently at night, and the men having the memory of our many narrow escapes in their minds, raised a cry that she had struck on a reef, and rushed on deck to get heartily laughed at by the watch. We reached Sydney January 6th, and found the public prints full of articles, which showed the interest taken in our late New Guinea work, and expressed hope for our future success, which it almost depressed me to read, knowing, as I did, the short time placed at my disposal by the Admiralty. My experience in former cruises had shown me that a steam pinnace was a necessity, and the Commodore being unable to supply me, I resolved to buy one here, hoping after our survey was over, to reimburse myself by selling it to the Dutch at Amboyna.

I was unable to see anything suitable, except one which belonged to the New South Wales Government, and this was lent me through the kindness of Sir Hercules Robinson, the governor, and Mr. Parkes, prime minister, on my making myself personally responsible in case of damage or loss, and undertaking to return her to Sydney after we had reached Singapore. I was but too glad to accept these or any conditions. The Government also supplied me with a deep-sea sounding apparatus, and by permission of the Commodore we were also provided with deep sea lines, and an abundance of saws and axes for cutting wood, which I foresaw would be often a necessity in the work before us. When the ship was docked for repairs, we found that our escape from the Figi coral-reef had been of the narrowest, as the planking had been all but ground through.

H.M. s. schooner "Sandfly" sailed for Possession Bay, New Guinea, January 30th, and next day the

"Basilisk," laden with provisions, and carrying fifty tons of coal on deck, was all ready for sailing. It was a wild day, blowing half a gale, but numbers of people came down to the rocky point of Farm Cove, off which we were anchored, to see us off; others came in boats, and the ship was crowded with friends, from whom we all felt it more or less painful to part. As soon as the anchor was at our bow, our men sprang aloft with flags, and running out on the yard-arms, and up to the mast-heads, waved them for farewell; this was answered with cheer on cheer from the shore, which the "Basilisk's" crew heartily returned, and then we steamed on our way—our homeward-bound pennant streaming eighty yards astern.

We were much delayed by contrary winds during our first week at sea, accompanied by such strong southerly currents that we were obliged to put into Brisbane to replenish coal, lest we should be crippled ere our surveying commenced. We shipped another deck load, and encouraged by the hearty interest taken in the work before us by Lord Normanby and his Government, finally left the Australian shores on February 9th, and steered for Teste Island. We occupied our time on the way by preparing for the survey; deep-sea lines were marked up to 3000 fathoms, the steam pinnace fitted with strong canvas upper works, and a hood over the bows to increase her safety in a sea-way, and give comfort to the men, and the other boats made ready for detached service.

On February 17th, when within 100 miles of Teste

Island, we met a strong north-west gale, accompanied by a heavy sea, in which the deep-laden "Basilisk" did not make her usual good weather. We were striking the top-gallant masts when she made a sudden plunge, a great sea swept over the forecastle, and with it went our gallant boatswain. The cry of "a man overboard!" roused every one. A boat's crew sprang at once into the quarter-boat to go to the rescue. For an instant I was agitated by as painful a doubt as can assail a seaman, as to whether I could permit the attempt to be made, the chances were so heavy against these nine lives in the quarter-boat; but a look to windward decided me, for Mr. Mudge was striking out bravely, and as he rose on the top of a great wave, he shouted out cheerily—"I am all right, sir!"—an unselfish speech, for he afterwards told me that he had thought by my face that I was about to jump overboard to save him, and wished to prevent it. I had no such thought, for I could not have saved myself in such a sea, and my duty was to look after the ship.

The boat was skilfully lowered away, and got clear safely, and the issue for life or death was watched breathlessly from the ship, for the boatswain was a favourite with all hands. A heavy sea disabled the oars for a space, and hope sank low, for our shipmate was exhausted, and lay floating deeply, and about to sink. At last the cry arose—"They have him!" and thank God it was true, though he had sunk below the surface ere rescued. Almost as anxiously we watched for the return of the boat, which came borne along on the crest of a great wave, and then appeared to be sinking stern foremost into the yawning abyss; but all were soon safe on board, and in a day or two we had the satisfaction of seeing Mr. Mudge at his duty.

On the 20th we passed Bell Rock, and through a grey watery mist made out the well-remembered peaks and outlines of our former discoveries with a thrill of gratification, remembering our work done, and feeling that we were returning to complete it under honourable circumstances. That evening we rode at anchor in our old haven, Hoop-iron Bay, surrounded by hundreds of natives, who recognised us with shouts of welcome, and Lieutenant Dawson and the new hands were enchanted with the exquisite scenery surrounding.

Six weeks only lay at our disposal, and I had anxiously considered how to make the most of them. We were ordered to commence the survey where we had left off last year, and carry it thence round East Cape, and along the unknown north coast of New Guinea, till the expiration of our time should arrest us; but I resolved to begin by making a trigonometrical survey of the space between Teste Island and East Cape, so as to decide at the outset the important question as to whether an available entrance to the new route existed here or not.

We remained at Teste Island till February 24th, rating the chronometers, and accurately fixing the position of O'Neill Island as a starting-point for our survey, and during this time our steam pinnace was an unceasing wonder to the natives. On one occasion Lieutenant Smith took about fourteen of their canoes in tow, and the owners shouted with pleasure and admiration, till he blew the steam whistle, when their consternation was extreme. They became convinced, however, that no ill was intended them, and after landing, collected their women on the beach, and made signs that they wished the whistle to be blown, which was done, and the men were highly amused by the terror of the women, who fled in dismay. Some time afterwards we had a native with us in the steam pinnace a whole day, and Lieutenant Dawson took pains in explaining the action of the engine to him, and found the man so interested and intelligent as apparently to grasp the principle by which it acted. Amongst our many necessary duties was one of making surveying stations on various lofty points, and except in the case of our first station under the lofty tree before mentioned, on O'Neill Island, all the required points were so thickly wooded that regular expeditions had to be made to clear a horizon for the theodolite. The summit of Glenton, a small island some three miles in circumference, and 400 feet high, four miles south-east of Moresby Island, was first attacked by a party, consisting of about forty men armed with axes and saws. The island rises so precipitously from the sea that landing is difficult, but we found a small sandy beach, and landing without a wetting, we chose the shoulder of a steep hill which seemed likely to lead to the top, and began to climb. It was easy at first, for we could pass between the trees; soon, however, the dense under-growth closed in, and every foot of way had to be cut through creepers and bushes. So thick was the entanglement, that we could only direct our progress to the top by sending men into the lofty tree-tops to guide us. Streaming with perspiration, and tormented with mosquitoes, we found ourselves at last on a narrow plateau, about a quarter of an acre in extent, dipping on its southern side to a precipice so wooded as to shut out every glimpse of the sea, the sun itself was almost hidden from our sight by the dense undergrowth in which we were buried, and the over-shrouding leafage. It seemed a task for Hercules to clear away such a mass of obstruction; but the strong arms of our men soon let in daylight: axes rang and saws grated cheerfully, and every now and then came the cry, "Stand clear!" and a big tree bowed its head and toppled over, crushing down the underwood in its fall, and thus doing good service. Below the plateau our men found foothold on projecting ledges, and felled the huge trees that grew up the face of the precipice. These, as they rolled over, were often caught in their descent by other trees, and remained provokingly obstructing the view, so that three trees had often to be felled to lower one. In the midst of our work a violent tropical storm burst over us, and was welcome indeed, for the water we had brought up with us was all expended, and we were all thirsty. As the rain ran in small water-spouts from the branches, every mouth was open to catch it, and we thought the refreshment cheaply purchased by a wetting.

In a few hours all the trees, except a giant which we left to crown the summit, had fallen, and the theodolite was free to sweep the horizon. We felt proud of our work, but gazed on it with some ruth as we thought of the years it would take nature to replace these leafy shades. Our thoughts were soon drawn away by the glorious panorama that stretched before us. Below us, at the foot of the precipice, the light waves curled on a snowy coral beach; to the west the wooded peaks of Moresby Island closed the view; but on every other side, island after island floated on the calm of an intense blue sea, volcanic, lofty and rugged, or coralline, low, white, and covered with graceful trees. Every variety of form, and tint of light and shadow, abounded in the near islands; whilst those beyond faded out, as they distanced, into dim shapes, faint clouds, very dreams of islands, giving one a sense of the profusion of creative power, that was almost overwhelming.

The summit of Glenton Island being cleared, we left Lieutenant Dawson to take his round of angles, and went to visit a group of islands about nine miles off the east end of Moresby Island, named by us Engineer Group, as a whole; and separately, Slade, Skelton, Watts, and Butchard, after our able engineers. The three first are lofty islands, from six to nine miles in circumference, and highly cultivated by their inhabitants: Slade Island has very large villages,

Lieutenant Smith and I finding that there was too much surf on for us to land from the steam pinnace on Slade Island, went on shore in native canoes, knowing that in case of treachery at the hands of these untried natives we could protect ourselves with our revolvers, and received a somewhat doubtful welcome from a large crowd on the beach. We gave them the salutation learned by us on our last cruise, and on this the people thawed a little, and led us to a cleared space in their village, where we sat down, and they all seated themselves round us, and commenced an animated conversation amongst themselves, of which we were evidently the subjects. Tired of waiting their pleasure, we rose presently, and began to walk about and investigate. They seemed to think we were going to steal their goods, and would not let us enter their houses, nor barter for anything, save a few nuts and yams; so that we left them with our bags of iron hoop pretty full. Going off in the canoe, I was upset for the second time that day, and being weighed down by the iron hoop, sank, and should have found a difficulty in getting to the surface again, had it not fallen out of the bag and allowed me to rise and gain the bottom of the canoe.

By March 3d, after unremitting hard work of officers and men, Lieutenant Dawson and I had satisfied ourselves that the passage round East Cape was not through China Straits, but round the east end of Moresby Island; and on this day I had the satisfaction of conning the ship from the foretop through the passage between Grant and Shortland Islands, and so through still narrower waters to an island near East Cape, seen by us last year, and named Lydia, about ten miles in circumference, and 1034 feet high. This was a great point gained, as it proved the existence of a channel navigable for large steamers round the East Cape of New Guinea; but as it led in one place between dangerous reefs, with a channel scarce 500 yards wide, I resolved to devote more time, and search for a safe channel for sailing-vessels. In the meantime the lofty razor-edge summit of Lydia Island was cleared for a station, and from this look-out we could discern more than fifty islands awaiting our survey and naming. I was struck by the conscientiousness displayed by a boy at Lydia Island, with whom I attempted to barter an axe for a handsome shell necklace he wore. He made signs that the necklace was not his, and refused to trade; his companions urged him vehemently, even trying to force it off his neck, and at last so far prevailed that he took the axe from my hand and half unfastened the necklace; conscience pricked him, and he hurriedly thrust back the axe, and making signs that he would go and get leave from the owner to sell it, paddled off amidst the jeers of his friends. The houses on Lydia Island were unusually small, and the natives seemed of a darker race than those in the vicinity.

On March 4th we paid our first and much desired visit to the D'Entrecasteaux group. These lofty islands, which culminate in 7000 feet of height, had been seen from a distance on their eastern side by the French navigator whose name they bear, but had not been visited by him or any white man. We had spent this day in surveying off the southern shores of the Prevost range, as we have named the lofty southern range of the islands, and observing a populous village at Cape Ventenat, resolved to land there. The people in the canoes near shore feared and avoided us, so we gave chase to some canoes which we saw to seaward, and coming up with them before they could reach the reef they were making for, threw them some strips of red cloth and lengths of iron hoop, and conciliated them; but we landed with caution, for all the women had been sent out of sight, and the men looked doubtful of us. Our precautions were happily needless; we were eagerly welcomed; the women and children soon reappeared, and we were offered hot and savoury food from their large earthen bowls. Here, for the first time, human figures painted on the gable-ends of the larger houses were seen by us; the artist's skill was of the rudest, and the subjects were unfit for reproduction. We did not meet with any other attempt to delineate the human form here, save in some small grotesque carvings at the ends of wooden knives, spoons, and ornamented clubs, of which many were pretty well executed.

On March 8th, so much surveying work had been accomplished that it became needful for Lieutenant Dawson to leave off active work, and plot or place the accumulated results on the chart, and as this would occupy our able surveyor a week, I determined to spend this time in making a running survey of the D'Entrecasteaux group. We took the "Basilisk" accordingly that evening round to the northern coast of New Guinea, and after much searching, the shore being "steep to," and the water very deep, found ground in twenty-two fathoms, with swinging room for the ship in a bay. Dropping anchor about five yards from the sounding, it sank into forty-five fathoms, whilst under our stern the depth was ninety-three fathoms. Next day we steered for the western shores of D'Entrecasteaux, passing several dangerous reefs, and anchored twenty-five miles north of East Cape, in a small cove, where the ship had barely room to swing clear of the reefs. Trap Bay, as we named it, is exposed to westerly winds, but the weather was fine, and it answered our requirements. The ship safe, I went away exploring the coast to the north, and found what I thought to be an extensive bay, but which proved afterwards to be broad straits separating the two southern islands of the D'Entrecasteaux group. It was dark when we returned to the ship, and a heavy swell was rolling in, precursor of bad weather, which kept us bound to our dangerous anchorage for two days. Only a few natives lived about Trap Bay, and their houses were so well hidden in the bush that we could not find them. They would not communicate with us on shore, but came freely off to the ship, with pigs and fruit. On the 10th we stood north, to look for an anchorage, and found ourselves in a wide strait, separating the two large southern islands which we have since named Normanby and Fergusson Islands. We kept along its southern shores, beneath the lofty volcanic peaks of Normanby Island, not knowing what any moment might reveal to us, and, being under its lee, were sailing in calm blue water. Before us rose a pyramidal mountain, about 4000 feet high, rounding which we could see the sea beyond, but almost shut out from view by a cluster of islets at this, the eastern entrance to the Straits. Our boats went now to search for anchorage, and soon we dropped anchor, and swung clear by a few yards of a dark sandy beach, through which a clear mountain stream cut its way to the sea.

The beach was fringed with jungle and forest trees, but casting our eyes up the precipitous mountain-side we saw abundant cultivation, and beyond us a cleared space where a number of women were standing gazing at us, but no village. Presently the men came crowding to the beach, armed with clubs and spears, and Mr. Bentley and I landed, and walking up to the astonished savages gave them some presents, and patted them on the back; in fact, by this time we had all attained such experience in the management of savages that we felt confident of succeeding with these, and they soon became friendly, and we presently returned to the ship, carrying our purchases of weapons, which had perhaps been brought to the beach to be used against us. From this time, during the week we spent here, the ship was besieged from dawn to sunset by hundreds of canoes, containing many hundreds of natives from far and near, eager to barter all they possessed for iron hoop—stone hatchets, ornaments, yams, fruit, and fish, which latter made an agreeable variety of food for the men.

These natives are similar to the New Guinea men, but seem more liable to loathsome skin diseases. Their weapons differ slightly, the spears here being made without barbs, and they use slings for stones made of hair or fibre.

Our seamen made themselves popular with their dusky friends by getting them on board and painting them with quaint devices in tar and red paint; and those thus ornamented became objects of an envy on shore that produced only too many candidates for the paint-brush. Our men gave these people an alarm unintentionally on one occasion, by running up suddenly to loose sails. In a moment their canoes began to fly, crushing against each other, the large overwhelming the small, till, when about 100 yards off, they turned, and seeing that no harm was intended, regained their confidence, and seemed immoderately amused at their fears. After a time we began to observe that none of the natives who wore cane bracelets on their arms would allow themselves to be painted, and by their signs we understood that they were in mourning for the dead. Some of the officers visited the village belonging to these people, which stood about 1500 feet above the sea, on the brow of a hill, and was surrounded by cultivation, but they were not received with cordiality. The women were kept out of sight, and the men were evidently relieved when their visitors took their departure. The young officers became, whilst here, the possessors of native canoes, in which, in spite of many capsizes, they used to cruise about, miles away from the ship. Wild duck were seen here, perched on the branches of lofty trees, and spiders were found with bodies 5½ inches in length.

Lieutenant Dawson now began to plot his work, Lieutenant Smith to wood and water the ship, and Navigating-Lieutenant Mourilyan, Mr. Watts, engineer, and I, started in the steam-pinnance to lay down the unknown coast-line of these D'Entrecasteaux Islands, having six men with us. We had a whale-boat in tow which carried coals and provisions for a week, and would be a means of escape in case of accident to the pinnace.

Steaming out of the new strait to which we had given the name of Dawson Strait, to the west, we passed close under the high mountains that form its northern boundary, the native villages built high up on the hills, with their patches of cultivated ground, contrasting well with the mass of sombre forest which, except where broken by ravines, overspread all. Our course lay for a projecting cape off Fergusson, the middle island of the group, about twenty miles distant, and as we passed on within a few yards of the shore, the excited natives who watched us, and who must have thought us gods moving rapidly on the water without the exertion of apparent power, raced along the beach after us, shouting their exclamation of surprise, "Hoo-ee, Hoo-ee!" We had not time to land, but pressing on found ourselves at the entrance of another broad noble strait, which proved to separate Fergusson from the northmost and loftiest island of the D'Entrecasteaux group, to which we have given the name of Goodenough. This—Moresby Strait—is from eight to ten miles wide and fifteen in length, and both its island shores are grandly picturesque, Mount Goodenough rising to a height of nearly 8000 feet. The sides of this great mountain are cultivated to a height of about 2000 feet; gradually its woods give place to barrenness, and its summits stand bare and knife-edged against the sky. Mountain torrents dash down its ravines, and flash out at times from their dark green setting like molten silver. Night now closing, we sought to anchor between a small islet and the shore; our draught of water was but twelve or fourteen inches, and yet we could obtain no anchorage, for the channel was full of mushroom coral, which rose like great pillars from a depth of twenty and thirty fathoms to within three or four inches of the surface, so close together, that after many a wearying trial off the entrance of lovely coves and delicious looking bays, we had to seek a precarious anchorage in twenty fathoms water, outside these coral pillars, on which a dangerous surf was breaking. The natives then crowded alongside us, but we were weary, and wanted to have our evening meal in peace, so blew the steam whistle, and they seized their paddles and glided off into the darkness; but all night long the village clamoured like a frightened rookery, and our look-out men were frequently startled by natives stealing out to within a few feet of us on the reef. At last, some sleep being needful, I caused a rifle to be fired to seaward, and this secured us some quiet. Next day we attempted to pass round the north-west side of Goodenough Island. Its south-western shores are low, and rise very gradually for a mile, till they meet the first swellings of Mount Goodenough. Villages are scattered all over this ample plain, and the dark sandy beach is cut through by many mountain streams. We failed to circumnavigate the island for want of fuel, and the labour of constantly filling the boiler with fresh water was very retarding. Our first stopping place was at a little creek, named by us Breakfast Cove, at the head of which was a brackish lagoon, and beyond that, in thick forest, a rock-strewn watercourse, with delicious pools of cool water, in which we bathed, to our great refreshment. Here we breakfasted, and enjoyed the shade and space, after our much cramping up, in the boat. A naturalist would have envied our position, surrounded as we were by strange trees and shrubs and beautiful birds, to which we unfortunately could give no name. We knew the Megapode, a bush turkey, and recognised it here—a bird like a small barndoor fowl, with long yellow legs. The nests each consisted of about thirty cartloads of dry leaves, sticks, and shells, formed into a great heap, the heat of which would hatch the eggs deposited. Leaving Breakfast Cove we continued our course along the south-west of the island for about fifteen miles, coasting along a fine belt of alluvial land, full of villages, and well cultivated, the cultivation running from the plain high up the precipitous sides of magnificent Mount Goodenough, which are broken into an endless variety of ravines and valleys overshadowed by the lofty peaks that pierce the clear blue air. As day closed in I found that the island extended too far to the north-west, and that our coal was too short for us to get round it, and we turned back, much regretting the necessity, and anchored for the night in Breakfast Cove, where we had some work as usual in filling the boiler before turning in. We were awakened in the morning by the discordant screams of many birds, and after a plunge into one of the clear pools, shaded over by great trees, we steered for Fergusson Island, and came opposite a large village at noon. Here a very pleasant-looking old lady paddled off to us in a catamaran; we gave her some strips of red cloth, and she became quite friendly. On our landing, strange to say the women were the first to come forward, the men appearing, but keeping back in a state of evident timidity. The presents we gave the women, however, soon brought the men round us, and so entire was my confidence in their peaceable disposition that I visited their inland plantations, accompanied only by a seaman. I found large enclosures, well fenced in with bamboo, producing tropical fruits, yams, sweet potatoes, Indian corn, and sugar-cane, and saw the sago-palm growing in rich abundance here. The natives mash the sago in immense troughs, which I at first thought to be worn-out canoes. We all enjoyed this food, and used it largely. The good feeling of these natives deserves mention. They had never seen the "Basilisk," and knew nothing of our possessing superior arms. We were but ten men amongst hundreds, and they knew that we carried iron hoop on our persons; but not only did they refrain from the least attempt to molest us, but they helped us over obstacles, showed us the best paths, and took care of our clothes whilst we bathed. Here, a mile from the beach, I saw large masses of coral rock cropping up at perhaps a hundred feet above the sea level, close to volcanic cliffs. Taking leave of our friends, we passed to the north between Fergusson and Goodenough Islands, and found ourselves on the north shore of Fergusson Island. Steering then to the east, we hoped to go down round this island to the "Basilisk" in Dawson Strait. There was a singular absence of coral formation on this north shore; and the beach and bottom of the sea, formed of black volcanic sand, offered many valuable anchorages, as they sloped gradually into deep water. No natives lived on this part of the island, and we could not find any fish in the bays. We anchored for the night in a snug bay on the north side of the island; and on landing shot a wallaby.

We discovered here some boiling mineral springs, strongly alkaline, which united themselves in a rivulet that offered any degree of temperature to our bathers. Other hot springs may exist here at the bottom of the

SHOOTING A WALLIBY, NEAR THE BOILING SPRINGS, ON THE D'ENTRECASTEAUX ISLANDS.

sea, which would account for the absence of fish in the bays. In the sand and mud thrown out by these springs we found very small specimens of rubies and amethysts, evidently chippings from larger stones. We enjoyed our bathing here under the shade of huge overhanging trees, with the comfortable faith that snakes and alligators were unlikely to tolerate such a temperature, and that we should have our bath to ourselves, and the steam kept the mosquitoes at a distance, so that our comfort was perfect. On getting outside, on the 15th, we were met by a strong south-east breeze, and had to take shelter in a large bay, named by us Hughes Bay, after our stoker, sheltered to the north by eight or ten lofty islets, which we named Amphlett Group. After filling our boiler with fresh water, and trading with the friendly natives, who regarded our colour and clothes with wonder, we made a second attempt to round the east end of the island; but the wind had now increased to a gale, accompanied by a heavy ocean sea, which placed us in considerable danger, and finding from the unexpected trend of the land that we were still thirty or forty miles from the ship, we bore up, and determined to make a fair wind of the gale by returning the way we came. We spent the night in a sheltering bay, abounding with turtle, on the north-east of the island; and next morning rose early, and our coal being now expended, cut wood, by the aid of which, and greased coal bags, we managed to make about twenty miles progress, and reach the village we had previously visited in Moresby Straits, where we anchored for the night.

On March 18th we made another attempt to reach the ship, and when just at the entrance of Dawson Straits we had the pleasure of seeing her come steaming towards us, Lieutenant Smith, according to orders, being on his way to look for us on account of our prolonged absence. The cleanliness, free space, and comfort of the ship was very welcome after our hardships, and we were able to feel with pleasure that we had done a good piece of work in laying down the principal part of the before unknown coast-line of these islands, which lie directly in the track of the new route, extending ninety miles in a N.W. and S.E. direction, with an average width of about fifteen miles.

Lieutenant Dawson had finished his plotting by our return, so we sailed at once for our old surveying-ground, resolving to strain every nerve in searching for a better passage from the south round the East Cape of New Guinea. I had found by experience that boats were too low in the water to be of much use in such work, and were only fit to verify the clearness of a channel for a few yards at either side. I have frequently passed within twenty yards of dangerous reefs in boats without observing them, whereas, from aloft in the ship, in fine weather, and in the absence of too strong a sun-glare on the water, a reef could be seen two or three miles off. Our plan was for the ship to start in the early morning and take a zig-zag course to avoid the level sun-rays, sounding as she went, whilst we despatched boats at intervals to carry out lines of soundings between two fixed points, and to fix the position of any dangers that might exist. During such work Lieutenant Dawson would be absent for a day or two, engaged in the more scientific work of fixing positions trigonometrically. We almost lived aloft those days; but the weather was generally fine, and our work went on well. The anxious moments came when a cloud no bigger than a man's hand appeared on the horizon, and growing and nearing us rapidly, enveloped us in a tropical tornado, which sometimes lasted two hours. Anxious hours they were indeed, as we drove across the rain-pitted sea, now over the safe blue of the deep water, now over the treacherous shoaling green of the reefs; the leadsmen, like messengers of fate in the chains, calling their soundings; shut in all round by a gloom which no eye could pierce; seeing nothing but the coral below, which seemed to lift itself up to meet us; forbearing to anchor till there was no other alternative, and drifting on we knew not whither. It was difficult as the man at the bowsprit end reported "water appears to be shoaling!" to answer with a sufficiently cheery "very well!" The men cowered in their light clothing from the pitiless rain, which was cold and sharp as hail; our ears were full of the confusion of the elements and the roar of the escaping steam—all in strange contrast with the sunny calm which had just preceded.

At other times, when wooding or making plans, we anchored the ship and were away in the boats for days, Lieutenants Sydney Smith and Deedes, Navigating-

S

Lieutenant Mourilyan, Mr. Mudge, and I, working in different directions; and on all occasions the tact of the officers and good behaviour of the men prevented trouble arising with the natives. Once Lieutenant Smith thought that the cupidity of the natives of Teste Island was excited by the sight of the fire-bars of the steam pinnace, and he prudently changed his position. Lieutenant Deeds was fortunate in witnessing a fight between the natives of Slade and those of East Cape and Moresby Island. The combined warriors approached Slade Island in about twenty canoes, containing some thirty men each, but remained thirty yards off shore, throwing spears and slinging stones at the Slade Islanders, who waded out and returned the discharge. They kept this safe distance for two hours, dodging each other's missiles so skilfully that nobody seemed seriously hurt. We rarely saw a wounded man amongst these people, and but few enemies' skulls adorned the outside of their houses.

On March 26th we were joined by H.M.S. "Sandfly," but, as she had unfortunately grounded on a reef and injured her rudder, her services were lost to us, and she returned to Possession Bay for repairs.

On April 1st it was necessary to cut a supply of wood, and we found an anchorage off Blackney Island, a low uninhabited coral islet, about fifteen miles to the north-east of Moresby Island, where there was an abundance of wood, and which seemed to be an ancient home of the megapodes, as they had nested here in great numbers. The poor birds were delicious food, and were sacrificed accordingly. When we had got our wood off, the "Basilisk" looked more like an Irish turf-boat than a man-of-war, her entire upper-deck being covered with great wood-stacks; but we were only too happy to see it there, fuel being everything towards the success of our work.

Our surveying, which was monotonous work enough, was sometimes diversified by little incidents; for instance, in surveying Fools Cap, an isolated rock, Lieutenant Smith espied a cave with some rare shells shining within, and working his way in to get at them, had just put his hand on one, when a large land-snake upreared itself and disputed possession; taken by surprise, he tumbled back with more haste than dignity, and summoned some of the boat's crew, when he returned to the attack and killed the snake, a dangerous-looking brute, about four feet long, with claws or teeth in its tail.

On April 8th we resumed our old position at Possession Bay to await the arrival of a vessel with coal and stores expected by us. The result of our work was that we had found a passage, the least width of which was two miles, leading from Teste Island to the north of New Guinea; but there was still much to be done, and our boats were kept detached on work which, when all summed up, resulted in the laying down of more than 2000 miles of fixed soundings in this survey off the East Cape and D'Entrecasteaux Islands.

The "Sandfly" was lying here on our arrival, and

we found that the natives had committed the bold act of stealing the barricoes and boat's crutches from one of her boats. I had always been ready to overlook the smaller delinquencies of the natives, but this was going a step too far, and I directed Lieutenant Nowell, her commander, to lay an ambush, and seize some natives, near the spot where the robbery had been committed. Two were accordingly secured after a long struggle, in which their smooth skin and supple limbs eluded the attempts of our strong seamen, and were taken on board the "Sandfly," where they seemed to expect instant death. Their wives and friends came off weeping and offering presents to buy them off, and the natives deserted the ship and kept close to the shore in their canoes, ready for instant flight into the bush. I went amongst them in a dingey, thinking that many of them would recognise me and be assured, and at last succeeded in making them understand that the prisoners should be set free when the property was brought back. On the second day they restored the articles and we released the men, to the intense joy of their friends, which it was quite affecting to witness, and presently a large hog was sent on board the "Sandfly" to show their gratitude. A few days afterwards our carpenters, working on a stage over the side, missed a saw, but before we could take any steps, we saw a large canoe coming off, in which an old man stood holding up the saw, and on reaching us he returned it and expressed his anger at the theft.

The coal barque arriving, we were gladdened by the receipt of news from home, five months old it is true, but still how welcome! On April 15th, having got our coal on board, and having found that the "Sandfly's" defects unfortunately rendered it necessary to send her to Sydney, we towed the two vessels out of Possession Bay, gave them a good offing, and after seeing them stand south for Sydney, anchored in Hoop-Iron Bay to rate our chronometers. The following ten days were devoted to perfecting our knowledge of the route we had discovered, which passed between the east end of Moresby Island and Engineer Group, with a depth of water varying from 30 to 500 fathoms. A still more roomy but longer route had also been found by us from Teste Island to the north side of New Guinea, running eastward of the whole Archipelago Islands lying off East Cape.

We felt that all our desires of last year in this respect had now been fulfilled, and that the "Basilisk" had opened a new and accurately surveyed highway for commerce between Australia, New Guinea, and China.

CHAPTER XVII.

PREPARE TO SURVEY THE UNKNOWN NORTH-EAST COAST OF NEW GUINEA—LOW FEVER—DISTINCTIVE CHARACTERISTICS OF THIS COAST—GOOD-ENOUGH BAY—WARD-HUNT STRAITS—COAST FROM EAST CAPE TO CAPE VOGEL—RICH LAND ABOUT BENTLEY BAY—MUTINY AMONGST THE PIGS—SHARP GRASSY HILLS—CAPE FRERE—PLATEAUX AND RIVER AT BARTLE BAY—COLLINGWOOD BAY—MOUNTS VICTORY AND TRAFALGAR—SUPPOSED TRACES OF THE RHINOSCEROS—NATIVES BECOME VERY SHY—STEAM PINNACE CHASED—NEW KIND OF CANOE—DYKE ACLAND BAY—TUMULTUOUS GATHERING OF NATIVES—WAR CHANT—REFRAIN FROM LANDING—NARROW ESCAPE OF A PARTY OF OFFICERS FROM THE NATIVES—RIVER CLYDE.

I WISHED to remain longer and carry our survey farther to the eastward; but I had already exceeded the time allowed me by a fortnight; and there remained a running survey of the unknown north-east coast for about 300 miles as the crow flies, to be accomplished, a length which was certain to be much extended by the irregularities of the coast-line. We therefore turned the "Basilisk's" head westward on April 27th, amidst great rejoicings, for every mile was now a mile nearer home. At this time we were attacked by a low fever of a mild type, which completely prostrated those it seized for the time, and rendered our subsequent work more arduous, the more so as we were already forty men short of complement.

The first striking differences between these northern and the southern shores of New Guinea are, that here there is no outlying Barrier Reef, and that the shores, instead of shelving outwards, are steep-to. The mountains here generally run down to the sea; then follows a shore reef, from which the plumb line may be thrown into fifty fathom water. The coast-line is, as a rule, but little broken up, and affords few harbours, but offers several anchorages. Speaking generally, the coast-line from East Cape to Cape Cretin, a distance of 300 miles, may be spoken of as a series of bold headlands, running out twenty to forty miles seaward, with deep bays between—a configuration which increased our work twofold.

It has already been said that the passage between East Cape and the D'Entrecasteaux islands was named by us "Goschen Straits." Passing East Cape to the westward, the islands and the mainland of New Guinea recede from each other, forming an extensive bay, which we named after our commodore, "Goodenough." At the western end of this bay New Guinea stretches out, a far projecting promontory, to within fifteen miles of Goodenough Island; the passage between we named after the first Lord of the Admiralty, "Ward-Hunt Straits;" and named the promontory Cape Vogel, after the Prime Minister of New Zealand.

Between East Cape and Cape Vogel there is a coast-line of about 100 miles, along with a depth of from 500 to 600 fathoms; and a muddy bottom prevails at about two miles from the shore. Villages abound here, and the valleys, not seen from the sea, on account of the lie of the hills, are well cultivated.

Our course now lay round the southern shores of Goodenough Bay; and twenty miles west of East Cape the "Basilisk" found a good anchorage in Bentley Bay, and remained there for a day to survey and explore the surrounding country. The natives had evidently heard of us from their fellow-countrymen to the eastward, for they received us joyfully, and brought us off numbers of pigs, one of which was large enough to give all the ship's company a dinner. Landing with a small party I climbed the precipitous hills, 2000 feet high, and looked across to Milne Bay, which lay at their southern base. The land between was fairly cultivated, and watered by many streams; and to the west we could see great mountains rising in the clear air perhaps a hundred miles distant.

After a long tiresome scramble through the thick forest, where we were indebted to the natives who met us for guidance, we got back to the village off which the ship was anchored, suffering a good deal from the severe stings of the tree ants that had attacked us in the trees we were compelled to climb in order to take observations.

That night on board was marked by a mutiny amongst our numerous pigs; they were securely penned amidships, and remained quiet enough till the middle watch, when they suddenly seemed to become as possessed as their Jewish brethren of old, leapt out of the pens, and rushed squealing and grunting to the gangways to jump overboard. The men, who were all sleeping on deck, were quickly on the alert to save their future dinners. The pigs rushed wildly between their legs, capsizing them in all directions at first, but numbers prevailed in the end, and the poor piggies were secured all but one, which had successfully charged the guardians of the gangways and plunged overboard.

On April 29th we left Bentley Bay and went westward. From this point commenced our running survey, during which the positions of every prominent point on the coast, at distances of from twenty to forty miles from each other, was exactly fixed, the coast-line between carefully sketched in, and soundings laid down. I also kept steadily to my custom of communicating with the natives whenever possible.

Beyond Cape Ducie and Chads Bay the forest ceases, and is succeeded by an openly-wooded plateau, full of villages, which is backed two miles inwards by a range of sharp grassy hills, bare of wood, each defined by a belt of dark brushwood at its base, and coming crowding down, hill upon hill, with such a curious effect, as to remind us strongly of the plate in Black's "Atlas" of all the mountains of the world. Above the height of 2000 feet the forest, singularly enough, springs up again, on higher peaks, and covers them to the very top, at a height of six or seven thousand feet. Cape Frere is a noble headland, dropping, in a huge buffalo-headed mass, almost perpendicularly to the deep blue sea; and the "Basilisk" looked like a mere cock-boat in its shadow, as, almost scraping her sides against the beetling mass, she stood in to seek for an anchorage in Bartle Bay. This bay has an extensive tract of comparatively low land, marked by terraced plateaus at its head, from which a stream debouches through a dark sandy beach, and this seemed to afford a certainty of a good anchorage being found for the night; but we were doomed to disappointment, nowhere within a cable's length of the beach would an eighty fathom line touch ground. At last, after much seeking, we anchored in forty-nine fathoms—a depth greater than that of the English Channel midway—with our stern just swinging clear of the beach. The soil about Bartle Bay is very rich; and the land runs back in a series of terraced elevations to a lofty inland range of mountains. The river which issues at the head of the bay has ploughed deeply through these terraces, so that its banks are exposed in sections from ten to thirty feet high; they are composed of smooth water-worn stones, embedded in a light gravelly soil. We searched, but could find no trace of gold here; nor was any seen by us on the north coast of New Guinea. Wild duck abounded.

About 120 unarmed natives streamed along the beach to meet us on our landing, the foremost carrying the sacrificial dog, and others a pig slung on bamboo poles; but they were very timid, and it was some time before we could succeed in inducing them to approach us. When they gained confidence they took the dog by the hind legs in the usual way, and dashed its brains out against the gunwale of our boat, and hailing a passing canoe, they sent the body on board the "Basilisk," where, by my orders, it was received with all respect. They then presented me with the pig, and I made a return present of a hatchet, which was received in a way that showed they had but little idea of its use.

Next day we fixed the position of Cape Bartle, and explored the country, but only to a small extent, as the tall coarse grass was a serious hindrance. We followed the trend of the river, taking advantage of occasional native tracks, which led to yam and sugar-cane plantations, and visited the villages, which stand in groves of trees, and are not visible from the beach. We were surprised to find that the houses here were not built on poles nor saddle-roofed, but thatched close down to the ground, and of an oval form. The canoes were somewhat differently constructed, and the language was wholly different. It seemed to us then that Cape Frere was the dividing point between the two languages and styles of house-building, but farther to the westward we observed that the Malay building on poles recurred.

On the morning of May 1st we lifted our anchor with some difficulty, so reduced was the effective ship's company, and sailed for the bight of Goodenough Bay, some thirty miles off, over a tranquil sea, for the monsoon blowing on the south side of New Guinea was arrested by the lofty Owen Stanley range, the summits of which were now always obscured with heavy clouds, that told of troubled waters at the south side of the peninsula.

Our track lay about two miles from shore, and our faithful little ally, the steam pinnace, kept abreast of us within half-a-mile of the beach—a plan followed through this whole remaining survey, as enabling us to lay down a double line of soundings simultaneously.

The villages are scattered along this part of the coast on a plateau of park-like land, which intervenes between the shore and the mountains within, which, rising by gradually higher undulations, terminate at a height of many thousand feet above the sea. There can be no doubt as to the capabilities of this land if cultivated. On the hills herds of cattle, and sheep innumerable, might find pasture, whilst from the cold summits to the hot plains all the products of wide extents of climate might be grown. At two miles from shore we found the depth of water to be 620 fathoms. The coast trends W.N.W. from Cape Frere for some thirty miles to the bight of Goodenough Bay, which is marked by some fine waterfalls, which flash down its dark green mountain sides. So much river water is here discharged that the surface of the bay near the shore is quite fresh. A mud flat offered us a good anchorage here; and on some small islets off the coast, we obtained an abundant supply of pigeons. The natives made every effort to be friendly, but, as it was nearly dark when we anchored, we did not see much of them; they are of a dark copper-colour, and look intelligent.

The bold promontory, named by us Cape Vogel,

which terminates Goodenough Bay to the north-west, and is separated from the D'Entrecasteaux Islands by Ward-Hunt Straits, being passed, we found anchorage on the night of May 2d amidst a small group of islets, ten miles west of it. These were named by us Jabbering Islets, because their natives surrounded the ship with their canoes at night, and kept up such a noise that we could get no rest, though we tried every persuasion to induce them to move off. At last, sleep being absolutely necessary, we fired a rifle over their heads, and they vanished away into the gloom.

From Cape Vogel the land trends again W.N.W. for nearly fifty miles, and shows the usual aspects of the low wooded plain, with great mountains running behind, when another lofty promontory runs out for forty miles to the north-east, and forms the southern enclosure of another great bay. A double peaked mountain rises 4000 feet high from this promontory, and shows to its full height above the plain of the sea, and the low land from which it springs. Altogether the features were so striking that I resolved to honour them with great names. The Cape is therefore Cape Nelson; the two summits of the mountain are Mounts Victory and Trafalgar, and the great bay thus formed, is now Collingwood Bay. At the head of Collingwood Bay we found a good anchorage, and remained two days cutting wood. Here Lieutenant Smith observed the droppings of some large grass-eating animal in a spot where the bushes had been heavily trampled and broken. Our opinion was decided that a rhinosceros had haunted there; and we were much surprised, as this animal has never been believed to exist in New Guinea. It would have been very satisfactory to have set the question thus started at rest, but time failed us. The natives here, a dark, dirty-looking people, wholly destitute of clothing, were very shy and difficult of approach, and threatened us with their spears; but by dint of laying presents on the ground, and making friendly gestures, we succeeded in winning them to trade a little. All along this coast we noticed that the inhabitants of the large and populous villages were more civilised and comfortable-looking than those of the small, doubtless because the most desirable sites had been chosen by the many, and they had prospered accordingly. These Collingwood Bay people gazed at us with such a blank astonishment, and held such consultation about us amongst themselves, that we were persuaded that they, in common with their neighbours on this coast, had never seen white men before. The steam pinnace, whilst surveying at the head of the bay, was chased by a large number of canoes holding thirty or forty men each; but the officer in command did not think it prudent to allow them to come at all near, and may therefore have been mistaken in supposing their intentions to be hostile.

We left Collingwood Bay on April 5th, having found its western waters studded with dangerous reefs, through which we had to pick our way with great caution, and rounded Cape Nelson before nightfall, when we were much impressed by the fine picturesque appearance of Mounts Victory and Trafalgar. These mountains, which are joined by a saddle-shaped ridge, descend to the sea in open grassy and wooded slopes, which have all the appearance of English parkland. Thence the land trended westward, a pretty undulating country, with a shore broken up by bays and still lagoons, protected by reefs. We anchored for the night about six miles west of Cape Nelson, near some small islets, and were disturbed by the natives singing and shouting round the ship; but they kept at a distance. We made every effort in the morning to get them to come alongside, but they would not. They were quite unclad, repulsive-looking, and of a darkish colour, and wore their hair in long ugly ringlets like pipe-stems. Their canoes were of a kind new to us, being forty or fifty feet long, but so exceedingly narrow that a man could barely squeeze into them; besides the usual out-rigger, they had balancing spars on the opposite side, supporting a fighting stage to hold five or six men. In hope of making friends I coaxed some natives to bring their canoes alongside my gig, and though they were much alarmed, should have succeeded, but that my coxswain unfortunately stood up and began to coil the lead-line, when they, thinking they were about to be made fast, paddled off in an instant. Having failed on the water, a party of us went on shore and visited the village, but the natives had fled. The houses, which stood in plantations, were built of light cane, with a fireplace in the centre, and appeared clean; but every article had been removed from them.

Returning to the ship we found that some canoes had ventured near enough to barter; that no idea had been shown as to the value of our axes and hoop-iron, but that strips of cloth had been highly valued. Lieutenant Dawson, whilst engaged in fixing the position of these islets had a spear thrown at him, hence we called them Spear Islets. These natives had no human bone ornaments like those of Milne Bay.

West of Cape Nelson lies another large bay, fringed by a low densely-wooded coast, backed by the usual lofty inland range, and in this bay, which I named Dyke Acland, after my revered friend the late Sir Thomas Dyke Acland, Bart., we anchored in thirty-three fathoms, at eight miles' distance from shore.

The morning of May 7th rose thick and gloomy, with heavy rain; but having had a good view of the trend of the land the evening before, we proceeded cautiously on, with the steam pinnace leading. The western extremity of this bay, which is fifty miles from Cape Nelson, is about twenty miles to the eastward of a point indistinctly seen at a distance by D'Entrecasteaux and named by him Cape Sud Est; but as this part of the coast is low, and no distinctly defined cape exists here, it is evident that he had mistaken the high inland range of mountains, on which the position called by him a cape actually falls, for the coast-line.

The weather now cleared, and we were able to send our steam pinnace to coast along the shore as usual, whilst we kept on abreast two miles outside. The trend of the land was now about N.W., and the average depth of water about twenty-five fathoms. The shore here is low and wooded, but the numerous villages we passed seemed to indicate that it was not swampy land. Huge wooded mountains were seen in the background, and were considered by us to be part of the Owen Stanley range. Towards sunset we had reached a point of land which projected about fifteen miles to sea, crowned with hills about 400 feet high on the southern part, in lat. 8° 10′ S., and long. 148° 12 E., and named it Caution Point, on account of the uncertain soundings we obtained. We found an anchorage about half-a-mile from the shore, opposite a considerable village, in which the wildest excitement began immediately to prevail. Conches were blown, and a tumultuous gathering of armed savages took place on the beach opposite the ship. It happened to be one of our penny-reading nights, and they evidently took the singing and loud chorus, borne to them across the water, for our defiance, for they chanted back a war song in return. All night this excitement continued amongst the natives, but they did not venture off. In the morning, I took a boat with five men, and made an attempt to be friendly; but, unfortunately, such a surf was running on the beach as made it imprudent to land, uncertain as we were of the dispositions of the natives, whose excitement became intense as we neared the beach. About 100 men awaited us there, armed with spears, stone clubs, and shields, ornamented with bird of paradise plumes on their shoulders, and with shell necklets, and bedaubed with white and red pigments on their bodies, which were quite naked. Many of them were springing into the air and brandishing their weapons; some waded out waist-deep shaking their spears at us, totally unaware of our power to hurt them. Selecting one of these bold fellows, we let the boat drift towards him, and stood with our arms wide open to show that we had no weapons, one of the men holding out a piece of red cloth on the end of a boat-hook as a present. In this way we succeeded in getting four or five to come close and take our presents, but they would give us nothing in return. Suddenly they seized the boat and tried to drag us on shore. Observing no friendly signs, however, and seeing that no women or children were present, I decided on not landing. The fellows holding the boat were very muscular, and we shook them off with some difficulty, on which they caught the yoke-lines, which we had to cut to get off, so resolved were they to detain us. It was evident that as we went westward our dealings would have to be held with a fiercer race of savages; but of this I had been forewarned by the foresight of the then hydrographer, Admiral Richards.

Leaving Caution Point, we kept a sharp look-out for a large island shown on the chart as Richie Island, so named by D'Entrecasteaux, after the naturalist of his expedition. The position assigned it on the chart was long. 147° 50′ E., lat. 8° 10′ S., but rounding a cape less striking than the preceding capes, we found that no such island existed, and that the position given it was twenty miles inland. I therefore wished to name the cape Ward-Hunt, but it still remains on the chart as Richie Island, out of compliment to D'Entrecasteaux. Rounding this cape the land trends again westward, and we saw before us a large river discharging itself over a dangerous bar; immediately to the west was a beautiful bay running up to a sandy beach, fringed with groves of a kind of fir tree, admirably adapted for firewood, of which we were now much in need. Choosing a position off the best-looking trees, we anchored about 100 yards from the beach, in thirteen fathoms water, and were rather glad that no villages were at hand. In the evening some large canoes came round a point and neared the ship, but refused to communicate. They slowly paddled round, the savages chanting a monotonous tune, and beating time with their paddles on the sides of their canoes. Our men, then enjoying their singing and smoking hour, replied by copying the chaunt, and the savages listened with a dignified silence that provoked roars of laughter from the "Basilisk." We found that they had no intention of retiring for the night, so fired a signal-rocket over their heads, on which they beat a hasty retreat.

The following morning the men were employed in wooding, and I was writing in my cabin, when it was reported to me that three of our officers had strayed away from the wooding party about a mile along the beach, and that a large number of armed natives had landed from canoes, and were stealing through the bush with the evident intention of attacking them. We, from the ship, could see the natives gliding through the underwood, but the imperilled officers could not, and were quite unaware of their approach. Sub-Lieutenant Shortland and I jumped into the dingey with some spare rifles, and gained the beach just in time to give our shipmates the rifles, and put them on their guard. Hoping to maintain friendly relations, I advanced for about twenty yards alone, armed with a rifle, but holding my arms over my head towards the bush where the natives were now lurking, quite concealed from view. Suddenly they sprang from the bush to the open beach, and formed in two regular lines ten yards in my front—the first line of men armed with spears, which they held, quivering to throw, whilst they moved with a short quick step from side to side, as if to distract an enemy's aim, guarding themselves with shields. The second line was armed with clubs. For some seconds I forbore to fire, hoping still to win them round, but finding this hopeless, and that in another second I should be a target for fifty spears, I fired with a snap-shot at the leading savage. The bullet pierced his shield and spun him round on his heel, but did not wound him; there was no need to fire again and take life, for the whole body of warriors turned instantly in consternation, and ran for the canoes, and we followed till we drove them on board.

The river which lay beyond was named by us the Clyde. Unfortunately the dangerous bar at its mouth prevented our entering to explore it, and the jungle on its banks was too thick to enable us to do so on foot. Its breadth was about sixty yards, and the current clear and steady; and it will probably be found by the explorer to lead into the interior, for the low and undulating land it cleaves stretches back fully twenty miles to the mountain ranges. The river banks abounded in pigeons. Having got about forty tons of wood on board, we left the bay on May 10th. This bay, which will prove to be one of the best anchorages on this coast, we named Traitors' Bay, on account of the attempt made by the natives to cut off the officers.

As I write these lines a telegram has arrived announcing the death of Commodore Goodenough, C.B., C.M.G., commanding on the Australian station, by the poisoned arrows of the natives of Santa Cruz Island. I desire to pay my humble tribute of sorrow and admiration to the memory of this man, with whom I am happy in having held a private friendship for twenty-five years. I do not speak of the loss his friends sustain in him, of the generous nature, full of large kindness and the power of sympathy, of the sound helpful judgment that was ever ready for any call that could be made on it, for this is sacred ground; I speak of him only as a public man, and would say that though I have warmly appreciated him all through, as he rose in our service, I never knew his full professional worth till I had the honour of serving under him in Australia. There, his grasp of mind in dealing with a subject, his self-reliance and readiness to take responsibility, his happy way of taking his captains into his confidence, whilst always holding the reins himself, of giving praise liberally where praise was due, and cordial support or advice where either was needed, produced an impression on my mind of greatness in store for him in the future, which can now never, alas! be made good. His fine scientific and sailor-like qualities, his promptitude, his iron nerve, combine with his other gifts to make his loss a national one, and as such it will doubtless be regarded, and this will be some consolation to his friends; but their best will lie in the knowledge that his pure and devout spirit was ever ready to enter the presence of its Maker.

JAMES GRAHAM GOODENOUGH,

COMMODORE.

THE sad ship hastened; but as "three bells" struck,
Its high recall the sailor's spirit heard,
He smiled, and from our hands that would have held,
He passed at once obedient to the word.

The sea soft-leaping at his vessel's side,
Its pulses beating boundless sympathy
With his that sank; its farewell in his ear,
Where should a seaman die but on the sea!

He failed of home; those dear last words that fall
Before the immortal silence as we part;
But home came round his pillow, fondly drawn
By strong compulsion of that faithful heart.

The spirit swift to plan, the manly will
  To follow on and do, the voice to lead
In war, or council; we must mourn for these:
  They had been ready at his country's need.

But most for him the man of childlike heart,
  Who rang so true to every test of good,
Whose nature held a rare heroic fire,
  With the soft mood of gentle Collingwood.

It was not his to tread a glorious deck,
  To stay its thunders ere his spirit passed,
And through the lifting murk of battle see
  The alien flag come slowly down the mast.

It was not his, the calm of ended toils,
  Thus called at noon, ere half his task was done,
The voice of children's children in the warmth,—
  The ripening warmth of life's low evening sun.

But fate was kind. He died upon his post,
  Holding the olive in his hand to draw
An unwon race, stubborn, unpurposed, blind,
  To the fair brotherhood of light and law.

Nor saint nor sailor died in vain, who strove
  This citadel of heathen hearts to reach,
Fresh hands shall lift the olive from the dust
  Where they have left their bodies in the breach.

Nay, not in vain; but they shall have a joy
  For every link they laid in the great plan
That seeks to draw the scattered nations home,
  And shape the perfect family of man.

JANE MORESBY.

CHAPTER XVIII.

THICKLY WOODED, ALLUVIAL, LEVEL SHORE—HERCULES BAY AND LUARD ISLETS—REACH LONGUERUE ISLAND, WHENCE THE FURTHER COAST-LINE HAS BEEN PRETTY ACCURATELY TRACED BY THE OLD NAVIGATORS—LAST WOOD-CUTTING—NEW GUINEA ANTS—PARSEE POINT—MARKHAM RIVER—MOUNTAIN SLOPES CLOTHED WITH PALM AND TREE-FERNS—MOUNTS GLADSTONE AND DISRAELI—ASTROLOBE GULF—SNAGS BORNE SEAWARD ON A VAST BODY OF FRESH WATER—DEEP-SEA SOUNDINGS—STRONG CURRENT SWEEPS US FROM THRESHOLD BAY—VISIT OF RAJAH OF SALWATTI—MEET MR. MIKLUCHO MAKLAY AT AMBOYNA—PENNANT COMES DOWN AT SHEERNESS.

LEAVING Traitors' Bay, May 10th, we stood west, Navigating-Lieutenant Mourilyan in the steam pinnace doing good service as usual by examining the coast in-shore. Passing the mouths of several small rivers, where alligators were seen basking, we coasted the thickly-wooded level shore for twenty miles, and opened a bay, where we anchored in five fathom water, at two miles from shore, near a group of islets. The former we named Hercules Bay, after Sir Hercules Robinson, S.C.M.G., and the latter after the captain of Sheerness dockyard, Luard Islets. Picking our way through this group in the morning, we found that the coast-line on the west side of Hercules Bay altered its character entirely, the low alluvial land giving place to volcanic hills, that came precipitously down to the water's edge. Numerous volcanic islands were scattered off the coast, and had a singular appearance, looking as though great morsels had been broken from the hills and thrown into the sea. Between them and the mainland a depth of fifty fathoms prevailed. We saw no sign of inhabitants here. Twenty miles farther to the north-west we reached the Longuerue Island of D'Entrecasteaux, at the southern entrance to Huon Gulf, from which point the coast-line has been more or less accurately traced by the old navigators. Our work now was virtually done, my great desire had been attained, and England had won the honour of exploring out the last extensive unknown coast-line in the habitable world, and completing the work begun by Dampier about 1699, and continued by D'Entrecasteaux a century later.

Our object now was to find a good place for firewood, and lay in such a stock as would supply us with fuel till we should reach Amboyna; so keeping close to the shore inside Longuerue Island, till we opened a bay where we saw a fine clump of tall mangrove trees, free from jungle, and growing on a point of land easy of access, we anchored in twenty-five fathoms, off the edge of a shore reef, in a well-sheltered position. Here we remained three days, engaged in our last wood-cutting service. The men divided as usual into axe-men, sawyers, and carriers; attacked the timber with their old spirit, trees fell in all directions, and our carriers, the marines, were kept briskly going, taking the wood on bearers to be measured into fathoms, and down to the boats, which lay moored off the white beach. The labour of wood-cutting, in itself arduous, was so exhausting under a tropical sun that everything was done on such occasions to excite a healthy emulation amongst the men; they were divided into parties according to the part of the ship to which they belonged, and always worked together, aided frequently by most of the officers, and myself, who felled and sawed with the rest. Many of the men received ugly wounds in our first wood-cutting expeditions, before becoming accustomed to the use of the tools, but our greatest annoyance all through was from the ants, with which the New Guinea trees swarmed. They are of various kinds and habits, some are yellow, and burrow tunnels through the branches; a green species glues large bunches of leaves and twigs together, and forms a nest as large as a bee-hive; and there are several brown sorts; but one and all attacked us so fiercely, that at times we had to leave the victory with them, and choose some other spot for wood. At times, where the trees were particularly suitable, and we could not afford to leave them, we had to screw up all our powers of endurance; the officers led the assault, as if it had been a boarding-party, and we came off triumphantly with our wood, but bleeding, and with skin full of the forceps of these creatures which had remained in the wound when we brushed them off. During the survey we cut about 700 tons of hard tropical wood to save our coal; this fact, when our small numbers are considered, as well the ceaseless boat work, and surveying, and deep-sea sounding work, in which they were engaged, will give some idea of the zeal shown by the "Basilisk's" fine crew.

To this bay, which our observations placed in lat. 7° 29′ S. and long. 147° 25′ E., we gave the name of Death Adder Bay; our men having met some death adders in cutting wood. We saw a few deserted native huts here, but no inhabitants. Ten miles to the west villages were seen by our exploring boats, but not communicated with.

A study of the chart having shown that the coast-line for 250 miles to the west, as far as Astrolobe Gulf, was but slightly known. I resolved to continue our coasting survey to that point. May 14th we left Death Adder Bay, and steered north-west along the southern shores of Huon Gulf, past undulating and alluvial land, which succeeded the mountain spurs, and was dotted with villages, and, thirty-five miles north-west of Death Adder Bay, passed a projecting point of land, which had been mistaken by D'Entrecasteaux for an island. It was almost covered with large villages, whose inhabitants crowded to the shore to see us, and paddled after us in canoes, making every sign of friendship, but we could not delay to visit them. We called this point Parsee Point, from the circumstance of the natives wearing singular conical caps, made of tappa. Next morning, May 15th, I went to examine a river which discharges a large body of water into the head of Huon Gulf, but a bar at the entrance prevented our boats passing up, and the banks were too swampy and thickly wooded to permit of our exploring them on foot in the time at our disposal. We named it Markham River, after the able secretary of the Royal Geographical Society. Half a cable's length from the bar we found twenty-six fathoms water, and at a cable's length no bottom with a sixty fathom line. A vessel seeking to anchor here should first send a boat in to pick up a berth. The land now trended for fifty miles due east, forming the north side of Huon Gulf, and making another of those far projecting promontories which we have found so characteristic of north-eastern New Guinea. The land is bold, mountainous, and rises to a height of 9000 feet. It was named by me Rawlinson Range, after the president of the Royal Geographical Society. The valleys here, and the mountain slopes clothed with palms and tree ferns are especially beautiful and well inhabited; and every valley appeared to be watered by a clear mountain stream. Many canoes came off, and boldly ventured alongside to barter tortoise shell, yams, and cocoa-nuts. They brought dogs also, but they were not sacrificed. These people, who were of a dark brown colour, with flat noses, and somewhat woolly hair—more approaching the negro type than any we had seen before, seemed to us to have a knowledge of white men, and did not hesitate to come on board freely. Their canoes were differently constructed from any we had seen before—the outrigger, instead of being a heavy spar as long as the canoe, running close to the side, and supported at each end, was here a light spar supported only at the centre, at such an increased distance from the canoe, as made up for the decreased weight by greater leverage. This 15th of May was marked as an unfortunate day, for our steam pinnace broke down, and was afterwards useless to us. We found a precarious anchorage for the night in forty-five fathoms, about a cable's length from shore.

Rounding Cape Cretin on May 16th, we stood north-west, having the high mountainous islands of New Britain in sight to the north, and from the tiny low islets off Cape Cretin, as well as from the mountainous mainland, we were chased by many canoes, whose rowers anxiously vociferated entreaties to us to stop and barter, but the wind was fresh and fair, and I was too anxious to economise fuel to be able to gratify them. From Cape Cretin to Dampier's Cape King William, a distance of forty miles, the coast line presents new features, for along the rear of the beach runs a narrow terrace of good soil, on which a few solitary huts are scattered, and behind this the land rises in rocky plateaux, as regular as the lines of a fortification, divided by ravines, and looming one above the other till they reach the inland Finisterre Mountains. The air being beautifully clear we were able to measure the altitude of the highest peaks of this range, which, facing each other boldly, lift their heads far above all compeers 11,400 feet above the sea. Their relative position and their greatness suggested irresistibly the names I gave them—Mounts Gladstone and Disraeli, and the wish that one of their great antitypes may emerge ere long from the clouds in which he has veiled his lofty brows, and front his rival as of old.

From Cape King William to Astrolobe Gulf, a distance of 100 miles, the coast runs in a W.N.W. line, and the shores are "steep-to," with a depth of 350 fathoms a mile from shore. The mountains are wooded to the beach, and are studded with many villages. We reached Astrolobe Gulf on May 18th, the western limit of our work, having successfully surveyed all the previously unknown coast of New Guinea, and proved that a clear passage exists to its northern shores and along them. A belt of volcanic islands extends off this part of New Guinea, at distances varying from twenty to fifty miles from the mainland. One of these—Lesson Island—passed by us May 20th, in lat. 3° 35′ S., and long. 144° 47′ E., was then belching out volumes of smoke from the crater at its summit. It appeared perfectly cone-shaped from a distance; but on near approach we found the western side flattened, crowded with cocoa-nut trees, and the home of a large population. The mountain is about 2200 feet high, by three miles and a half in circumference. Vegetation climbs for 800 or 1000 feet up its sides; above which arid rocks, and precipices riven by deep fissures, form a strange crown to the slopes of feathery palm and tropical trees beneath. From the parched lips of the crater a silver stream came leaping; and surely never water looked brighter than this, now spreading itself out in tiny threads of silver against the dark background, now gathering itself into white cascades, and plunging into fissure after fissure till it reached the world of green below, and leaped from a ledge of dark rock into the sea. Large numbers of the natives came off to us, and showed the utmost anxiety for iron hoop. Their hair was dressed in the most preposterous fashion—it had been suffered to grow long as a woman's, and was drawn through a conical cane case, over the end of which it curled. This case, which was about a foot long, and highly ornamented with feathers and shells, was worn at the back of the head, at right angles to it, and looked like a horn. These people, who were of a dark copper colour and very intelligent in manner, seemed cheerful and friendly, and I regretted much that time did not permit us to improve our acquaintance with them.

Nine miles north-west of Lesson Island we found bottom at 820 fathoms, and shortly afterwards got entangled in a vast crowd of snags, huge uprooted trunks of trees, borne on a great body of fresh water which forced its way seaward. We had to get steam up to clear ourselves of these obstructions, which gave us some heavy blows, spite of care. This water, doubtless, is the outcome of a large river somewhere in the neighbourhood of Cape Della Torre, and is worth the attention of explorers. On May 22d, in latitude 2° 37′ S., and longitude 142° 7′ E., we found bottom at 2000 fathoms. Our deep-sea soundings were very laborious to the men, as we had no fittings, and all the work had to be done by hand. It took our reduced company three hours to haul in these 2000 fathoms of line. We tried for deep-sea soundings every day—no small trial to the patience of as willing a ship's company as ever sailed.

We anchored in Humboldt Bay, May 23d, wishing to learn if the Dutch had made a settlement here, a report to which effect had reached Sydney before we left. The bay is very large, and contains deep capacious bights, up one of which we steered, and anchored over a coral reef in eight fathoms, where we were presently surrounded by scores of canoes full of wild vociferating savages, armed with formidable bows and arrows, here first seen by us in East New Guinea. They showed no sign of fear nor reverence; and knowing their reputation for making sudden attacks, we kept our rifles ready. It seems singular that the nearer we came to the seat of the Malay race proper, in New Guinea, the more unlike the coast native became to the Malay type, the Humboldt Bay people being almost black, with hair inclining to be woolly, and nose and lips verging towards the negro formation. The women were but little ornamented, and wore the ti-ti, or grass petticoat; the men, who were unclad, were profusely decorated with barbaric finery, some of which, particularly a breast-plate of boar's tusks laid flat, and sewn on to plaited cane-work, on which a ground-work of brilliant red seeds was gummed, had quite a fine effect. Once or twice there was every prospect of a free fight amongst the men in the canoes, bows were bent, spears brandished, amidst furious shouting in some dispute over their trading; and all our skill as peace-makers was tasked. On one occasion a man parted with some sago for a smaller quantity of iron hoop than his better half thought due; and without more ado she seized her paddle and belaboured him heartily over the head and shoulders; his friends, instead of pitying his plight, shouted with merriment; he did not retaliate, but slunk away, looking foolish.

The houses here are of a conical form, and thatched close down to the ground, or to the platform on which they stand, if built on a reef. There was no trace of a Dutch settlement; and we stood west again after a narrow escape over a coral reef off Providence Isle, on which the Dutch flag is flying, finding no greater depth than 2000 fathoms in our deep-sea soundings.

On May 27th we had reached the western extreme of New Guinea, about a week's sail from Amboyna, with our old ship in a very rusty condition from her long sea work, and her decks dyed a dark mahogany colour from the stacks of wood they had continuously borne; so it was needful to take a little time and put her so to rights as to do herself credit beside the Dutch men-of-war she might meet at Amboyna. Threshold Bay, 46 miles south of the equator, in 131° 25′ east longitude, seemed a likely place for our purpose, so taking up a convenient position at

U

nightfall, we waited for daylight to find the anchorage.

During the night, however, we were swept 55 miles to the north-west, at the rate of five knots an hour, by the strongest ocean current we had any of us ever met. It was therefore the evening of May 28th when we anchored off a delicious little cove of this large open bay, before a large village, through which a mountain stream was running; and here we saw the Dutch flag flying.

The inhabitants are pure Malays, descendants of those who have driven the aboriginal inhabitants back into the interior, and now hold their own by the use of firearms. The Rajah of Salwatti, who is supreme ruler at this extreme of New Guinea, came off to visit us on the following day in a large prahu, rowed by about twenty men, and ornamented with various banners, and an enormous Dutch ensign. A huge gong, slung in the bow, was beaten continually as he approached, seated under a large blue silk umbrella spread in the stern, and we received him in conformity with such pomp. We found him a well-informed gentlemanly man, able to speak a few words of English; in which he told us that we were the first English man-of-war he had seen on this coast, and expressed a hope that many English ships would follow. We went to quarters and showed him the power and range of our great guns, which seemed to astonish him not a little: and he then exchanged gifts with me, presenting me with some live cassowaries,* a tree kangaroo,

* One of these is now in the Zoological Gardens, London.

and some beautiful bird of paradise skins, which I returned with a regulation sword, giving him also a quantity of tea and sugar, which he said was the greatest luxury he could have. He then took his leave with much ceremony, and landed at the village, where the prahu was hauled above high-water mark, and we thought we had done with him; but no, the Rajah doffed his robe of state, and launching in a small canoe, with two men to paddle, came off to the ship as a trader of bird skins. Very keen bargains he drove, coaxing fowling-pieces, powder, shot, and pistols from the officers for his skins, over which we repented afterwards at our leisure. The Dutch, or Hollanders, as the Malays termed them, seemed to be in small repute here.

Having completed our painting and smartening-up on May 30th, we bade our last adieu to New Guinea, and passing through Pitt Straits between the islands of Battanta and Salwatti, where the scenery is very beautiful, found the tide so fierce against us that, steaming seven knots, we barely held our own. We arrived at Amboyna on June 2d, where we experienced every attention from the governor and from Lieutenant-Commander Doorman, H.N.M.S. "Bali," and greatly enjoyed our return to the comforts of civilised life. Here we met the zealous Russian traveller Mr. Miklucko Macklay, who had spent eighteen months amongst the New Guinea people at Astrolobe Gulf, and concerning whose fate I had been instructed to make inquiries. He was able to clear up some of our perplexities, amongst others, our ignorance as to the natives' manner of disposing of their dead, we having seen no graves but those at Discovery Bay and Skelton Island. He told us that they bury their dead in the houses they have lived in, and disinter the remains at the expiration of six months, when they hang the skull up, destitute of the lower jaw, which is kept as an ornament. But at the eastern end of New Guinea the skulls we saw hung up were all perfect, and the jaw-bones worn as bracelets by the men were, by unmistakable signs, described to us as those of enemies whom they had killed and eaten.

Mr. Macklay's experiences generally corroborated ours, and went to prove that the Papuans lead a quiet sort of life—the men fishing, hunting, and making canoes and weapons, and the women tilling the ground, carrying burthens, and doing the housework. He did not speak of any wars or fightings, and the solitary bloodless engagement seen by us seems to show that they know the value of their lives. Mr. Macklay had been brought off from Astrolobe Gulf by the Russian corvette "Izumrud." The "Izumrud," after five days' stay on the coast of New Guinea, had 130 sick on arrival at Amboyna. The "Basilisk," during her many months there, spent in ceaseless labour, had almost an immunity from sickness; a difference consequent, in my opinion, on the superior cleanliness of our English seamen, who, besides bathing in the sea nearly every day, enjoyed after each day's work a freshwater tub in the forecastle.

The traveller was in a deplorable state of health, and not expected to survive when we left; but I have since heard welcome news of his recovery.

It will easily be supposed that our men greatly enjoyed their run on shore at Amboyna; the morals of the place were, however, in a very low state, and we left it with anything but favourable ideas of the Dutch as colonists. The absence of energy, the number of government monopolies, and the dislike with which their rulers are regarded by the native population, forced themselves on the attention.

Fanned by a gentle monsoon, we sailed through the Molucca Sea—every sail set—not a cloud in the sky—not the sign of a squall in the horizon—as if over charmed waters. We postponed all drills, and gave the men perfect rest; pleasant indeed to them after their unusually trying work. The thought of "home" filled, I think, every heart. These days were full of the feeling that most of us would wish the last days of life to bring with them—that of labour done—done to the full of all our powers—of rest in the present—of hope of speedy reunion with friends long unseen.

Beautiful islands succeeded each other, rising like faint blue clouds on the horizon, gradually filling out and warming in form and colour, and sinking behind us again, to be forgotten soon, for our thoughts flew all before us now.

We arrived at Singapore on June 29th, and here our able surveyor, Lieutenant Dawson, left us for

Sydney, taking with him our faithful little steam cutter, now put in good repair, to be returned to the New South Wales Government.

Our pennant was hauled down at Sheerness after an eventful commission, thirty-nine days short of four years, on December 15, 1874.

SUPPLEMENTARY CHAPTER.

OUR DUTY TO NEW GUINEA AND POLYNESIA.

Most men who have pondered on the future of the islands lying on the north and east Australian shores, and our concern in it, have felt that sooner or later we shall find ourselves called on to decide on a plan of action with regard to the races that inhabit them, which, working perhaps from small beginnings at a few points, will by force of natural expansion eventually cover the whole ground. How shall we treat the South Sea Islands and that part of New Guinea which is not Dutch? The question is not a new one—it sleeps at times, as other affairs of the Empire press, and again awakens; it has just received an answer at Fiji; it asks for one at present in New Guinea—it sleeps, but never dies; for the causes that prompt it, the issues depending, give it a sure vitality. It may be asked hastily by some "Why is this question ours?" but a little thought will bring it home. England, as represented by Australia and New Zealand, being the great power lying nearest to these islands, holds the primary advantage of easy access and proximity; English subjects have settled themselves on many of these islands, and on some have established thriving industries, which are increasing in importance. Lawless Englishmen have made themselves a curse in some, and to an extent which has obliged us to establish a sort of undeclared protectorate, by turning our cruisers into a sea-police, charged with the repression of the more overt acts of violence. These islands, which lay hidden for centuries, visited alone by a chance Spaniard or English navigator, are emerging fast from their seclusion. We want labour, cotton, sugar, tobacco, coffee, sago, spices, cocoa-nut oil, jute, shell, bêche-de-mer, sandal-wood—a hundred commodities which we find they can give us, and we are determined to have these things; we demand them with a yearly increasing avidity. Surely then we are called on to protect these people to the uttermost in the discharge of their good offices to us, and to do them what good we can in return. They have seen so much of our heathenism that we are bound in fairness to show them something of our Christianity. We are the best colonists in the world; we do not claim the merit of perfection for our laws and system of government, but we believe them to be the best extant. Our residence amongst these races, and the prevalence of our laws, are therefore rather to be desired for them according to our own belief, than the like connection with any other nation. Lastly, if examination proves that strategic weakness—that political complications with other powers may follow our neglect to move—that alien hands may reap a rich harvest that might have been ours, we shall, I think, be ready to confess that this question has some affinity to us. Suppose, however, that we could draw an arbitrary line round these islands, and determine that across a certain space of sea no European flag should ever float—that there should be a break here in the circulation of the world's commerce, a non-conducting link in the chain of human thought, would not such an enactment be a sin against the economy of nature—be inevitably self-punished?

There are of course two ways of dealing with this question, we can either annex Polynesia and East New Guinea, or we can leave the matter to the mercy of chance. The argument against annexation may be stated briefly thus: We have ground enough for our emigrants to appropriate now, and for a long time to come. The climate of a large part of New Guinea, and some of the islands, is such that Europeans could not hope to be manual workers there. The English character is found too often to deteriorate when Englishmen are brought into contact with aboriginal races, and it is therefore undesirable to increase the extent of contact. The empire is already so large that the central governing body is sometimes unable to find leisure to acquaint itself with the nature and gravity of important questions at the proper time. These island races are now happy in their own way, and should be left so. Why should we seek to force our "fire-water" on them, along with our Manchester calicoes—perhaps our opium, as we did on the Chinese? May not our occupation of these islands lead to the very extinction of these races? Have we money over and above our present engagements to spend? Does not Australia need all her public funds for her internal development? Is not England saddled with the largest national debt in the world? Do not fresh responsibilities bring with them fresh possibilities of danger and difficulty?

The argument against annexation is strong, but before measuring it with the counter-plea, we should remind ourselves of the precept that "the right," not "the expedient," should be the guide of national as well as of individual conduct. All Christian philosophy teaches us that "the right" will be found to have been "the expedient," in the end. Woe to the nation that palters with its conscience! its punishment is prepared; the blunted susceptibilities, the lower standard of honour, the cruel all-slaying lust of wealth, the coward cringing to any power that may hurt its lower interests, which follow national faithlessness to duty, are the causes and signs of decadence, and prelude national death.

It is advanced that there is room for the present and future requirements of our out-goers in existing colonies, and to spare, but is a sufficiency of this space available for their purposes? Sugar-cane, cotton, and tobacco, require conditions for their growth, which are only to be found in a small part of Australia. The great Australian industry of sheep-farming is largely crippled at times for want of watered land, and suffers certain restrictions. The interior of that great island is an arid territory, presenting difficulties in the way of habitation which it will task the future energies of a more matured Australia to overcome. Our possession of vast tracts of country in North Canada all but unpeopled —of waste lands in Ireland and Scotland, has not been allowed to stand in the way of our appropriation of territory that has seemed desirable. The arid Australian centre, nay the steppes of Russia, the very desert of Sahara itself, will doubtless be subdued and peopled, should the world last long enough; but whilst fruitful well-watered tracts of territory await us, it is surely impolitic to throw ourselves upon a stern grapple with nature when all the odds are against us. All waste of time and strength is surely a mistake, nay a sin, against political economy, which desires to apply every atom of useful force at its due time and place.

But it is as vain as it is impolitic to attempt to prescribe a field for emigration, for it will be guided not only by expediency, but by natural instinct. As truly as Goth and Hun, coming forth from their birthplaces and swarming southward, were led by an instinct which obeyed a hidden law, so truly do these solitary forerunners of the dominant race in the South Seas, these expeditionary bodies to New Guinea, obey a law they wot not of,—a law stronger in action then the greed of gain, the love of adventure, the impatience of restraint, which they recognise in themselves.

Let it be granted that we have room for ourselves and our children, but we have our grand-children to think for—the time when Australia and New Zealand as well as England will be constrained to throw off their thousands to find fresh homes. It would be selfish to resolve that we will only take thought for the needs of our own generations. It would be Quixotic to forego present interests in favour of a possible future—it is but justice to remember that we are as truly curators of the inheritance of coming generations as we are heirs of the past, bound not only to transmit what we have received but to develope it by faithful fosterage, and to leave it as free of danger and encumbrance looming in the future, as we can make it.

The climate of a great part of New Guinea would not be prejudicial to Europeans. High land, possessing every degree of temperature, abounds there; and the Europeans who already inhabit islands in Polynesia appear to enjoy perfect health. The malarias that prevail in unhealthy spots would probably depart with the too dense growth of tropic vegetation, as ague has vanished under the hand of the drainer in many parts of our Lincolnshire fen-country. But unhealthy spots might surely be avoided. The inhabitants of Queensland, who will doubtless be among the first settlers in New Guinea, are already accustomed to a range of temperature that will have prepared them for a warmer climate. White men may certainly find themselves unable to undertake much manual labour on the lower levels in New Guinea and the islands, but they should be able to find abundant employment as directors of coloured toilers, till such time as their descendants shall have grown acclimatised, as the Portuguese and Spaniard in the Brazils and Mexico, and the Englishman at New Orleans. Such a relative position involves no more injury or degradation to the coloured operative than it does to the English, who puts his hand to work to which other men have applied brain and gold. We may admit that it is an unfortunate fact that the character of the Englishman often deteriorates when he lives among savages, but this is not inevitable. The Englishman, however, is determined to pitch his tent amongst them, and it is our business to prevent this deterioration, and to protect his savage neighbour, by applying early safe-guards of law and supervision. We have been tardy in doing this in various parts of the world. We have too often held aloof till matters have grown so bad as to force our attention, and have then learned that lawlessness is a costly evil—costly in money, blood, and honour, to those who are forced to charge themselves with its extinction. But if many of our countrymen have brought a stigma on the national honour by their evil deeds, others are already living and dying for these people, and a flood of philanthropy lies ready in England and Australia to be poured out on these islands when opportunity is given.

From the suggested difficulty of governing an empire greater than our present no argument rises, for the burden of governing the islands would doubtless be arranged to fall on the parliament of a great Australian dominion, privileged to deal with all questions not strictly imperial.

It is argued that the islanders appear sufficiently happy without our intervention, but perhaps their happiness is not so real as is supposed. Some of them suffer from famines, which a little knowledge, forethought, or communication with mankind would have prevented. They have no ease in old age, no comfort in sickness, no skill in dealing with any sort of physical evil. Violence, fraud, and bloodshed, prevail in many places; the women are everywhere more or less slaves; cruel customs, some too dreadful for mention—infanticide, self-mutilation, human sacrifices, cannibalism, are the customs of some islands; and, from an intelligence dwarfed to the narrow range of its surroundings, from animal instincts and childish fears, hideous religions are evolved, which keep these human souls in a most wretched bondage. Suppose, however, these people to be content with such things as they have for want of knowledge of better, is their ignorance to be the boundary of our duty? Are these countless lives to drop away like leaves from autumnal forests, to come new again with a perpetual spring of life, and drop, and leave no sign? Are these men to rise so far, and no further, above the level of the brute? to build their rude huts, and bask in the sun, as they did in the days of Quiros and Captain Cook, to the end? never to have part and lot with the rest of the human race, to share its toils, its victories, its rewards? If Christianity is a good thing, have we not a right to go out into the highways and hedges and bring in these people who are lying in the very shadow of the empire, how and when we can? Our task in leading them into membership with the human family would not be a difficult one. They have not been degraded by generations of slavery, as in Jamaica or St. Domingo; they are not possessed by a satisfying faith in the traditions of Brahminical lore, biassed by prejudices of caste, saturated with the antipathies of Mohammedanism, nor imbued with the polite scepticism that follows on the surrender of these. We should have little to undo. These races offer an almost virgin page on which we are free to write the whole moral code. Our acts of colonisation, the necessities of our commerce, are bringing us into a yearly-increasing relationship with them, and it is much within our power at present to decide the character of this relationship—nay, to decide on their fate; on the question of their very existence. An issue how momentous! No single aboriginal inhabitant of Van Diemen's Land is alive to-day; the natives of Australia are perishing fast, and will soon be extinct. We would save the poor remnant if we could, but it is to be feared that its doom cannot now be averted. The type was low, and all experience proves that the lower the type the more antagonistic is the approach of civilisation to the immediate interests of the savage. The hunter who requires to possess a tract of land on which a city might stand that he may fill a few mouths, will probably starve before there is time to absorb him into the body politic, by teaching him the ways and uses of our civilisation.

Have we no atonement to make for all the innocent blood that has lain at our door from the time that we began to drive the red man from his hunting-grounds till now? And what other form of atonement can we find than this of making ourselves tutors of the childhood of these races that lie directly within our influence, and leading them up to moral and intellectual manhood. It is no law of nature that the aboriginal shall melt away before the civilised race. Nature has not committed the gigantic folly of creating millions of creatures in the form and with all the powers of man, who are yet needless to her purposes, and for whom there is no room in her economy. Yet some will tell us that the extinction of the less noble races has been contemplated. The very suitability of a race to labour in the climate in which it is found proves the intention to perpetuate it and to use it, whilst attaining its own highest elevation, to contribute its quota to the general good of the world. Aboriginal races have not perished by Nature's decree, but because of our weakness, ignorance, and sin. Our first colonists in Australia were few, weak, and isolated by special difficulties of inter-communication; they led a hard-working and precarious life, and were so absorbed in their own concerns as to be unable to take due steps to reconcile the natives to their intrusion. They consequently met violence by violence, till the breach between the old and new dwellers of the soil had grown too vast to be bridged across, and the extinction of the weaker began almost to assume the form of a seeming necessity. Again, almost within the memory of living men, we were ignorant of much of our duty, and our moral standard was very low. We not only tolerated slavery; we legislated for it; we hung for petty theft; and these things seemed right in our eyes. Men who prided themselves on being models of honour at home, too often forgot all the ten commandments when they had to deal with credulous and passionate aborigines, and thought no more shame of wringing rupees from a Hindoo, or shooting a thieving black, than our early kings did of fleecing the Jews. Our century is characterised by an increase of moral light co-equal with its advance in physical power, as a glance will show. It demands the mercy of reformatory treatment for the criminal, and education for the masses, as zealously as it plies the steam-engine and the telegraph wire. We know our duty in a broad way, and are daily working out its minutiæ. We are strong enough to perform much of it, and are growing stronger; are we wanting alone in the possession of an honest will to make our simple neighbours friends to us and a blessing to themselves? They are capable of receiving good at our hands; they take kindly to Christianity, as all who have visited the Christianised islands can testify. Many of these men are leading noble lives at this moment; some have died martyrs to their convictions as truly as Stephen or Paul.

It is easy to say that they are incapable of benefiting much by us. It would be just as easy to say that a great future awaits these undeveloped races, that they are destined to take up the torch of progress after we have laid it down. But our commission is not to speculate; it is to do our duty to people whose acquaintance we have made, and intend to prosecute, without their will or against it, for our own purposes. It seems to me that the broad containing lines of our duty are evident, whilst the filling in must be, and may be, left to time. Perhaps I have no right to any opinion; be it so. I am conscious of my own ignorance and short-sightedness; conscious that these native races have so touched my heart that I have become their partizan, and perhaps a partial reasoner. I will express no opinion. I will but say that I hope to see my country take up what I conceive to be her duty, and annex New Guinea and the islands, and thus have it in her power to start right with the aborigines from the first; to prevent the first occasions of mistrust, disgust, and anger, which would at once and for ever stamp an image of greed, perfidy, and cruelty, as our likeness on the native heart. It would seem that no great money expense is involved at the outset in recognising our legitimate position, and that islands rich by nature would soon become self-supporting with respect to religion and government. The act of annexation would cost nothing, and would but need to be followed up gradually, as circumstances should indicate and enable, beginning of course with the islands on which Europeans have established themselves.

Missionaries have done much in many of these islands, and are doing more. Would it not be possible to acknowledge and assist them publicly, in view of the fact that both politically and commercially we reap a material benefit from their efforts, and so accelerate their success? Would it not be possible, for example, to give a grant to the Milanesian College on Norfolk Island, the most powerful instrument for good in the South Seas, and thus enable it to extend itself, and send out ten instructed native teachers for every one that it now elaborates?

On any island where a small white community has begun to form itself, might not a man of good repute be selected, and endued with some degree of magisterial power, for the due exercise of which he might be made answerable to the captain of the next visiting man-of-war? The very routine and form of order has a most beneficial influence, and men often acquire a higher tone and steadiness of purpose from a sense of responsibility. A small reward would probably go a long way in securing the services of such men, and they might easily by degrees become recognised by the natives as holding the balance between English and native interests. There may be nothing in this proposition; it is only prompted by the feeling that it may be wise to use the material that lies to hand at first, as far as it will reach. The possession of the islands once accepted, a power of statesmanship would be directed towards them sufficient to meet all necessities—suggestions are therefore idle.

The responsibilities that we should have to undertake with regard to New Guinea and the islands would be small at first, and would only increase with our ability to meet them. We should, doubtless, be bound by a new obligation to labour in the direction of Christianising, and making them law-abiding; but this is a responsibility which it is not only our direct self-interest to assume, but one which would deliver us from the greater, of perpetually putting down lawless English ruffianism and unmeasured native reprisals, with a strong hand. I need, I think, add nothing to what I have said in the body of the book as to the value of the commodities that await us in New Guinea and some of the islands, and the capabilities of soil for growing various crops. I have spoken of what I have seen simply and briefly, and not ventured to express much opinion as to future possibilities, feeling that my opinion is of no account, whilst my testimony as an eye-witness may be of some little value to intending settlers. On the political aspects of the annexation question I have no right or inclination to say a word. I know that the fact of Australia's strength and peace, lying in the circumstance of her isolation and the absence of near contending interests, is as patent to all as it is to me, as also the knowledge that a foreign power established in New Guinea might easily prove a troublesome neighbour, especially in the event of its home government being at war with the mother country. But I also know that the attention of our statesmen has been turned to this question of annexation, and I have the happy faith of an Englishman in their judgment. Another view of the subject has more attraction for me. Of the three great islands that lie in a line, Van Diemen's Land, Australia, and New Guinea, we have long known that the geological formation is continuous from Victoria to Van Diemen's Land; we now know that it is equally continuous in Queensland and New Guinea. Can any one think without emotion of the possibilities which such a range of latitude presents? Is it not as though Nature herself has striven to show us that she has here laid down the noble proportions of an empire, and bids us not curtail it for our children.

APPENDIX.

My attention having been called of late to several schemes for colonising New Guinea, and to a very natural want of knowledge on the part of the public press as to what localities are fit or unfit for white settlement, I was induced to write the following letter to the *Times*, with the hope that the information it contains might be useful. I now reprint it, with the intention of making such slight additions as the simultaneous appearance of a letter from the Rev. S. M'Farlane, containing debateable matter, seems to have rendered necessary.

NEW GUINEA.

To the Editor of the "Times."

Sir—I did not expect to have to request you to grant the favour of inserting a first and last letter from me on the New Guinea question, as I have no direct or indirect personal interest in any attempt to colonise New Guinea, my sole connection with the subject lying in the accident of my having been the volunteer explorer whose work has opened out an unknown coast to enterprise ; but I find myself compelled to write, because such constant applications for information are made to me as render me anxious to deliver myself by answering, according to the best of my knowledge, once for all. Since sending you some remarks on Mr. Stone's letter, too, I have been addressed by some of the promoters of a new Association for colonising New Guinea with respect to the reflections thrown on Her Majesty's ship "Basilisk's" charts, and requested to make some statement which may restore a confidence to their public, which they declare to have been appreciably shaken. Lastly, being conscious that I have spoken in strong terms before the Royal Geographical Society and Colonial Institute of the richness of portions of the country in question, and seeing that some confusion exists in the minds of intending settlers as to which are the desirable parts, I think a few words of explanation and warning are perhaps due.

As to the character of this country, I can only speak generally within the limits of a letter. The New Guinea coast north of Torres

Straits, as far east as Yule Island, appears to be an almost unbroken level, of swampy, mangrove-covered, and probably malarious country, on the low dreary shores of which the surf breaks unchecked by any barrier reef; a home of the black Papuan race, and wholly unsuited for white occupation.

Reaching Yule Island, some thirty miles west of Redscar Bay, we find a change. The Owen Stanley range approaches the coast to within twenty or twenty-five miles; but the high and healthy land of their slopes is cut off from the sea-board by a belt of this same low, mangrove-covered swamp, through which the rivers discovered by Her Majesty's ship "Basilisk" will in time afford steam-water ways, for their currents are too rapid for sail or oar, to the high lands within. At Redscar Head, thirty-five miles east of Yule Island, an entire change is found to have obtained; the shore is sheltered by a great barrier reef, which uprears itself from bottomless depths, at a distance of from four to ten miles from the shore, inside which lies calm navigable water, which ripples up to a coral beach, backed by round-topped swelling hills, openly timbered with rich tropical valleys between. From this point to the extreme east of New Guinea, the coast, as far as my knowledge and judgment go, is suitable for white settlement, and it is peopled by a mild Malayan race, with which it seems possible to live on terms of easy friendship.

The three considerable islands, Hayter, Basilisk, and Moresby, which lie off the east end of New Guinea, and command the new route, are, I think, suitable for white habitation, especially the last, which attains an elevation of 1500 feet, and is larger and more fertile than the others. The sago palm is particularly prolific on this island, and its harbours are numerous. The north-eastern shores of New Guinea are apparently more tropically luxuriant than the south-eastern, and their lofty mountains, where a cool temperature is obtainable, appear more accessible. There is no barrier reef to create a succession of secure harbours, but the anchorages are sufficiently good and numerous. It must, however, be remembered that the natives, after passing Cape Vogel, appear to be a treacherous and savage race.

With regard to the natural wealth of this country, some certainties, probabilities, and possibilities, exist, which should not be confounded, but disentangled and rated according to their value. First, then, as to the certainties:—

New Guinea is rich in timber, which ought to form an immediate article of export—and here I would speak a word of warning against indiscriminate and wasteful felling, by pointing attention to the New Hebrides group, where the supply of sandal wood, once bountiful, has been all but exhausted by wasteful treatment.

New Guinea is fruitful in the sago palm, and the yield might be increased so as to form a permanent and paying export. Yams and roots are abundant, and might be cultivated to any extent for food or export ; but the main source of wealth in New Guinea at present is the cocoa-nut, of which the supply appeared to me to be practically unlimited. I can scarcely give a better idea of the value of the cocoa-nut harvest than by quoting from a late Report of Consul Miller, of Tahiti, who says that the value of the coprah (dried cocoa-nut kernels) exported from Tahiti in 1874 was £20,191, and that of the cocoa-nut oil (311 tons) £11,190. These products, actually in existence, would doubtless be the first support of an infant colony, and to them I think its immediate attention should be directed.

The probabilities are as follows :—Pearl-shell, bêche-de-mer, and tortoise-shell fisheries would doubtless offer a paying return, but would need time and material for their development.

Tens of thousands of acres of low land could probably be cultivated for rice, cotton, and sugar-cane with profit. On my late visit to the New Hebrides group I was struck by the excellence of its increasing cotton plantations, and felt the importance of English industry in this direction as tending to make us sufficiently independent of the American supply. The cultivation of such crops is not, however, a task for European labour, and would doubtless fall to the lot of the Chinese in New Guinea, whose importation would be a matter of time. Jute and other fibres are also among the products existent in New Guinea. We found steel sand in Hall Sound and Milne Bay. The high grass lands, which, as far as my observation went, seemed to be better watered than the generality of Australian pastures, would doubtless afford runs to millions of sheep and cattle, and much of the high land appears suitable for coffee culture.

On the possible sources of wealth in New Guinea, by which I intend the mineral, too much stress has in my opinion been laid, and this with the risk of attracting the least valuable, because the least plodding, class of colonists. The only sign of mineral wealth seen by the "Basilisk's" company were the fragments of gold quartz picked up by us at Fairfax Harbour, Port Moresby. It is probable, for several reasons, that a mountainous country like New Guinea has not been forgotten by Nature in respect of minerals ; but we must await the verdict of a geological survey as to the accessibility and amount of such deposits before we allow a consideration of them to enter into any calculation. The postponement of the discovery of gold in New Guinea is doubtless to be desired, for the restraint and assuredness of established law, the existence of easy inter-communication, the creation of a sufficient food supply, and the presence of a large balance of population engaged in the regular industry of civilised life are needed to mitigate the evils attending a gold rush, and to turn the new wealth with least delay into its true channels. The wish that no gold may be found in New Guinea can be indulged in only by those who do not travel beyond first aspects, who fail to perceive that solvent and purifying forces exist in a healthy body politic, which, working by natural laws, transmute such evils as may be dreaded here into final good, and who fail to consider the impetus that such an accidental force must give to the development of a country.

I heartily wish the expedition success, but do not feel myself in a position to speak with any authority as to its prospects. Success or disaster will wait on the venture, as the conditions for prosperity are complied with or despised. It will suggest itself that a thorough understanding with the natives is the first essential. The colony should have good staying power in the shape of adequate support from its English and Australian founders for the first two years of its existence; after which, supposing the organisation to be good and a system of mercantile connection with the required markets to have been established, the colony ought to be able to stand alone.

As to the surveying work done by Her Majesty's ship "Basilisk" I need say nothing to sailors, but if it be in any way necessary that I should come forward for the satisfaction of the special public interested, I am willing to specify what the "Basilisk" has done and not done.

It must be understood that no chart is ever implicitly relied on by navigators unless it is shown to be in all its parts the results of a triangulated survey, and not even then in any part which is left destitute of soundings. A running survey of a coast professes only to delineate the coast-line, and mark such dangers as the surveyors may have been able to discover, and does not claim to be an exhaustive survey. A chart is only incorrect when the coast-line is inaccurately drawn, when soundings are given and clear water indicated where reefs or other obstructions are afterwards found to exist, or where dangers are shown but not accurately fixed.

The triangulated, sounded-out surveys of the "Basilisk" embrace about 50 miles of the south coast of New Guinea in Torres Straits, including the islands of Saibai, Talbot, and Cornwallis, and the Great Warrior reef; also a space at the east end of New Guinea, containing about 50 miles of latitude and 75 of longitude, which includes the gateway of the new Australian-Chinese route round the east end of New Guinea, together with the archipelago of islands and reefs there brought to light, and a portion of the south and western shores of the D'Entrecasteaux islands. The "Basilisk's" running survey of the previously unknown coast of New Guinea extends from East Cape to Huon Gulf, a distance of 278 miles as the crow flies, and further runs on from Huon Gulf to Astrolobe Bay, between which two latter points the coast-line was partially known, making here a total of 480 miles as the crow flies, or a real coast-line (in consequence of its irregularities) of about 700 miles. These are the "Basilisk's" surveys proper, the other work consisting merely in the making of some additions to the existing New Guinea charts, of which the work done at Yule Island, lately alluded to, was an instance.—I am, Sir, yours faithfully,

J. MORESBY, Captain, R.N.

The Glen, Queenstown.

Mr. M'Farlane's letter is as follows:—

To the Editor of the "Times."

Sir—I have just read the report, in the *Sydney Morning Herald*, of a large and influential meeting held in that town with reference to a contemplated expedition to New Guinea, consisting of a number of persons who are emigrating thither with their families, intending to settle on Yule Island, "with a view to opening up a trade with the Australian ports in the products of the island." These products are, according to their statement, "Cocoa-nut oil, palm oil, sandal wood, mahogany, cedar, ebony, cinnamon, cloves, nutmegs, mace, arrowroot, sago, and sugar-cane." The marine products are also stated to be "bêche-de-mer, pearl-shell, turtle-shell, and trepang."

Now, Sir, let it be distinctly understood that I very heartily sympathise with all attempts to open up New Guinea and develope its resources, whether those efforts be of a missionary, scientific, or commercial character. Although a missionary, and convinced that missionaries make the best pioneers among savages, and that there can be little real civilisation or improvement of the natives without the religious element, still I do not desire to see the civilisation of numerous tribes left to missionaries alone, although the improved social condition of the South Sea Islanders abundantly proves that the missionary pioneer does not confine himself to teaching the natives to say prayers and sing psalms.

I rejoice in the efforts of such enterprising men as M. D'Alberte, the Italian naturalist, and such expeditions as that fitted out by the distinguished colonist who has just arrived among us from Sydney. These gentlemen have the means of supplying themselves with provisions, etc., and of moving from one part of the island to another, or leaving it altogether, when they please; and, moreover, every part of the island is attractive to the naturalist, as every little village is to the missionary. My object in writing is to offer a little information, advice, and warning to those who contemplate emigrating to New Guinea, for I consider that silence would be as culpable and cruel on the part of those who, like myself are acquainted with the facts of the case, as the statements are outrageously misleading contained in the "programme" from which the Rev. Dr. Lang quoted the above extracts. It is evident that the emigrants expect to find on their arrival at Yule Island the products mentioned in that "prospectus or programme." I pity them if they come relying upon anything of the kind, for they will not be able to obtain any one of them. Even cocoa-nuts and sugar-cane are very scarce on the island, and both are dear. The natives wanted from us an axe for two cocoa-nuts. All may be had on the mainland, I have no doubt; but will it pay to collect them? For cocoa-nuts they must go to the west; for sago, to the head of the gulf; for spices, round to the west and north ; for ebony, round to the eastern side of the peninsula, whence I got some curiosities carved in that wood ; for sandal wood and mahogany I don't know where they must go ; we have not yet seen any on the island. Fancy a few persons settling in Cornwall to trade in articles which are only to be had in Hull, Aberdeen, and more distant places, the only way of getting at these ports being by sea, round a dangerous and unsurveyed coast !

The emigrants further state in their prospectus that "It is their intention on landing to at once place themselves on friendly terms with the natives," which I think may be easily done. We have not yet found any difficulty in accomplishing this desirable end. They must, of course, be prepared to submit to a good deal of annoyance and pilfering, or choose the much worse alternative of coming to open hostility with the natives. Those at and about Yule Island, however, are much more honest and friendly than the people of Port Moresby.

They also state that it is their intention "to keep up a direct and constant communication, viâ Somerset, to Sydney by the Torres Straits mail. It is understood that no difficulty will arise in accomplishing the same." Certainly not between Somerset and Sydney, but how about the communication between Yule Island and Somerset ? Dr. Lang says "that the plan of going by the Torres Straits mail steamer as far as Somerset is a very good one ; and if a small steam launch were carried on the deck of the steamer, the little party could get over to New Guinea with great facility, and at small expense." It is evident that the good old doctor has not crossed the Gulf during the S.-E. season ; had he been with us last week he would have found that it is dangerous crossing in ordinary S.-E. weather, even in the steamship "Ellengowan," the mission steamer of the London Missionary Society, which is 80 feet long, and has proved her sea-going qualities by steaming out from England. When we first came here, four years ago, we found it impossible to beat to windward in the gulf, although the vessel we had chartered was a smart schooner of 100 tons. After "hammering at it" for four days without gaining a mile, we were obliged to enter and beat up inside the Great Barrier Reef of Australia. During the N.-W. season there are times when "a small steam launch" might cross the gulf.

There is one product of the country not mentioned by the emigrants, but which they are likely to get before any of the others—viz. fever. We have not yet found any part of the coast, or any island in Torres Straits free from the dangerous malady, Cape York and Port Moresby not excepted. Our Polynesian teachers and their families have been sadly reduced; they cannot stand the climate as well as Europeans. Although our mission is still young, we have lost no less than 21 of our number —17 by the diseases of the climate, and four by the clubs of the savages. These are facts which it may be well for those proposing to emigrate to New Guinea to consider. It is true that a few of the 17 had diseases in their system which this climate rapidly developed and brought to a fatal termination; humanly speaking they would have lived long in their own country.

There is positively nothing to be had on the south-east peninsula, so far as we know, which is of any commercial value. Pearl-shell and bêche-de-mer may be found on the coast, and gold in the interior, as in Australia.

Cotton, coffee, etc., may be cultivated, but labour would have to be imported. Missionaries, scientific, and prospecting expeditions, are the only persons who should visit New Guinea for some time to come. None should come here who are not well supplied with provisions, and with the means of leaving the island if necessary. I know that many will not be disposed to give this letter the consideration to which it is entitled, because it proceeds from a missionary, supposing that we are anxious to prevent traders from settling in New Guinea. It will certainly be very unfortunate for the future of New Guinea if a number of reckless fellows come here, determined to make their way with the "almighty revolver," and so frustrate their own ends and endanger our lives. The natives are quiet and friendly all along the coast; they know very little of foreigners, and are disposed to regard us as their friends; it would be a pity to alter that impression and create one of hostility.

When I arrived in Sydney from our first visit to Redscar Bay I found the unfortunate "Maria" preparing to leave for that place, and learnt something of the party from a gentleman who contemplated forming one of their number. I was requested to visit the "Maria," and meet some of the leading members of the expedition, which I did, giving them what information I could about the place and people. Knowing that the captain was ignorant of the locality, and that it was the worst season which they could have selected, I advised them not to go. I am now offering the same advice to those contemplating emigrating to Yule Island, who are more likely to find their graves than the treasures they anticipate. The time for emigration has not yet arrived. Wait at least till the result of the Macleay expedition is known. I can only advise such to emigrate as are in a position which the natives declare us to be in—viz. obliged to leave our own country.—Yours very truly,

S. M'FARLANE.

On board the "Ellengowan," Yule Island, July 11.

Mr. M'Farlane's letter, evidently written with the best intentions, is to be respected accordingly; but whilst sympathising with the spirit in which he writes, and agreeing with some of his statements, I cannot but see that he falls into some mistakes that call for notice.

He commences in a way calculated to produce an erroneous impression, when he states "that he had just read the report, in the *Sydney Morning Herald*, of a large and influential meeting held in that town, with reference to a contemplated expedition to New Guinea, consisting of a number of persons who are emigrating thither with their families, intending to settle on *Yule Island*." Now the meeting at Sydney was fully aware that Yule Island is but a tiny islet about two miles long by three-quarters of a mile broad, situated off a low malarious part of the coast; it could not and did not therefore confine its attention to Yule Island, but dealt with a series of resolutions in favour of the annexation of New Guinea, and the colonisation of that vast island. Mr. M'Farlane having thus placed the colonists in a locality where they will certainly never settle as a body, goes on to say that these emigrants are prepared to find on their arrival at Yule Island "Cocoa-nut oil, palm oil, sandal wood, mahogany, cedar, ebony, cinnamons, cloves, nutmegs, mace, arrowroot, sago, sugar-cane," ready for their enrichment. It is scarcely likely that any assemblage of commonly informed people would have expected this islet to prove such a garden of the Hesperides, but if any man in England has been bitten by such a wild idea, Mr. M'Farlane's letter may help to cure him.

He proceeds to state that sugar-cane and cocoa-nuts are so dear on Yule Island that an axe was asked by the natives in payment for two cocoa-nuts. We in the "Basilisk" found them fairly plentiful there, though Yule Island is not a seat of the cocoa-nut, but we observed that whilst the natives refused to take our axes as barter, being then totally ignorant of the value of iron, they were willing to part with anything they had in exchange for polished pearl-shell ornaments.

Mr. M'Farlane must surely see that the poverty,—the very extinction of this little island, would have no effect on a scheme for the colonisation of New Guinea. Why, therefore, should he give his ideas of its poverty such prominence?

He continues—"All" (*i.e.* the produce specified) "may be had on the mainland, no doubt, but will it pay to collect them? For cocoa-nuts they must go to the west" (where does the vague "west" lie?); "for sago to the head of the gulf" (Papua); "for spices round to the west and north; for ebony round to the eastern side of the peninsula."

Here Mr. M'Farlane commits himself to certain authoritative statements, leaving his readers to take for granted that he is fully competent to make them.

But *do* Mr. M'Farlane's experiences in New Guinea warrant this? Does he possess any acquaintance at all with the great island, beyond that acquired in visiting the mission-stations of Katow in Torres Straits, and those at Yule Island, Redscar Bay, and Port Moresby, which latter lie within sixty miles of each other? Has he ever visited the eastern shores of New Guinea, which stretch about 260 miles to the east from Port Moresby, or the northern shores of the island? Had he done this, or even conversed with any one who has, he would have written—"For cocoa-nuts they must go to the EAST; for sago, also to the *East;* for spices, as yet nowhere in New Guinea; for ebony, probably to all the great tropical forests." The cocoa-nut and sago palm were found by us to be more plentiful at the extreme East Cape of New Guinea than anywhere else.

The difficulties Mr. M'Farlane speaks of in crossing from Somerset to Eastern New Guinea do not appear to me to be such as are inevitable. We found that the meteorology of the east coast during the months of February, March, April, and May 1873, differed materially from that of Torres Straits.

Leaving Torres Straits in the first week in February, when heavy rains and strong north-west gales prevailed, the "Basilisk" remained in the vicinity of Redscar Bay till the first week in March, and experienced calm clear weather, with the exception of one strong breeze from the N.W., with rain. On our return to Torres Straits in March, constant winds from the N.W. and rain prevailed, which were left behind as we retraced our way to Eastern New Guinea, where, from March 20th to May 8th, we again experienced continuous fine weather. It seems therefore early to express a decided opinion on the meteorology of New Guinea. I agree with Mr. M'Farlane that some risk would be run in attempting to cross the Gulf of Papua in a small steam launch during the south-east monsoon; but the distance is only 250 miles, and taking the opportunity of fine weather, I should not hesitate to undertake the crossing during the monsoon, whilst I should at all times feel perfectly safe in attempting it in a good seaworthy decked boat. The passage between Somerset and East New Guinea is not in fact so much to be dreaded as much of the navigation of the English Channel.

Mr. M'Farlane descants on the unhealthiness of New Guinea, and supports his opinion by making a statement as to the mortality of the native Polynesian Christian teachers employed by the London Missionary Society in New Guinea, but he instances no case of a white man suffering from climatic causes.

It has already been seen that Mr. M'Farlane, except at Port Moresby (which the missionaries have publicly announced to be a healthy locality), has no knowledge of the high and presumably healthy parts of New Guinea, which are alone fitted for the white man's occupation; but his facts are so striking, that I would fain direct his attention to some of their causes. I am satisfied, from the evidence which came under my own eyes, as I think he will be on consideration, that influences other than climatic arrayed themselves against the lives of these poor creatures.

During the first four years which passed after the native teachers were established in New Guinea, they were unwisely scattered at stations in Torres Straits and at Redscar Bay, whilst the agent of the London Missionary Society residing at Cape York (Somerset), had no adequate means of visiting and supplying them with necessary food. The teachers and their families were left unguided and unprovided amongst savages, who refused to supply them with food gratis, and in a country whose produce was different from that of their native islands. The result was that when, in 1872-3, the "Basilisk" visited these poor creatures, she found them in such a deplorable state from want of sufficient food and medicines that several had died, and others were only saved by being brought on board, and given nourishing food and proper medicines. These facts, together with the opinion of the surgeon of the "Basilisk," were officially reported by me to the agent of the London Missionary Society at the time. By the possession of the "Ellengowan" missionary steamer, the mission is now placed on a more satisfactory footing, and it is probable that we shall henceforth cease to hear of so heavy a death-rate amongst the native teachers, even in the unhealthy parts, where they have, in my opinion, been unwisely settled. It should also be remembered that these native teachers came from various South Sea Islands, more than a thousand miles distant, where all the conditions of their lives were different.

The general health of the men of the "Basilisk" ship's company during the eight months spent in New Guinea, when they were exposed to all the vicissitudes of climate, in open boats, on detached service up rivers, on shore-work, surveying, visiting natives, and cutting 700 tons of wood for steaming purposes, was exceptionally good. The men occasionally suffered from boils, caused by a scarcity of fresh provisions; and whilst on the *North* coast of New Guinea a low fever prevailed amongst us for a time, but it was of a mild type, soon passing over, and leaving no bad effects.

The allusion made by Mr. M'Farlane to the loss of the "Maria" is not fortunate, as that vessel was wrecked about 800 miles from New Guinea. Nor can the results of the Macleay Expedition affect the question of the colonisation of East New Guinea, as Mr. Macleay has only attempted to explore the shores and rivers of the malarious coast north of Torres Straits, inhabited by the black, naked, hostile Papuan.

The following information was supplied to me by Mr. Edwin Redlich, master of the schooner "Franz," who went to search for pearl-shell on the extreme west of New Guinea, where the Dutch have so long held nominal sway.

It has since been published, for the information of seamen, by the Admiralty, and I introduce it here in order that the reader may contrast what it tells of the fierce bloody nature of the black Papuans of West New Guinea, with the mild, comparatively inoffensive, manners of the races inhabiting the eastern end of the great island.

Galewo Strait separates the considerable island of Salwatti from the west end of New Guinea. The Rajah of Salwatti, afterwards, in conversation with me, confirmed the truth of Captain Redlich's statement:—

GALEWO STRAIT AND SALWATTI ISLANDS.

On the 10th November came to an anchor off a small island, which the natives called "Soron." There is a large settlement of Malayas and Papuans, who fly the Dutch colours, and are the immediate subjects of the Rajah of Salwatti. On the 12th November sent the two large boats, with eighteen men all told, for a three weeks' cruize, fitted out with all necessaries. My chief mate, Mr. H. Schluetor, a native of Hamburg, had the command. I could not send more men, as eleven were laid up with the climatic fever.

Friday, 6th December.—Boats not back, which made me very uneasy, all the more as I had received tidings that the two boats had been seen three days ago not far from Soron; which information, however, proved to be erroneous afterwards.

Saturday, 7th December.—Boats not back. To-day a Soron native told me that a canoe had come from the southward with the news that the boats had been seen steering towards a place on the mainland of New Guinea, where the natives are very treacherous, and known to be very dangerous. The same Soron man told me that a man-of-war was lying at Gillolo. I concluded at once to man a boat and send it in search of the two missing ones. I engaged two natives from Soron island to act as pilots.

Thursday, 12th December.—Late in the evening the whaleboat returned; they had not seen anything of the boats. I had given the man in charge of this boat a letter, in which all the particulars are stated to the captain of the man-of-war, but the ship had left when my messenger arrived at Gillolo. Found out afterwards that it was an Italian man-of-war. Friendly natives had told the men that the two boats had been seen steering towards the land, and that they had not returned. They all expressed their opinion that the men must have been murdered. I could not leave this place without having tried all and every means to ascertain the fate of my men, and I concluded to ask the Rajah of Salwatti for his aid. Weighed on the 13th December, and arrived at Salwatti on the same day, but found that the rajah was away on a cruize.

Sunday, 15th December.—The rajah returned, and from the account he gave me respecting the ferociousness of the Papuans, I lost the last hope for the safety of my unfortunate men. The rajah granted me every assistance, and I supplied him with fire-arms, but he declined my company, as he thought it would place his weak party in danger.

Saturday, 21st December.—The rajah returned and brought back six guns, a double-barrelled breech-loader, one revolver, the mate's watch, totally broken, his jacket, a compass, and a cartridge-pouch. He had recovered them in the bush, and expressed an opinion that the men had been cooked and eaten. I could not make up my mind to leave this place without having been on the spot myself, and tried to persuade the rajah to render me his assistance. At last I succeeded, and the day for starting was fixed for that day week. In the meantime we prepared for the expedition, made cartridges, and practised our blacks with firearms.

Monday, 30th December.—The rajah came on board with three proas containing forty-five natives, and all their war implements. I went in the chief's proa, my steward, a Singapore Malaya, and a Fiji boy. The second mate with two men went in another proa; and another Fiji man in a third proa. All had joined the expedition voluntarily, and the firearms were equally distributed. In the evening we anchored at English or Saili point.

Tuesday, 31st December.—Went from Saili point about twelve miles farther down the coast. In going down several proas belonging to different places under the rajah's authority had joined our party, which now amounted to nine proas and about 120 men.

Wednesday, 1st January 1873.—Went along the coast for at least twenty miles to small islands about eight miles distant from the mainland. The native name for these islands is "Efmatal." This part of New Guinea is greatly obstructed by shoals and reefs. At about midnight got under weigh from there, and steered eastward towards the mainland.

Thursday, 2d January 1873.—We have made now at least two degrees from Salwatti, and we are now steering into a large and beautiful river named "Crabara," pulling very fast till 11 o'clock at night, when we anchored, and I presume we were then at least thirty miles up the river; which must go a long way inland. It is here half-a-mile wide; the banks are adorned with luxuriant vegetation.

Here the whole party divided, some remained at anchor, and some went farther up the river.

Friday, 3d January.—This morning two of the proas, with three bush natives whom they had caught, returned. One of them, according to his own confession, had been actually engaged in the murder of my men, and boasted of having killed the "white man." He said that the two boats had been seen lying at anchor at Efmatal island. Three canoes from the mainland, in each canoe fifteen men, had gone off with bananas, pine-apples, etc., which they gave to my men in the boats, and then quietly paddled off to the coast. They had behaved quite friendly, and put the mate and men off their guard. The New Guinea men had counted the number of men in the boats, the arms, etc.

The next night the savages returned and landed at the back of Efmatal island. They found the men, with the exception of two boys who had been left in the boats, camped on shore by their fires. They had divided into two parties, a little apart. The New Guinea men crawled upon them and killed them in the twinkling of an eye, without even a cry being raised by the victims; after that, they killed the two boys in the boats, and then brought the latter to a place which nearly dries at low water, and here they burnt the boats. The savages took all the bodies up the river Crabara. There they cut off their heads, kept them for trophies, and sold the bodies to a neighbouring tribe, who had cooked and eaten them.

The three prisoners were horrible-looking fellows, especially the one who had helped to murder my men. They are a different race to that inhabiting the more civilised parts of New Guinea, and easily distinguished, and if I ever go there again I will not give them a chance of coming near me if I can help it. After the prisoners were well secured, all the proas went farther up the river, and I hoped that we should go to the village "Crabara," which is about twelve miles farther up. After having gone up for about six miles, we heard the shells and drums right and left in the bushes. The rajah then commanded a retreat, for he said they might come down on us by the thousands, and we made the best of our way down the river.

Saturday, 4th January 1873.—In the morning we anchored at Efmatal island. The cannibal was brought on shore to the exact spot where he had killed the mate, and in front of where the boats had been lying at anchor. He was lashed to the very tree under which he had killed the mate, and was shot there and then. I fired the first shot and the second mate the second, with which he dropped down dead. As soon as he was dead the natives cut his head off, and strapped the body to the branch of a tree as a warning example to other cannibals who will certainly visit here now and then. All the men had witnessed the execution, and the rajah had given his sanction to it.

The two other savages remained in the rajah's hands, and both died a most horrible death. I witnessed the execution of one of them. He was in the true sense of the word cut to pieces by women and children, the widows and orphans of those who were killed in the first expedition when the rajah went out and recovered my guns, etc.

Monday, 6th January 1873.—Arrived at Salwatti. Stated the whole affair in several letters, and left them in the rajah's hands. One letter directed to the captain of the first man-of-war calling there; the second to the Prussian Consul-General in Hamburg; the third to the Sultan of Ternate; and the fourth to my present owners, Messrs. Barron and Austin, of Sydney.

When Captain Lawson's book on New Guinea appeared, I was requested to criticise it. This I refused to do from delicacy, as I was then engaged in the preparation of my own book, and my feeling was to wait and simply state in that what I had myself seen in New Guinea. Finding, however, that Captain Lawson's book was beginning to be accepted in some quarters as an authority; and being further appealed to for information, I sent the following letter to the *Athenæum*, of May 29th, 1875:—

THE INTERIOR OF NEW GUINEA.

My attention has just been directed to Captain Lawson's book on New Guinea, and I have been called on by my geographical friends to express my opinion as to the credibility of the narration. This I can scarcely do becomingly, lest I should be for a moment misconceived as claiming the status of an explorer, whose assent or dissent must be final for the time. I am, however, ready to state the principal points on which my experience is opposed to that of Captain Lawson, and to indicate instances where I meet with difficulties in his book, and should require explanation or parallel proof for my own satisfaction.

Captain Lawson tells us that, between November 1871 and May 1872, he formed an intention of exploring New Guinea, and organised a small expedition for that purpose, which sailed in the brig "Nautilus," from Sydney, on May 24th. H.M.S. "Basilisk," under my command, arrived at Sydney on December 14th, 1871, sailed for Torres Straits, January 15th, 1872, returned from thence to Sydney April 5th, 1872, and left it on May 14th. I feel a surprise that, between these dates, no word of Captain Lawson's expedition should have reached me; nay, that he did not come to me for information, as public attention was largely attracted to the New Guinea coast at the time, in consequence of the "Basilisk's" new discoveries in that quarter, and of the disastrous fate attending the brig "Maria" expedition, which left Sydney in January" 1872, for New Guinea.

Captain Lawson says (page 2), "I accidentally met (at Sydney) with a merchant captain who was in the habit of making trading voyages to New Guinea." Then (page 3) "He had himself been engaged in a bartering trade with them for several years, and could speak their language fluently."—I must unhesitatingly state that no vessel from Sydney was in the habit of trading to the mainland of New Guinea. Some black Papuans, inhabiting islands in Torres Straits, are engaged in diving for pearl-shell, and paid in kind and money, but with these islanders only has any commercial communication been had.

Page 12. "Houtree is situated on Torres Straits, in long. 143° 17′ 8″ E., lat. 9° 8′ 18″ S."—This position is *in the sea*, about one mile from the west end of Bristow Island, and six miles from the low wooded coast of New Guinea, touching a locality marked in the Admiralty charts "shallow flats" and "heavy rollers," surveyed by the late Captain Blackwood, R.N., and the present hydrographer of the navy. Of those dangers Captain Lawson takes no notice. The boats of H.M.S. "Basilisk," by my direction, surveyed this part of the coast of New Guinea within ten miles of the alleged position of "Houtree," but they never heard of such a place, or of any "bay" or "harbour" near there.

Page 4. "Fifteen or sixteen native proas put off from the shore."—Proas do not exist in Torres Straits. The ordinary canoe is used, hollowed out of the trunk of trees.

Page 4. "The joint property of half-a-dozen Chinese adventurers, who had settled in the village."—Chinamen have no communication whatever with this part of New Guinea; neither have they ever settled or owned property of any kind within 600 miles of the position assigned to Houtree.

Page 5. "Papuans, very repulsive looking. . . . exceedingly short, squat bodies, black, matted, and dirty hair, and a lithe, monkeyish manner."—The Papuans of this part of New Guinea are jet black, remarkably tall muscular men, their hair is frizzled, and the men usually shave their heads, and wear *wigs* so artistically constructed that we were days amongst them without discovering the deception.

Page 5. "Curious looking fowls."—No tame fowl were seen by us in New Guinea.

Page 5. "Twelve dollars a month" (for Papuan guides).—The mainland Papuans have no knowledge of the value of money; and why "dollars," when the current coin of all Australian vessels engaged in Polynesian trade is pounds, shillings, and pence? No currency but English is used by the pearl-shellers in Torres Straits.

Page 5. "I selected two who had a knowledge of the English

language, and who were further recommended to me as having spent the greatest part of their lives in the interior of the island. They were sailors, and had been in the habit of making voyages to the islands of the Indian Archipelago, in the course of which they had picked up information; besides English, they spoke a smattering of French, Dutch, and Portuguese, as well as several dialects of Malays."—I can but say that this part of New Guinea has been till now unknown to white races, and that its inhabitants had certainly not seen a white face between the time of the surveying voyage by H.M.S. "Fly," in 1845, and the advent of the pearl-shellers in Torres Straits in 1865, or thereabouts. To speak of native Papuans being "sailors," "making voyages to the Indian Archipelago," and speaking several languages, is the wildest flight of imagination possible, according to my experience.

Page 8. "Criminals who had become slaves."—We saw no trace of slavery amongst them.

Page 8. "They (at Houtree) were mostly engaged in fishing, and trading with Dutch and Chinese merchants who frequented them, and they also made voyages to the neighbouring islands, which are colonised principally by the Dutch."—As senior naval officer on two occasions in Torres Straits, it was my duty to acquaint myself with all particulars relating to the various islands; I must therefore state the fact that the Dutch have not colonised one single island, or any ground within 600 miles of the position given to Houtree.

Page 8. "The articles they have to dispose of are spices, drugs, gums, several kinds of wood and bark, the well-known birds of paradise, some inferior pearls, cocoa-nuts, and monkey skins, and many other articles of a like nature. . . From what I heard and saw, I should say that they (the exports and imports), are very considerable."—I have already said that no traffic has been had with the southern mainland of New Guinea, nor do any of the above-named commodities exist as articles of commerce in the Torres Straits Islands. Cocoa-nuts grow there, of course, and a few soiled bird of paradise plumes can be had as curiosities; we obtained a few pearls from the divers, but they were found in very small quantity. *Bêche-de-mer*, pearl-shell, and tortoise-shell are raised to a large amount by the natives of the Torres Straits Islands, employed by Europeans.

Page 9. "I ascertained that three or four small Dutch vessels generally called at Houtree in the course of the year, but that some hundreds of Malay and Chinese boats visited the place in the same period." During my command in these waters not one Dutch, Malay, or Chinese vessel visited Torres Straits for the purpose of commerce. A Chinese boat to reach Houtree would have to sail about 3000 miles, and circumnavigate New Guinea. The idea of a voyage of such extent and audacity shocks the sense of probability. The Malay proas are unknown in Torres Straits, but visit the Arrow Islands, about 600 miles west of the supposed Houtree.

Page 10. "Fields enclosed with railings."—Their cultivation is of the rudest kind. Fields cannot be said to exist; there are rough enclosures kept from the attacks of pigs by close set stakes.

Page 10. "Principal crops . . . . nutmegs . . . . occupied and cultivated by the Chinamen."—Nutmegs are not cultivated in this part of New Guinea; but the tree doubtless grows wild, as we shot pigeons with the wild nutmeg in their crops.

Page 11. "And the skin of a tanned yellowish hue."—The colour of the natives is pure ebony black.

Page 12. "They were well acquainted with the value of money, and Dutch coins were in circulation amongst them."—I have already said that the Dutch and Dutch coin are utterly unknown to the Papuans in this part of New Guinea.

Page 16. "The natives from the villages from great distances round frequented the marsh to procure salt."—We frequently tried, and always found the New Guinea natives most adverse to the taste of salt.

Page 19. "He said a goat."—We never saw traces of such an animal in New Guinea, and the frightened astonishment of the natives, on seeing a sheep on board the "Basilisk," indicated that to the coast natives, at all events, an animal of such a size was a novelty.

Page 19. "Boiled rice was set before us, followed by roast monkey." —Rice is unknown amongst the Papuans, and no trace of monkeys was ever seen by us.

Page 20. "The property . . . . pots, kettles of European manufacture, tools, knives . . . . skins cured for trading purposes, fancy buttons, china ornaments . . . . some hundreds of marbles," etc.—We never saw any such articles in Papuan huts; indeed, there must be a touch of sarcasm here. "Fancy buttons" for naked Papuans! The Papuan household effects seen by us were bows and arrows, spears, stone clubs, fishing-spears, cocoa-nut bowls, mats, shell ornaments, bird of paradise feathers of a worthless sort, and never prepared for trading purposes, stone adzes for agriculture, dogs, and cassowaries occasionally, as house pets.

Page 21. "Huts divided into two apartments . . . . the inner one devoted to the use of the ladies."—We never saw such an arrangement; the Papuan huts are large and often of two floors, the upper one being principally used for sleeping purposes, but we never saw any sign of the women possessing any privacy; in fact the habits of these people are against the idea.

Page 21. "Toddy prepared from the sap of the cocoa-nut tree."—We never saw any intoxicating drink amongst the Papuans, and were struck by the peculiarity, as the making of ava is general amongst the South Sea Islanders.

Page 25. Captain Lawson speaks of grass growing five or six feet over his head as bending easily to the weight of the body and yielding passage. We found it exhausting work to get through this grass, and only succeeded in doing a mile by about three hours' effort.

Pages 31, 32. Extraordinary quietude between the hours of ten and four in the forest is spoken of, but at daybreak a humming of insects, screaming of parrots, chattering of monkeys, with a thousand other sounds from birds and beasts, was heard, insomuch that Captain Lawson "had to shout when talking." We ascended New Guinea rivers for about twenty miles, running through the heart of dense forests, and were impressed with the solemn, almost painful, silence which prevailed at all hours, unbroken save by the scream of a parrot or other wild-bird note.

Page 32. "Heard the report of fire-arms."—Strange, at some eighteen days' journey from the coast, where we had never beheld a Papuan with fire-arms.

Page 39. "Deer and Moolah."—The "Basilisk," though on the look-out for traces of sport, never saw a sign of such animals, nor of some others mentioned through the book.

Page 53. "Mount Misty rises to a height of 10,672 feet," and two other peaks near it respectively to "12,580 feet," and "12,945."—These mountains, by Captain Lawson's map, appear to be but ninety miles from the coast, and it is difficult to understand how they could have remained unseen by the officers of H.M.S. "Basilisk," or those of H.M.S. "Fly," in 1845, who were within 100 miles of them, with a flat, low country, and (in our case) a clear atmosphere between.

Page 61. "An old man . . . smoking a long Dutch pipe."—The people of our acquaintance used the large bamboo pipe only, from which each man of a party takes a whiff and passes it on.

Page 62. "Fights and murders were frequent . . . traders landed and burnt the Papuan villages."—The only murder that has ever taken place here within my knowledge was that of three native teachers, placed by the London Missionary Society on Bampton Island, about fifteen miles from the position Captain Lawson assigns to Houtree.

Page 63. A native (Taa) is said to possess "a hundred head of cattle."—If cattle had been known by Australian traders to exist so near Cape York, the Jardine Brothers would have been aware, and not have undertaken the expense and risk of driving a herd of cattle from Brisbane to Cape York, a distance of 1000 miles, through an unknown country, full of hostile natives.

Page 70. "Natives sold into slavery to the Dutch, who transport them to their settlement."—I have visited the Dutch settlements in the east, but have failed to observe any form of slavery.

Page 72. "The women and children take their meals after the men have finished."—In our experience they always ate together, and we regarded it as one sign of their good treatment of the women.

Page 78. "It (a scorpion) had stung him through the linen breeches he wore."—I know not how to conceive of a Papuan wearing "linen breeches," and again, the sting of the scorpion is here spoken of as producing certain death, a statement opposed to all experience.

Pages 101 and 102. The trap-door spider is here mentioned as seen, enormous in size and poisonous in bite. This kind of spider is common enough in Jamaica, but was never seen by us here. Now we were frequently engaged in cutting wood for fuel to a gross amount of 600 or 700 tons, and were brought into the closest and, at times, most distressing contact with insect life. We recognised several varieties of spider, and it seems singular that this remarkable one should have escaped our notice.

Page 205. Natives on the river are here stated to possess "daggers . . . curved swords, pikes, and flint muskets . . . horse pistols 100 years old."—How came such arms to be amongst savages 200 miles inland, when none are to be seen on the coast.

Page 209. "The sea, he (a chief) said, could easily be reached by water in a day and a half or two days . . . he had never seen a European before, nor a black man, but had heard of both. Malay and Chinese vessels frequented the northern coast to trade."—From this statement, coupled with Captain Lawson's map and account, he must have been somewhere near Astrolobe Gulf. In this part of the country the eminent Russian traveller, Mr. Macklay, spent eighteen months, and on my meeting him at Amboyna, in June 1874, he gave me an account of the natives, which, more or less, has since been published in Europe, showing that the natives of north-east New Guinea are wholly savage and destitute of fire-arms, and have no communication whatever with Chinese, Dutch, or Malay races, and this account accords with our observations in the "Basilisk."

Page 236. "There are no distinct tribes in New Guinea."—All our experience goes to prove that distinct tribes do exist.

Page 273. "Nine Malay and two Chinese vessels in the Bay of Houtree."—Captain Lawson says he reached Houtree, on his return from the interior, February 1873, at which time the boats of the "Basilisk" were from ten to twenty miles from the given position of Houtree, and the "Basilisk" herself was at Warrior Island, not forty miles distant. Certainly then no Malay or Chinese vessel was near Houtree.

Page 278. "There are certain parts of the coast, especially the east coast, which have no villages or fixed inhabitants, and these places are the favourite harbours of refuge for the pirates and robbers who infest the eastern seas."—We found villages and fixed inhabitants everywhere on the east coast, and we are at a loss to know what pirates or robbers Captain Lawson refers to.

Page 280. "Gold and silver, the latter common . . . copper, lead, iron, tin, abundant."—Not a sign of any of these metals, excepting gold, was ever seen by the "Basilisk."

Captain Lawson states that he left Houtree on the 24th of February, in a Chinese junk of forty or fifty tons, and reached Banda on the 1st of March, making thus a distance of about 1000 miles in five days, and this during the prevalence of the north-west monsoon. This, to my mind, is almost the most surprising statement in the book.

Page 282. "Granted permission to reside in Banda until I could obtain a passage in a Dutch vessel."—Why wait for a *Dutch* vessel when a regular line of mail steamers runs monthly between Banda, Batavia, and Singapore? Neither is it now necessary for an Englishman to "ask permission" to reside in Banda, so long as he conducts himself within the laws.

J. MORESBY, Captain, R.N.

Printed by R. & R. CLARK, *Edinburgh.*

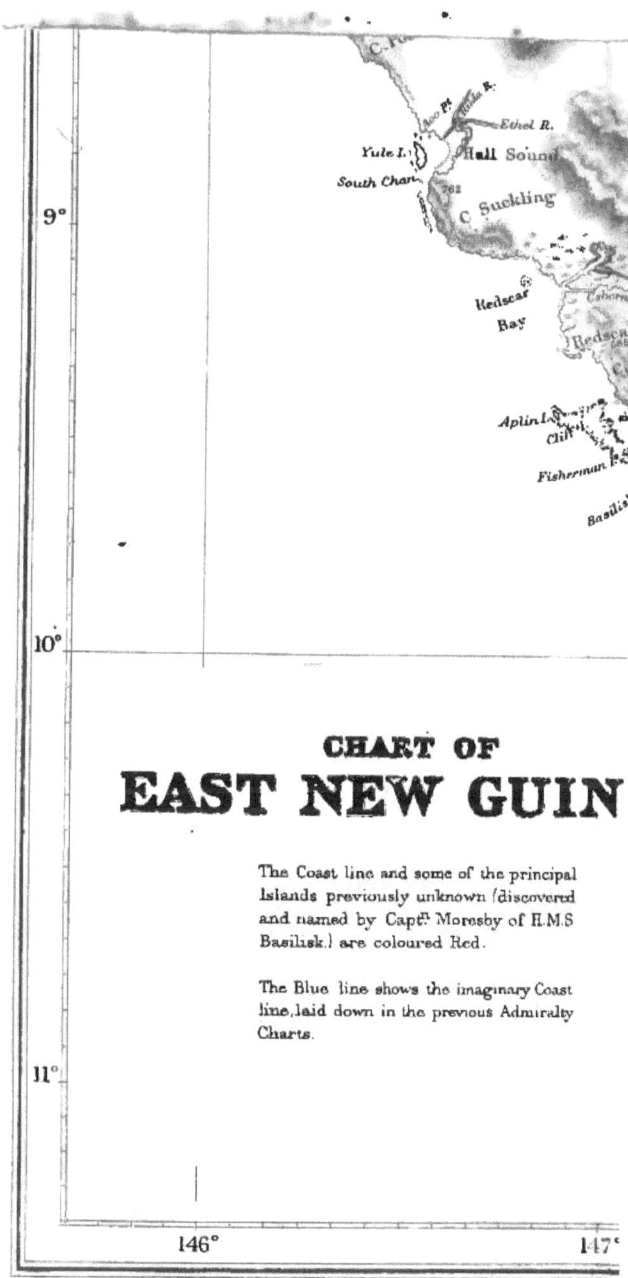
Ethel R.
Yule I.
Hall Sound
C Suckling
Redscar Bay
9°
10°
11°
146°
CHART OF
EAST NEW GUIN
The Coast line and some of the principal Islands previously unknown (discovered and named by Captn. Moresby of H.M.S Basilisk.) are coloured Red.
The Blue line shows the imaginary Coast line, laid down in the previous Admiralty Charts.

ALBEMARLE STREET, LONDON,
January, 1875.

MR. MURRAY'S

GENERAL LIST OF WORKS.

ALBERT (THE) MEMORIAL. A Descriptive and Illustrated Account of the National Monument erected to the PRINCE CONSORT at Kensington. Illustrated by Engravings of its Architecture, Decorations, Sculptured Groups, Statues, Mosaics, Metalwork, &c. With Descriptive Text. By DOYNE C. BELL. With 24 Plates. Folio. 12*l*. 12*s*.

——— (PRINCE) SPEECHES AND ADDRESSES with an Introduction, giving some outline of his Character. With Portrait. 8vo. 10*s*. 6*d*.; or *Popular Edition*, fcap. 8vo. 1*s*.

ABBOTT'S (REV. J.) Memoirs of a Church of England Missionary in the North American Colonies. Post 8vo. 2*s*.

ABERCROMBIE'S (JOHN) Enquiries concerning the Intellectual Powers and the Investigation of Truth. 19*th Edition*. Fcap. 8vo. 3*s*. 6*d*.

——— Philosophy of the Moral Feelings. 14*th Edition*. Fcap. 8vo. 2*s*. 6*d*.

ACLAND'S (REV. CHARLES) Popular Account of the Manners and Customs of India. Post 8vo. 2*s*.

ÆSOP'S FABLES. A New Version. With Historical Preface. By Rev. THOMAS JAMES. With 100 Woodcuts, by TENNIEL and WOLF. 64*th Thousand*. Post 8vo. 2*s*. 6*d*.

AGRICULTURAL (ROYAL) JOURNAL. (*Published half yearly.*)

AIDS TO FAITH: a Series of Theological Essays. 8vo. 9*s*.

CONTENTS.

Miracles	DEAN MANSEL.
Evidences of Christianity	BISHOP FITZGERALD.
Prophecy & Mosaic Record of Creation	DR. MCCAUL.
Ideology and Subscription	Canon COOK.
The Pentateuch	Canon RAWLINSON.
Inspiration	BISHOP HAROLD BROWNE.
Death of Christ	ARCHBISHOP THOMSON.
Scripture and its Interpretation	BISHOP ELLICOTT.

AMBER-WITCH (THE). A most interesting Trial for Witchcraft. Translated by LADY DUFF GORDON. Post 8vo. 2*s*.

ARMY LIST (THE). *Published Monthly by Authority.*

ARTHUR'S (LITTLE) History of England. By LADY CALLCOTT. *New and Cheaper Edition, continued to* 1872. With 36 Woodcuts. Fcap. 8vo. 1*s*. 6*d*.

AUSTIN'S (JOHN) LECTURES ON GENERAL JURISPRUDENCE; or, the Philosophy of Positive Law. 5*th Edition*. Edited by ROBERT CAMPBELL. 2 Vols. 8vo. 32*s*.

——— Student's Edition, compiled from the above work. By ROBERT CAMPBELL. Post 8vo.

ARNOLD'S (THOS.) Ecclesiastical and Secular Architecture of Scotland: The Abbeys, Churches, Castles, and Mansions. With Illustrations. Medium 8vo. [*In Preparation*.

B

ADMIRALTY PUBLICATIONS; Issued by direction of the Lords Commissioners of the Admiralty:—

A MANUAL OF SCIENTIFIC ENQUIRY, for the Use of Travellers. Edited by Sir JOHN F. HERSCHEL and ROBERT MAIN, M.A. *Fourth Edition.* Woodcuts. Post 8vo. 3s. 6d.

GREENWICH ASTRONOMICAL OBSERVATIONS 1841 to 1846, and 1847 to 1871. Royal 4to. 20s. each.

MAGNETICAL AND METEOROLOGICAL OBSERVATIONS. 1840 to 1847. Royal 4to. 20s. each.

APPENDICES TO OBSERVATIONS.

1837. Logarithms of Sines and Cosines in Time. 3s.
1842. Catalogue of 1439 Stars, from Observations made in 1836 to 1841. 4s.
1845. Longitude of Valentia (Chronometrical). 3s.
1847. Description of Altazimuth. 3s.
Twelve Years' Catalogue of Stars, from Observations made in 1836 to 1847. 4s.
Description of Photographic Apparatus. 2s.
1851. Maskelyne's Ledger of Stars. 3s.
1852. I. Description of the Transit Circle. 3s.
1853. Refraction Tables. 3s.
1854. Description of the Zenith Tube. 3s.
Six Years' Catalogue of Stars, from Observations. 1848 to 1853. 4s.
1862. Seven Years' Catalogue of Stars, from Observations. 1854 to 1860. 10s.
Plan of Ground Buildings. 3s.
Longitude of Valentia (Galvanic). 2s.
1864. Moon's Semid. from Occultations. 2s.
Planetary Observations, 1831 to 1835. 2s.
1868. Corrections of Elements of Jupiter and Saturn. 2s.
Second Seven Years' Catalogue of 2760 Stars for 1861 to 1867. 4s.
Description of the Great Equatorial. 3s.
1856. Descriptive Chronograph. 3s.
1860. Reduction of Deep Thermometer Observations. 2s.
1871. History and Description of Water Telescope. 3s.

Cape of Good Hope Observations (Star Ledgers). 1856 to 1863. 2s.
———— 1856. 5s.
———— Astronomical Results. 1857 to 1858. 5s.
Report on Teneriffe Astronomical Experiment. 1856. 5s.
Paramatta Catalogue of 7385 Stars. 1822 to 1826. 4s.

ASTRONOMICAL RESULTS. 1847 to 1871. 4to. 3s. each.

MAGNETICAL AND METEOROLOGICAL RESULTS. 1847 to 1871. 4to. 3s. each.

REDUCTION OF THE OBSERVATIONS OF PLANETS. 1750 to 1830. Royal 4to. 20s. each.

———— LUNAR OBSERVATIONS. 1750 to 1830. 2 Vols. Royal 4to. 20s. each.

———— 1831 to 1851. 4to. 10s. each.

BERNOULLI'S SEXCENTENARY TABLE. 1779. 4to. 5s.

BESSEL'S AUXILIARY TABLES FOR HIS METHOD OF CLEARING LUNAR DISTANCES. 8vo. 2s.

ENCKE'S BERLINER JAHRBUCH, for 1830. *Berlin*, 1828. 8vo. 9s.

HANSEN'S TABLES DE LA LUNE. 4to. 20s.

LAX'S TABLES FOR FINDING THE LATITUDE AND LONGITUDE. 1821. 8vo. 10s.

ADMIRALTY PUBLICATIONS—*continued.*

LUNAR OBSERVATIONS at GREENWICH. 1783 to 1819. Compared with the Tables, 1821. 4to. 7*s.* 6*d.*

MACLEAR ON LACAILLE'S ARC OF MERIDIAN. 2 Vols. 20*s.* each.

MAYER'S DISTANCES of the MOON'S CENTRE from the PLANETS. 1822, 3*s.*; 1823, 4*s.* 6*d.* 1824 to 1835. 8vo. 4*s.* each.

——— TABULÆ MOTUUM SOLIS ET LUNÆ. 1770. 5*s.*

——— ASTRONOMICAL OBSERVATIONS MADE AT GOTTINGEN, from 1756 to 1761. 1826. Folio. 7*s.* 6*d.*

NAUTICAL ALMANACS, from 1767 to 1877. 2*s.* 6*d.* each.

——— SELECTIONS FROM, up to 1812. 8vo. 5*s.* 1834-54. 5*s.*

——— SUPPLEMENTS, 1828 to 1833, 1837 and 1838. 2*s.* each.

——— TABLE requisite to be used with the N.A. 1781. 8vo. 5*s.*

SABINE'S PENDULUM EXPERIMENTS to DETERMINE THE FIGURE OF THE EARTH. 1825. 4to. 40*s.*

SHEPHERD'S TABLES for CORRECTING LUNAR DISTANCES. 1772. Royal 4to. 21*s.*

——— TABLES, GENERAL, of the MOON'S DISTANCE from the SUN, and 10 STARS. 1787. Folio. 5*s.* 6*d.*

TAYLOR'S SEXAGESIMAL TABLE. 1780. 4to. 15*s.*

——— TABLES OF LOGARITHMS. 4to. 60*s.*

TIARK'S ASTRONOMICAL OBSERVATIONS for the LONGITUDE of MADEIRA. 1822. 4to. 5*s.*

——— CHRONOMETRICAL OBSERVATIONS for DIFFERENCES of LONGITUDE between DOVER, PORTSMOUTH, and FALMOUTH. 1823. 4to. 5*s.*

VENUS and JUPITER: OBSERVATIONS of, compared with the TABLES. *London*, 1822. 4to. 2*s.*

WALES' AND BAYLY'S ASTRONOMICAL OBSERVATIONS. 1777. 4to. 21*s.*

——— REDUCTION OF ASTRONOMICAL OBSERVATIONS MADE IN THE SOUTHERN HEMISPHERE. 1764—1771. 1788. 4to. 10*s.* 6*d.*

BARBAULD'S (MRS.) Hymns in Prose for Children. With 112 Illustrations. Crown 8vo. 5*s.*

BARROW'S (SIR JOHN) Autobiographical Memoir, from Early Life to Advanced Age. Portrait. 8vo. 16*s.*

——— (JOHN) Life, Exploits, and Voyages of Sir Francis Drake. Post 8vo. 2*s.*

BARRY'S (SIR CHARLES) Life and Works. By CANON BARRY. *Second Edition.* With Portrait and Illustrations. Medium 8vo. 15*s.*

BATES' (H. W.) Records of a Naturalist on the River Amazon during eleven years of Adventure and Travel. *Third Edition.* Illustrations. Post 8vo. 7*s.* 6*d.*

BEAUCLERK'S (LADY DIANA) Summer and Winter in Norway. *Third Edition.* With Illustrations. Small 8vo. 6*s.*

BELCHER'S (LADY) Account of the Mutineers of the 'Bounty,' and their Descendants; with their Settlements in Pitcairn and Norfolk Islands. With Illustrations. Post 8vo. 12*s.*

BELL'S (SIR CHAS.) Familiar Letters. Portrait. Post 8vo. 12*s.*

B 2

BELT'S (THOS.) Naturalist in Nicaragua, including a Residence at the Gold Mines of Chontales; with Journeys in the Savannahs and Forests; and Observations on Animals and Plants. Illustrations. Post 8vo. 12*s*.

BERTRAM'S (JAS. G.) Harvest of the Sea: an Account of British Food Fishes, including sketches of Fisheries and Fisher Folk. *Third Edition*. With 50 Illustrations. 8vo. 9*s*.

BIBLE COMMENTARY. EXPLANATORY and CRITICAL. With a REVISION of the TRANSLATION. By BISHOPS and CLERGY of the ANGLICAN CHURCH. Edited by F. C. COOK, M.A., Canon of Exeter. Medium 8vo. VOL. I., 30*s*. VOLS. II. and III., 36*s*. VOL. IV., 24*s*.

Vol. I.	GENESIS	Bishop of Ely.
	EXODUS	Canon Cook; Rev. Sam. Clark.
	LEVITICUS	Rev. Samuel Clark.
	NUMBERS	Canon Espin; Rev. J. F. Thrupp.
	DEUTERONOMY	Canon Espin.
Vols. II. and III.	JOSHUA	Canon Espin.
	JUDGES, RUTH, SAMUEL	Bishop of Bath and Wells.
	KINGS, CHRONICLES, EZRA, NEHEMIAH, ESTHER	Canon Rawlinson.
VOL. IV.	JOB	Canon Cook.
	PSALMS	Dean of Wells, Canon Cook Rev. C. J. Elliott.
	PROVERBS	Rev. E. H. Plumptre.
	ECCLESIASTES	Rev. W. T. Bullock.
	SONG OF SOLOMON	Rev. T. Kingsbury.
Vol. V.	ISAIAH	Rev. W. Kay, D.D.
	JEREMIAH	Dean of Canterbury.

BICKMORE'S (A. S.) Travels in the Eastern Archipelago, 1865-6; a Popular Description of the Islands, with their Natural History, Geography, Manners and Customs of the People, &c. With Maps and Illustrations. 8vo. 21*s*.

BIRCH'S (SAMUEL) History of Ancient Pottery and Porcelain: Egyptian, Assyrian, Greek, Roman, and Etruscan. *Second Edition*. With Coloured Plates and 200 Illustrations. Medium 8vo. 42*s*.

BIRD'S (ISABELLA) Hawaiian Archipelago; or Six Months Among the Palm Groves, Coral Reefs, and Volcanoes of the Sandwich Islands. With Illustrations. Crown 8vo.

BISSET'S (ANDREW) History of the Commonwealth of England, from the Death of Charles I. to the Expulsion of the Long Parliament by Cromwell. Chiefly from the MSS. in the State Paper Office. 2 vols. 8vo. 30*s*.

BLUNT'S (REV. J. J.) Undesigned Coincidences in the Writings of the Old and New Testament, an Argument of their Veracity: containing the Books of Moses, Historical and Prophetical Scriptures, and the Gospels and Acts. *Eleventh Edition*. Post 8vo. 6*s*.

——— History of the Church in the First Three Centuries. *Fifth Edition*. Post 8vo. 6*s*.

——— Parish Priest; His Duties, Acquirements and Obligations. *Sixth Edition*. Post 8vo. 6*s*.

——— Lectures on the Right Use of the Early Fathers. *Third Edition*. 8vo. 9*s*.

——— University Sermons. *Second Edition*. Post 8vo. 6*s*.

——— Plain Sermons. *Sixth Edition*. 2 vols. Post 8vo. 12*s*.

BLOMFIELD'S (BISHOP) Memoir, with Selections from his Correspondence. By his Son. *Second Edition*. Portrait, post 8vo. 12*s*.

BOSWELL'S (JAMES) Life of Samuel Johnson, LL.D. Including the Tour to the Hebrides. By Mr. CROKER. *A new and revised Library Edition*. Portraits. 4 vols. 8vo. [*In Preparation*.

BRACE'S (C. L.) Manual of Ethnology; or the Races of the Old World. Post 8vo. 6s.

BOOK OF COMMON PRAYER. Illustrated with Coloured Borders, Initial Letters, and Woodcuts. 8vo. 18s.

BORROW'S (GEORGE) Bible in Spain; or the Journeys, Adventures, and Imprisonments of an Englishman in an Attempt to circulate the Scriptures in the Peninsula. Post 8vo. 5s.

——— Zincali, or the Gypsies of Spain; their Manners, Customs, Religion, and Language. With Portrait. Post 8vo. 5s.

——— Lavengro; The Scholar—The Gypsy—and the Priest. Post 8vo. 5s.

——— Romany Rye—a Sequel to "Lavengro." Post 8vo. 5s.

——— WILD WALES: its People, Language, and Scenery. Post 8vo. 5s.

——— Romano Lavo-Lil; Word-Book of the Romany, or English Gypsy Language; with Specimens of their Poetry, and an account of certain Gypsyries. Post 8vo. 10s. 6d.

BRAY'S (MRS.) Life of Thomas Stothard, R.A. With Portrait and 60 Woodcuts. 4to. 21s.

——— Revolt of the Protestants in the Cevennes. With some Account of the Huguénots in the Seventeenth Century. Post 8vo. 10s. 6d.

BRITISH ASSOCIATION REPORTS. 8vo.

York and Oxford, 1831-32, 13s. 6d.
Cambridge, 1833, 12s.
Edinburgh, 1834, 15s.
Dublin, 1835, 13s. 6d.
Bristol, 1836, 12s.
Liverpool, 1837, 16s. 6d.
Newcastle, 1838, 15s.
Birmingham, 1839, 13s. 6d.
Glasgow, 1840, 16s.
Plymouth, 1841, 13s. 6d.
Manchester, 1842, 10s. 6d.
Cork, 1843, 12s.
York, 1844, 20s.
Cambridge, 1845, 12s.
Southampton, 1846, 15s.
Oxford, 1847, 18s.
Swansea, 1848, 9s.
Birmingham, 1849, 10s.
Edinburgh, 1850, 15s.
Ipswich, 1851, 16s. 6d.
Belfast, 1852, 15s.
Hull, 1853, 10s. 6d.
Liverpool, 1854, 18s.
Glasgow, 1855, 15s.
Cheltenham, 1856, 18s.
Dublin, 1857, 15s.
Leeds, 1858, 20s.
Aberdeen, 1859, 15s.
Oxford, 1860, 25s.
Manchester, 1861, 15s.
Cambridge, 1862, 20s.
Newcastle, 1863, 25s.
Bath, 1864, 18s.
Birmingham, 1865, 25s
Nottingham, 1866, 24s.
Dundee, 1867, 26s.
Norwich, 1868, 25s.
Exeter, 1869, 22s.
Liverpool, 1870, 18s.
Edinburgh, 1871, 16s.
Brighton, 1872, 24s.
Bradford, 1873, 25s.

BROUGHTON'S (LORD) Journey through Albania, Turkey in Europe and Asia, to Constantinople. Illustrations. 2 Vols. 8vo. 30s.

——— Visits to Italy. 2 Vols. Post 8vo. 18s.

BROWNLOW'S (LADY) Reminiscences of a Septuagenarian. From the year 1802 to 1815. *Third Edition.* Post 8vo. 7s. 6d.

BRUGSCH'S (PROFESSOR) History of Ancient Egypt. Derived from Monuments and Inscriptions. *New Edition.* Translated by H. DANBY SEYMOUR. 8vo. [*In Preparation.*

BURGON'S (REV. J. W.) Christian Gentleman; or, Memoir of Patrick Fraser Tytler. *Second Edition.* Post 8vo. 9s.

——— Letters from Rome. Post 8vo. 12s.

BURN'S (COL.) Dictionary of Naval and Military Technical Terms, English and French—French and English. *Fourth Edition.* Crown 8vo. 15s.

BURROW'S (MONTAGU) Constitutional Progress. A Series of Lectures delivered before the University of Oxford. *2nd Edition.* Post 8vo. 5s.

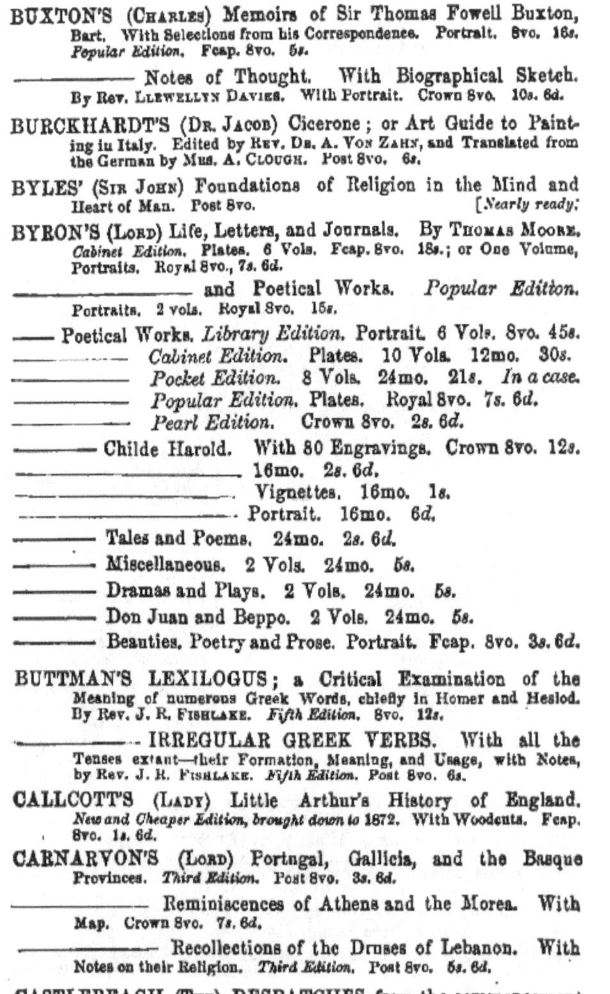

BUXTON'S (Charles) Memoirs of Sir Thomas Fowell Buxton, Bart. With Selections from his Correspondence. Portrait. 8vo. 16s. *Popular Edition.* Fcap. 8vo. 5s.

——— Notes of Thought. With Biographical Sketch. By Rev. Llewellyn Davies. With Portrait. Crown 8vo. 10s. 6d.

BURCKHARDT'S (Dr. Jacob) Cicerone; or Art Guide to Painting in Italy. Edited by Rev. Dr. A. Von Zahn, and Translated from the German by Mrs. A. Clough. Post 8vo. 6s.

BYLES' (Sir John) Foundations of Religion in the Mind and Heart of Man. Post 8vo. [*Nearly ready.*

BYRON'S (Lord) Life, Letters, and Journals. By Thomas Moore. *Cabinet Edition.* Plates. 6 Vols. Fcap. 8vo. 18s.; or One Volume, Portraits. Royal 8vo., 7s. 6d.

——— and Poetical Works. *Popular Edition.* Portraits. 2 vols. Royal 8vo. 15s.

——— Poetical Works. *Library Edition.* Portrait. 6 Vols. 8vo. 45s.

——— *Cabinet Edition.* Plates. 10 Vols. 12mo. 30s.

——— *Pocket Edition.* 8 Vols. 24mo. 21s. *In a case.*

——— *Popular Edition.* Plates. Royal 8vo. 7s. 6d.

——— *Pearl Edition.* Crown 8vo. 2s. 6d.

——— Childe Harold. With 80 Engravings. Crown 8vo. 12s.

——— 16mo. 2s. 6d.

——— Vignettes. 16mo. 1s.

——— Portrait. 16mo. 6d.

——— Tales and Poems. 24mo. 2s. 6d.

——— Miscellaneous. 2 Vols. 24mo. 5s.

——— Dramas and Plays. 2 Vols. 24mo. 5s.

——— Don Juan and Beppo. 2 Vols. 24mo. 5s.

——— Beauties. Poetry and Prose. Portrait. Fcap. 8vo. 3s. 6d.

BUTTMAN'S LEXILOGUS; a Critical Examination of the Meaning of numerous Greek Words, chiefly in Homer and Hesiod. By Rev. J. R. Fishlake. *Fifth Edition.* 8vo. 12s.

——— IRREGULAR GREEK VERBS. With all the Tenses extant—their Formation, Meaning, and Usage, with Notes, by Rev. J. R. Fishlake. *Fifth Edition.* Post 8vo. 6s.

CALLCOTT'S (Lady) Little Arthur's History of England. *New and Cheaper Edition, brought down to* 1872. With Woodcuts. Fcap. 8vo. 1s. 6d.

CARNARVON'S (Lord) Portugal, Gallicia, and the Basque Provinces. *Third Edition.* Post 8vo. 3s. 6d.

——— Reminiscences of Athens and the Morea. With Map. Crown 8vo. 7s. 6d.

——— Recollections of the Druses of Lebanon. With Notes on their Religion. *Third Edition.* Post 8vo. 5s. 6d.

CASTLEREAGH (The) DESPATCHES, from the commencement of the official career of Viscount Castlereagh to the close of his life. 12 Vols. 8vo. 14s. each.

CAMPBELL'S (LORD) Lord Chancellors and Keepers of the Great Seal of England. From the Earliest Times to the Death of Lord Eldon in 1838. *Fifth Edition.* 10 Vols. Crown 8vo. 6s. each.

——— Chief Justices of England. From the Norman Conquest to the Death of Lord Tenterden. *Third Edition.* 4 Vols. Crown 8vo. 6s. each.

——— Lords Lyndhurst and Brougham. 8vo. 16s.

——— Shakspeare's Legal Acquirements. 8vo. 5s. 6d.

——— Lord Bacon. Fcap. 8vo. 2s. 6d.

——— (SIR NEIL) Account of Napoleon at Fontainebleau and Elba. Being a Journal of Occurrences and Notes of his Conversations, &c. Portrait. 8vo. 15s.

——— (SIR GEORGE) India as it may be: an Outline of a proposed Government and Policy. 8vo.

——— (THOS.) Essay on English Poetry. With Short Lives of the British Poets. Post 8vo. 3s. 6d.

CATHCART'S (SIR GEORGE) Commentaries on the War in Russia and Germany, 1812-13. Plans. 8vo. 14s.

CAVALCASELLE AND CROWE'S History of Painting in Italy, from the 2nd to the 16th Century. With Illustrations. 5 Vols. 8vo. 21s. each.

——— Early Flemish Painters, their Lives and Works. Illustrations. Post 8vo. 10s. 6d.; or Large Paper, 8vo. 15s.

CHILD'S (G. CHAPLIN, M.D.) Benedicite; or, Song of the Three Children; being Illustrations of the Power, Beneficence, and Design manifested by the Creator in his works. *10th Thousand.* Post 8vo. 6s.

CHISHOLM'S (MRS.) Perils of the Polar Seas; True Stories of Arctic Discovery and Adventure. Illustrations. Post 8vo. 6s.

CHURTON'S (ARCHDEACON) Gongora. An Historical Essay on the Age of Philip III. and IV. of Spain. With Translations. Portrait. 2 Vols. Small 8vo. 12s.

——— New Testament. Edited with a Plain Practical Commentary for the use of Families and General Readers. With 100 Panoramic and other Views, from Sketches and Photographs made on the Spot. 2 vols. 8vo. 21s.

CICERO'S LIFE AND TIMES. His Character as a Statesman, Orator, and Friend, with a Selection from his Correspondence and Orations. By WILLIAM FORSYTH, M.P. *Third Edition.* With Illustrations. 8vo. 10s. 6d.

CLARK'S (SIR JAMES) Memoir of Dr. John Conolly. Comprising a Sketch of the Treatment of the Insane in Europe and America. With Portrait. Post 8vo. 10s. 6d.

CLIVE'S (LORD) Life. By REV. G. R. GLEIG. Post 8vo. 3s. 6d.

CLODE'S (C. M.) Military Forces of the Crown; their Administration and Government. 2 Vols. 8vo. 21s. each.

——— Administration of Justice under Military and Martial Law, as applicable to the Army, Navy, Marine, and Auxiliary Forces. *2nd Edition.* 8vo. 12s.

COLCHESTER (THE) PAPERS. The Diary and Correspondence of Charles Abbott, Lord Colchester, Speaker of the House of Commons 1802-1817. Portrait. 3 Vols. 8vo. 42s.

CHURCH (THE) & THE AGE. Essays on the Principles and Present Position of the Anglican Church. 2 vols. 8vo. 26*s*. Contents:—

VOL. I.

Anglican Principles.—Dean Hook.
Modern Religious Thought.—Bishop Ellicott.
State, Church, and Synods.—Rev. Dr. Irons.
Religious Use of Taste.—Rev. R. St. John Tyrwhitt.
Place of the Laity.—Professor Burrows
Parish Priest.—Rev. Walsham How.
Divines of 16th and 17th Centuries.—Rev. A. W. Haddan.
Liturgies and Ritual, Rev. M. F. Sadler.
Church & Education.—Canon Barry.
Indian Missions.—Sir Bartle Frere.
Church and the People.—Rev. W. D. Maclagan.
Conciliation and Comprehension.—Rev. Dr. Weir.

VOL. II.

Church and Pauperism.—Earl Nelson.
American Church.—Bishop of Western New York.
Church and Science. — Prebendary Clark.
Ecclesiastical Law.—Isambard Brunel.
Church & National Education.—Canon Norris.
Church and Universities.—John G. Talbot.
Toleration.—Dean Cowie.
Eastern Church and Anglican Communion.—Rev. Geo. Williams.
A Disestablished Church.—Dean of Cashel.
Christian Tradition.—Rev. Dr. Irons.
Dogma.—Rev. Dr. Weir.
Parochial Councils. — Archdeacon Chapman.

COLERIDGE'S (SAMUEL TAYLOR) Table-Talk. Portrait. 12mo. 3*s*. 6*d*.

COLLINGWOOD'S (CUTHBERT) Rambles of a Naturalist on the Shores and Waters of the China Sea. Being Observations in Natural History during a Voyage to China, &c. With Illustrations. 8vo. 16*s*.

COLONIAL LIBRARY. [See Home and Colonial Library.]

COOK'S (Canon) Sermons Preached at Lincoln's Inn. 8vo. 9*s*.

COOKERY (MODERN DOMESTIC). Founded on Principles of Economy and Practical Knowledge, and adapted for Private Families. By a Lady. Woodcuts. Fcap. 8vo. 5*s*.

COOPER'S (T. T.) Travels of a Pioneer of Commerce on an Overland Journey from China towards India. Illustrations. 8vo. 16*s*.

CORNWALLIS (THE) Papers and Correspondence during the American War,—Administrations in India,—Union with Ireland, and Peace of Amiens. *Second Edition*. 3 Vols. 8vo. 63*s*.

COWPER'S (COUNTESS) Diary while Lady of the Bedchamber to Caroline Princess of Wales, 1714—20. Edited by Hon. SPENCER COWPER. *Second Edition*. Portrait. 8vo. 10*s*. 6*d*.

CRABBE'S (REV. GEORGE) Life and Poetical Works. With Illustrations. Royal 8vo. 7*s*.

CROKER'S (J. W.) Progressive Geography for Children. *Fifth Edition*. 18mo. 1*s*. 6*d*.

——— Stories for Children, Selected from the History of England. *Fifteenth Edition*. Woodcuts. 16mo. 2*s*. 6*d*.

——— Boswell's Life of Johnson. Including the Tour to the Hebrides. *New and revised Library Edition*. Portraits. 4 vols. 8vo. [*In Preparation*.

——— Essays on the Early Period of the French Revolution. 8vo. 15*s*.

——— Historical Essay on the Guillotine. Fcap. 8vo. 1*s*.

CUMMING'S (R. GORDON) Five Years of a Hunter's Life in the Far Interior of South Africa. *Sixth Edition.* Woodcuts. Post 8vo. 6s.

CROWE'S AND CAVALCASELLE'S Lives of the Early Flemish Painters. Woodcuts. Post 8vo, 10s. 6d.; or Large Paper, 8vo, 15s.

——— History of Painting in Italy, from 2nd to 16th Century. Derived from Researches into the Works of Art in that Country. With 100 Illustrations. 5 Vols. 8vo. 21s. each.

CUNYNGHAME'S (SIR ARTHUR) Travels in the Eastern Caucasus, on the Caspian, and Black Seas, in Daghestan and the Frontiers of Persia and Turkey. With Map and Illustrations. 8vo. 18s.

CURTIUS' (PROFESSOR) Student's Greek Grammar, for the Upper Forms. Edited by DR. WM. SMITH. Post 8vo. 6s.

——— Elucidations of the above Grammar. Translated by EVELYN ABBOT. Post 8vo. 7s. 6d.

——— Smaller Greek Grammar for the Middle and Lower Forms. Abridged from the larger work. 12mo. 3s. 6d.

——— Accidence of the Greek Language. Extracted from the above work. 12mo. 2s. 6d.

——— Principles of Greek Etymology. Translated by A. S. WILKINS, M.A., and E. B. ENGLAND, B.A. 8vo. *Nearly Ready.*

CURZON'S (HON. ROBERT) ARMENIA AND ERZEROUM. A Year on the Frontiers of Russia, Turkey, and Persia. *Third Edition.* Woodcuts. Post 8vo. 7s. 6d.

——— Visits to the Monasteries of the Levant. *Fifth Edition.* Illustrations. Post 8vo. 7s. 6d.

CUST'S (GENERAL) Lives of the Warriors of the 17th Century—The Thirty Years' War. 2 Vols. 16s. Civil Wars of France and England. 2 Vols. 16s. Commanders of Fleets and Armies before the Enemy. 2 Vols. 18s.

——— Annals of the Wars—18th & 19th Century, 1700—1815. With Maps. 9 Vols. Post 8vo. 5s. each.

DAVIS'S (NATHAN) Ruined Cities of Numidia and Carthaginia. Illustrations. 8vo. 16s.

DAVY'S (SIR HUMPHRY) Consolations in Travel; or, Last Days of a Philosopher. *Seventh Edition.* Woodcuts. Fcap. 8vo. 3s 6d.

——— Salmonia; or, Days of Fly Fishing. *Fifth Edition.* Woodcuts. Fcap. 8vo. 3s. 6d.

DARWIN'S (CHARLES) Journal of Researches into the Natural History of the Countries visited during a Voyage round the World. *Eleventh Thousand.* Post 8vo. 9s.

——— Origin of Species by Means of Natural Selection; or, the Preservation of Favoured Races in the Struggle for Life. *Sixth Edition.* Post 8vo. 7s. 6d.

——— Variation of Animals and Plants under Domestication. With Illustrations. 2 Vols. 8vo. 28s.

——— Descent of Man, and Selection in Relation to Sex. With Illustrations. Crown 8vo. 9s.

——— Expressions of the Emotions in Man and Animals. With Illustrations. Crown 8vo. 12s.

——— Fertilization of Orchids through Insect Agency, and as to the good of Intercrossing. Woodcuts. Post 8vo. 9s.

——— Fact and Argument for Darwin. By FRITZ MÜLLER. With numerous Illustrations and Additions by the Author. Translated from the German by W. S. DALLAS. Woodcuts. Post 8vo. 6s.

DELEPIERRE'S (OCTAVE) History of Flemish Literature. 8vo. 9*s.*

———— Historic Difficulties & Contested Events. Post 8vo. 6*s.*

DENISON'S (E. B.) Life of Bishop Lonsdale. With Selections from his Writings. With Portrait. Crown 8vo. 10*s.* 6*d.*

DERBY'S (EARL OF) Iliad of Homer rendered into English Blank Verse. *7th Edition.* 2 Vols. Post 8vo. 10*s.*

DE ROS'S (LORD) Young Officer's Companion; or, Essays on Military Duties and Qualities: with Examples and Illustrations from History. Post 8vo. 9*s.*

DEUTSCH'S (EMANUEL) Talmud, Islam, The Targums and other Literary Remains. 8vo. 12*s.*

DOG-BREAKING; the Most Expeditious, Certain, and Easy Method, whether great excellence or only mediocrity be required. With a Few Hints for those who Love the Dog and the Gun. By LIEUT.-GEN. HUTCHINSON. *Fifth Edition.* With 40 Woodcuts. Crown 8vo. 9*s.*

DOMESTIC MODERN COOKERY. Founded on Principles of Economy and Practical Knowledge, and adapted for Private Families. Woodcuts. Fcap. 8vo. 5*s.*

DOUGLAS'S (SIR HOWARD) Life and Adventures. Portrait. 8vo. 15*s.*

———— Theory and Practice of Gunnery. Plates. 8vo. 21*s.*

———— Construction of Bridges and the Passage of Rivers, in Military Operations. Plates. 8vo. 21*s.*

———— (WM.) Horse-Shoeing; As it Is, and As it Should be. Illustrations. Post 8vo. 7*s.* 6*d.*

DRAKE'S (SIR FRANCIS) Life, Voyages, and Exploits, by Sea and Land. By JOHN BARROW. *Third Edition.* Post 8vo. 2*s.*

DRINKWATER'S (JOHN) History of the Siege of Gibraltar, 1779-1783. With a Description and Account of that Garrison from the Earliest Periods. Post 8vo. 2*s.*

DUCANGE'S MEDIÆVAL LATIN-ENGLISH DICTIONARY. Translated by Rev. E. A. DAYMAN, M.A. Small 4to. (*In preparation.*

DU CHAILLU'S (PAUL B.) EQUATORIAL AFRICA, with Accounts of the Gorilla, the Nest-building Ape, Chimpanzee, Crocodile, &c. Illustrations. 8vo. 21*s.*

———— Journey to Ashango Land; and Further Penetration into Equatorial Africa. Illustrations. 8vo. 21*s.*

DUFFERIN'S (LORD) Letters from High Latitudes; an Account of a Yacht Voyage to Iceland, Jan Mayen, and Spitzbergen. *Fifth Edition.* Woodcuts. Post 8vo. 7*s.* 6*d.*

DUNCAN'S (MAJOR) History of the Royal Artillery. Compiled from the Original Records. *Second Edition.* With Portraits. 2 Vols. 8vo. 30*s.*

DYER'S (THOS. H.) History of Modern Europe, from the taking of Constantinople by the Turks to the close of the War in the Crimea. With Index. 4 Vols. 8vo. 42*s.*

EASTLAKE'S (SIR CHARLES) Contributions to the Literature of the Fine Arts. With Memoir of the Author, and Selections from his Correspondence. By LADY EASTLAKE. 2 Vols. 8vo. 24*s.*

EDWARDS' (W. H.) Voyage up the River Amazons, including a Visit to Para. Post 8vo. 2*s.*

ELDON'S (LORD) Public and Private Life, with Selections from his Correspondence and Diaries. By HORACE TWISS. *Third Edition.* Portrait. 2 Vols. Post 8vo. 21*s.*

ELGIN'S (LORD) Letters and Journals. Edited by THEODORE WALROND. With Preface by Dean Stanley. *Second Edition.* 8vo. 14*s.*

ELLESMERE'S (LORD) Two Sieges of Vienna by the Turks. Translated from the German. Post 8vo. 2*s.*

ELLIS'S (W.) Madagascar, including a Journey to the Capital, with notices of Natural History and the People. Woodcuts. 8vo. 16*s.*

——— Madagascar Revisited. Setting forth the Persecutions and Heroic Sufferings of the Native Christians. Illustrations. 8vo. 16*s.*

——— Memoir. By HIS SON. With his Character and Work. By REV. HENRY ALLON, D.D. Portrait. 8vo. 10*s.* 6*d.*

——— (ROBINSON) Poems and Fragments of Catullus. 16mo. 5*s.*

ELPHINSTONE'S (HON. MOUNTSTUART) History of India—the Hindoo and Mahomedan Periods. *Sixth Edition.* Map. 8vo. 18*s.*

——— (H. W.) Patterns for Turning; Comprising Elliptical and other Figures cut on the Lathe without the use of any Ornamental Chuck. With 70 Illustrations. Small 4to. 15*s.*

ENGEL'S (CARL) Music of the Most Ancient Nations; particularly of the Assyrians, Egyptians, and Hebrews; with Special Reference to the Discoveries in Western Asia and in Egypt. *Second Edition.* With 100 Illustrations. 8vo. 10*s.* 6*d.*

ENGLAND. See CALLCOTT, CROKER, HUME, MARKHAM, SMITH, and STANHOPE.

ENGLISHWOMAN IN AMERICA. Post 8vo. 10*s.* 6*d.*

ESSAYS ON CATHEDRALS. With an Introduction. By DEAN HOWSON. 8vo. 12*s.*

CONTENTS.

Recollections of a Dean.—Bishop of Carlisle.
Cathedral Canons and their Work.—Canon Norris.
Cathedrals in Ireland, Past and Future.—Dean of Cashel.
Cathedrals in their Missionary Aspect.—A. J. B. Beresford Hope.
Cathedral Foundations in Relation to Religious Thought.—Canon Westcott.
Cathedral Churches of the Old Foundation.—Edward A. Freeman.
Welsh Cathedrals.—Canon Perowne.
Education of Choristers.—Sir F. Gore Ouseley.
Cathedral Schools.—Canon Durham.
Cathedral Reform.—Chancellor Massingberd.
Relation of the Chapter to the Bishop. Chancellor Benson.
Architecture of the Cathedral Churches.—Canon Venables.

ETHNOLOGICAL SOCIETY'S TRANSACTIONS. Vols. I. to VI. 8vo.

ELZE'S (KARL) Life of Lord Byron. With a Critical Essay on his Place in Literature. Translated from the German, and Edited with Notes. With Original Portrait and Facsimile. 8vo. 16*s.*

FAMILY RECEIPT-BOOK. A Collection of a Thousand Valuable and Useful Receipts. Fcap. 8vo. 5*s.* 6*d.*

FARRAR'S (A. S.) Critical History of Free Thought in reference to the Christian Religion. 8vo. 16*s.*

——— (F. W.) Origin of Language, based on Modern Researches. Fcap. 8vo. 5*s.*

FERGUSSON'S (JAMES) History of Architecture in all Countries from the Earliest Times. Vols. I. and II. Ancient and Mediæval. With 1,000 Illustrations. Medium 8vo. 63s.

——— Vol. III. Indian and Eastern. With 300 Illustrations. Medium 8vo. [In the Press.

——— Vol. IV. Modern. With 330 Illustrations. Medium 8vo. 31s. 6d.

——— Rude Stone Monuments in all Countries; their Age and Uses. With 230 Illustrations. Medium 8vo. 24s.

——— Holy Sepulchre and the Temple at Jerusalem. Woodcuts. 8vo. 7s. 6d.

FLEMING'S (PROFESSOR) Student's Manual of Moral Philosophy. With Quotations and References. Post 8vo. 7s. 6d.

FLOWER GARDEN. By REV. THOS. JAMES. Fcap. 8vo. 1s.

FORD'S (RICHARD) Gatherings from Spain. Post 8vo. 3s. 6d.

FORSYTH'S (WILLIAM) Life and Times of Cicero. With Selections from his Correspondence and Orations. *Third Edition.* Illustrations. 8vo. 10s. 6d.

——— Hortensius; an Historical Essay on the Office and Duties of an Advocate. *Second Edition.* Illustrations. 8vo. 12s.

——— History of Ancient Manuscripts. Post 8vo. 2s. 6d.

——— Novels and Novelists of the 18th Century, in Illustration of the Manners and Morals of the Age. Post 8vo. 10s. 6d.

FORTUNE'S (ROBERT) Narrative of Two Visits to the Tea Countries of China, 1843-52. *Third Edition.* Woodcuts. 2 Vols. Post 8vo. 18s.

FOSS' (Edward) Biographia Juridica, or Biographical Dictionary of the Judges of England, from the Conquest to the Present Time, 1066-1870. Medium 8vo. 21s.

——— Tabulæ Curiales; or, Tables of the Superior Courts of Westminster Hall. Showing the Judges who sat in them from 1066 to 1864. 8vo. 10s. 6d.

FRANCE. *** See MARKHAM, SMITH, Student's.

FRENCH (THE) in Algiers; The Soldier of the Foreign Legion—and the Prisoners of Abd-el-Kadir. Translated by Lady DUFF GORDON. Post 8vo. 2s.

FRERE'S (SIR BARTLE) Indian Missions. *Third Edition.* Small 8vo. 2s. 6d.

——— Eastern Africa as a field for Missionary Labour. With Map. Crown 8vo. 5s.

——— Bengal Famine. How it will be Met and How to Prevent Future Famines in India. With Maps. Crown 8vo. 5s.

——— (M.) Old Deccan Days; or Fairy Legends Current in Southern India. With Notes, by SIR BARTLE FRERE. With Illustrations. Fcap. 8vo. 6s.

GALTON'S (FRANCIS) Art of Travel; or, Hints on the Shifts and Contrivances available in Wild Countries. *Fifth Edition.* Woodcuts. Post 8vo. 7s. 6d.

GEOGRAPHICAL SOCIETY'S JOURNAL. (*Published Yearly.*)

GEORGE'S (ERNEST) Mosel; a Series of Twenty Etchings, with Descriptive Letterpress. Imperial 4to. 42s.

——— Loire and South of France; a Series of Twenty Etchings, with Descriptive Text. Folio. 42s.

GERMANY (HISTORY OF). See MARKHAM.

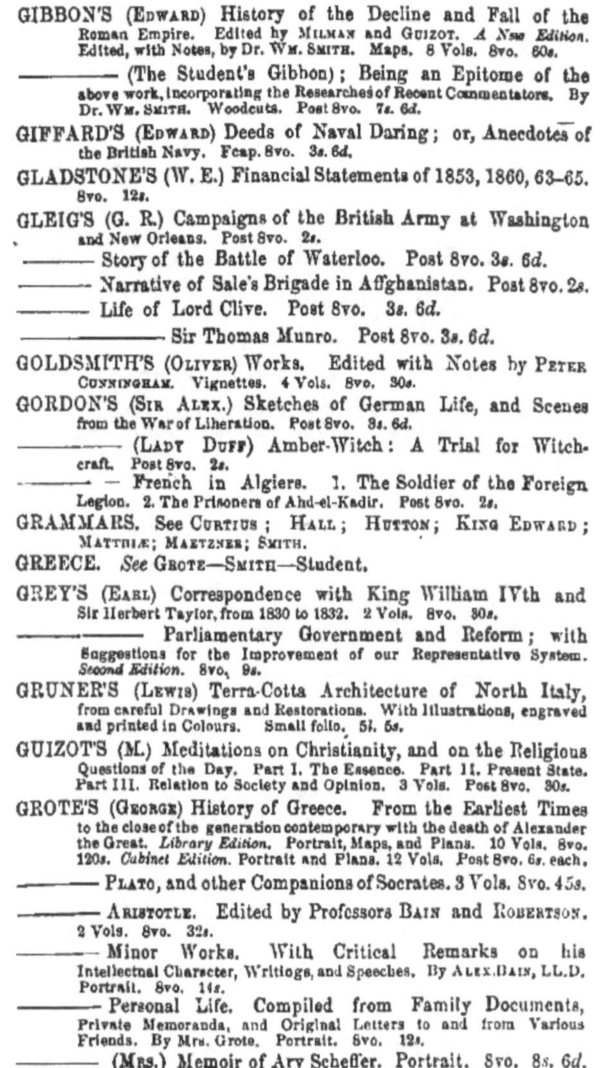

GIBBON'S (EDWARD) History of the Decline and Fall of the Roman Empire. Edited by MILMAN and GUIZOT. *A New Edition.* Edited, with Notes, by Dr. WM. SMITH. Maps. 8 Vols. 8vo. 60*s.*

——— (The Student's Gibbon); Being an Epitome of the above work, incorporating the Researches of Recent Commentators. By Dr. WM. SMITH. Woodcuts. Post 8vo. 7*s.* 6*d.*

GIFFARD'S (EDWARD) Deeds of Naval Daring; or, Anecdotes of the British Navy. Fcap. 8vo. 3*s.* 6*d.*

GLADSTONE'S (W. E.) Financial Statements of 1853, 1860, 63–65. 8vo. 12*s.*

GLEIG'S (G. R.) Campaigns of the British Army at Washington and New Orleans. Post 8vo. 2*s.*

——— Story of the Battle of Waterloo. Post 8vo. 3*s.* 6*d.*

——— Narrative of Sale's Brigade in Affghanistan. Post 8vo. 2*s.*

——— Life of Lord Clive. Post 8vo. 3*s.* 6*d.*

——— Sir Thomas Munro. Post 8vo. 3*s.* 6*d.*

GOLDSMITH'S (OLIVER) Works. Edited with Notes by PETER CUNNINGHAM. Vignettes. 4 Vols. 8vo. 30*s.*

GORDON'S (SIR ALEX.) Sketches of German Life, and Scenes from the War of Liberation. Post 8vo. 3*s.* 6*d.*

——— (LADY DUFF) Amber-Witch: A Trial for Witchcraft. Post 8vo. 2*s.*

——— French in Algiers. 1. The Soldier of the Foreign Legion. 2. The Prisoners of Abd-el-Kadir. Post 8vo. 2*s.*

GRAMMARS. See CURTIUS; HALL; HUTTON; KING EDWARD; MATTHIÆ; MAETZNER; SMITH.

GREECE. *See* GROTE—SMITH—Student.

GREY'S (EARL) Correspondence with King William IVth and Sir Herbert Taylor, from 1830 to 1832. 2 Vols. 8vo. 30*s.*

——— Parliamentary Government and Reform; with Suggestions for the Improvement of our Representative System. *Second Edition.* 8vo. 9*s.*

GRUNER'S (LEWIS) Terra-Cotta Architecture of North Italy, from careful Drawings and Restorations. With Illustrations, engraved and printed in Colours. Small folio. 5*l.* 5*s.*

GUIZOT'S (M.) Meditations on Christianity, and on the Religious Questions of the Day. Part I. The Essence. Part II. Present State. Part III. Relation to Society and Opinion. 3 Vols. Post 8vo. 30*s.*

GROTE'S (GEORGE) History of Greece. From the Earliest Times to the close of the generation contemporary with the death of Alexander the Great. *Library Edition.* Portrait, Maps, and Plans. 10 Vols. 8vo. 120*s.* *Cabinet Edition.* Portrait and Plans. 12 Vols. Post 8vo. 6*s.* each.

——— PLATO, and other Companions of Socrates. 3 Vols. 8vo. 45*s.*

——— ARISTOTLE. Edited by Professors BAIN and ROBERTSON. 2 Vols. 8vo. 32*s.*

——— Minor Works. With Critical Remarks on his Intellectual Character, Writings, and Speeches. By ALEX. BAIN, LL.D. Portrait. 8vo. 14*s.*

——— Personal Life. Compiled from Family Documents, Private Memoranda, and Original Letters to and from Various Friends. By Mrs. Grote. Portrait. 8vo. 12*s.*

——— (MRS.) Memoir of Ary Scheffer. Portrait. 8vo. 8*s.* 6*d.*

HALL'S (T. D.) School Manual of English Grammar. With Copious Exercises. 12mo. 3*s*. 6*d*.

——— Primary English Grammar for Elementary Schools. 16mo. 1*s*.

——— Child's First Latin Book, including a Systematic Treatment of the New Pronunciation, and a full Praxis of Nouns, Adjectives, and Pronouns. 16mo. 1*s*. 6*d*.

HALLAM'S (HENRY) Constitutional History of England, from the Accession of Henry the Seventh to the Death of George the Second. *Library Edition*. 3 Vols. 8vo. 30*s*. *Cabinet Edition*. 3 Vols. Post 8vo. 12*s*.

——— Student's Edition of the above work. Edited by WM. SMITH, D.C.L. Post 8vo. 7*s*. 6*d*.

——— History of Europe during the Middle Ages. *Library Edition*. 3 Vols. 8vo. 30*s*. *Cabinet Edition*, 3 Vols. Post 8vo. 12*s*.

——— Student's Edition of the above work. Edited by WM. SMITH, D.C.L. Post 8vo. 7*s*. 6*d*.

——— Literary History of Europe, during the 15th, 16th and 17th Centuries. *Library Edition*. 3 Vols. 8vo. 36*s*. *Cabinet Edition*. 4 Vols. Post 8vo. 16*s*.

——— (ARTHUR) Literary Remains; in Verse and Prose. Portrait. Fcap. 8vo. 3*s*. 6*d*.

HAMILTON'S (GEN. SIR F. W.) History of the Grenadier Guards. From Original Documents in the Rolls' Records, War Office, Regimental Records, &c. With Illustrations. 3 Vols. 8vo. 63*s*.

HANNAH'S (REV. DR.) Divine and Human Elements in Holy Scripture. 8vo. 10*s*. 6*d*.

HART'S ARMY LIST. (*Published Quarterly and Annually*.)

HAY'S (SIR J. H. DRUMMOND) Western Barbary, its Wild Tribes and Savage Animals. Post 8vo. 2*s*.

HEAD'S (SIR FRANCIS) Royal Engineer. Illustrations. 8vo. 12*s*.

——— Life of Sir John Burgoyne. Post 8vo. 1*s*.

——— Rapid Journeys across the Pampas. Post 8vo. 2*s*.

——— Bubbles from the Brunnen of Nassau. Illustrations. Post 8vo. 7*s*. 6*d*.

——— Emigrant. Fcap. 8vo. 2*s*. 6*d*.

——— Stokers and Pokers; or, the London and North Western Railway. Post 8vo. 2*s*.

——— (SIR EDMUND) Shall and Will; or, Future Auxiliary Verbs. Fcap. 8vo. 4*s*.

HEBER'S (BISHOP) Journals in India. 2 Vols. Post 8vo. 7*s*.

——— Poetical Works. Portrait. Fcap. 8vo. 3*s*. 6*d*.

——— Hymns adapted to the Church Service. 16mo. 1*s*. 6*d*.

HERODOTUS. A New English Version. Edited, with Notes and Essays, historical, ethnographical, and geographical, by CANON RAWLINSON, assisted by SIR HENRY RAWLINSON and SIR J. G. WILKINSON. *Third Edition*. Maps and Woodcuts. 4 Vols. 8vo.

HATHERLEY'S (LORD) Continuity of Scripture, as Declared by the Testimony of our Lord and of the Evangelists and Apostles. *Fourth Edition*. 8vo. 6*s*. *Popular Edition*. Post 8vo. 2*s*. 6*d*.

HOLLWAY'S (J. G.) Month in Norway. Fcap. 8vo. 2*s*.

HONEY BEE. By REV. THOMAS JAMES. Fcap. 8vo. 1*s*.

HOOK'S (DEAN) Church Dictionary. *Tenth Edition*. 8vo. 16*s*.

——— (THEODORE) Life. By J. G. LOCKHART. Fcap. 8vo. 1*s*.

HOPE'S (T. C.) ARCHITECTURE OF AHMEDABAD, with Historical Sketch and Architectural Notes. With Maps, Photographs, and Woodcuts. 4to. 5*l.* 5*s.*

——— (A. J. BERESFORD) Worship in the Church of England. 8vo. 9*s.*

FOREIGN HANDBOOKS.

HAND-BOOK—TRAVEL-TALK. English, French, German, and Italian. 18mo. 3*s.* 6*d.*

——— HOLLAND,—BELGIUM, and the Rhine to Mayence. Map and Plans. Post 8vo. 6*s.*

——— NORTH GERMANY,—PRUSSIA, SAXONY, HANOVER, and the Rhine from Mayence to Switzerland. Map and Plans. Post 8vo. 6*s.*

——— SOUTH GERMANY,—Bavaria, Austria, Styria, Salzburg, the Austrian and Bavarian Alps, the Tyrol, Hungary, and the Danube, from Ulm to the Black Sea. Map. Post 8vo. 10*s.*

——— KNAPSACK GUIDE TO THE TYROL. 16mo. 6*s.*

——— PAINTING. German, Flemish, and Dutch Schools. Illustrations. 2 Vols. Post 8vo. 24*s.*

——— LIVES OF EARLY FLEMISH PAINTERS. By CROWE and CAVALCASELLE. Illustrations. Post 8vo. 10*s.* 6*d.*

——— SWITZERLAND, Alps of Savoy, and Piedmont. Maps. Post 8vo. 9*s.*

——— FRANCE, Normandy, Brittany, the French Alps, the Rivers Loire, Seine, Rhone, and Garonne, Dauphiné, Provence, and the Pyrenees. Maps. 2 Parts. Post 8vo. 12*s.*

——— ISLANDS OF THE MEDITERRANEAN—Malta, Corsica, Sardinia, and Sicily. Maps. Post 8vo.

——— ALGERIA. Map. Post 8vo. 9*s.*

——— PARIS, and its Environs. Map. 16mo. 3*s.* 6*d.*

*** MURRAY'S PLAN OF PARIS, mounted on canvas. 3*s.* 6*d.*

——— SPAIN, Madrid, The Castiles, The Basque Provinces, Leon, The Asturias, Galicia, Estremadura, Andalusia, Ronda, Granada, Murcia, Valencia, Catalonia, Aragon, Navarre, The Balearic Islands, &c. &c. Maps. 2 Vols. Post 8vo. 24*s.*

——— PORTUGAL, LISBON, Porto, Cintra, Mafra, &c. Map. Post 8vo. 9*s.*

——— NORTH ITALY, Piedmont, Liguria, Venetia, Lombardy, Parma, Modena, and Romagna. Map. Post 8vo. 10*s.*

——— CENTRAL ITALY, Lucca, Tuscany, Florence, The Marches, Umbria, and the Patrimony of St. Peter's. Map. Post 8vo. 10*s.*

——— ROME AND ITS ENVIRONS. Map. Post 8vo. 10*s.*

——— SOUTH ITALY, Two Sicilies, Naples, Pompeii, Herculaneum, and Vesuvius. Map. Post 8vo. 10*s.*

——— KNAPSACK GUIDE TO ITALY. 16mo.

——— PAINTING. The Italian Schools. Illustrations. 2 Vols. Post 8vo. 30*s.*

——— LIVES OF ITALIAN PAINTERS, FROM CIMABUE to BASSANO. By Mrs. JAMESON. Portraits. Post 8vo. 12*s.*

——— RUSSIA, ST. PETERSBURG, MOSCOW, POLAND, and FINLAND. Maps. Post 8vo. 15*s.*

——— DENMARK. Map. Post 8vo. 6*s.*

HAND-BOOK—SWEDEN. Map. Post 8vo. 6s.

——— NORWAY. Map. 6s.

——— GREECE, the Ionian Islands, Continental Greece, Athens, the Peloponnesus, the Islands of the Ægean Sea, Albania, Thessaly, and Macedonia. Maps. Post 8vo. 15s.

——— TURKEY IN ASIA—CONSTANTINOPLE, the Bosphorus, Dardanelles, Broussa, Plain of Troy, Crete, Cyprus, Smyrna, Ephesus, the Seven Churches, Coasts of the Black Sea, Armenia, Mesopotamia, &c. Maps. Post 8vo. 15s.

——— EGYPT, including Descriptions of the Course of the Nile through Egypt and Nubia, Alexandria, Cairo, and Thebes, the Suez Canal, the Pyramids, the Peninsula of Sinai, the Oases, the Fyoom, &c. Map. Post 8vo. 15s

——— HOLY LAND—SYRIA PALESTINE, Peninsula of Sinai, Edom, Syrian Desert, &c. Maps. Post 8vo.

——— INDIA — BOMBAY AND MADRAS. Map. 2 Vols. Post 8vo. 12s. each.

ENGLISH HANDBOOKS.

HAND-BOOK—MODERN LONDON. Map. 16mo. 3s. 6d.

——— ESSEX, CAMBRIDGE, SUFFOLK, AND NORFOLK, Chelmsford, Colchester, Maldon, Cambridge, Ely, Newmarket, Bury, Ipswich, Woodbridge, Felixstowe, Lowestoft, Norwich, Yarmouth, Cromer, &c. Map and Plans. Post 8vo. 12s.

——— CATHEDRALS of Oxford, Peterborough, Norwich, Ely, and Lincoln. With 90 Illustrations. Crown 8vo. 18s.

——— KENT AND SUSSEX, Canterbury, Dover, Ramsgate, Sheerness, Rochester, Chatham, Woolwich, Brighton, Chichester, Worthing, Hastings, Lewes, Arundel, &c. Map. Post 8vo. 10s.

——— SURREY AND HANTS, Kingston, Croydon, Reigate, Guildford, Dorking, Boxhill, Winchester, Southampton, New Forest, Portsmouth, and ISLE OF WIGHT. Maps. Post 8vo. 10s.

——— BERKS, BUCKS, AND OXON, Windsor, Eton, Reading, Aylesbury, Uxbridge, Wycombe, Henley, the City and University of Oxford, Blenheim, and the Descent of the Thames. Map. Post 8vo. 7s. 6d.

——— WILTS, DORSET, AND SOMERSET, Salisbury, Chippenham, Weymouth, Sherborne, Wells, Bath, Bristol, Taunton, &c. Map. Post 8vo. 10s.

——— DEVON AND CORNWALL, Exeter, Ilfracombe, Linton, Sidmouth, Dawlish, Teignmouth, Plymouth, Devonport, Torquay, Launceston, Truro, Penzance, Falmouth, the Lizard, Land's End, &c. Maps. Post 8vo. 12s.

——— CATHEDRALS of Winchester, Salisbury, Exeter, Wells, Chichester, Rochester, Canterbury. With 110 Illustrations. 2 Vols. Crown 8vo. 24s.

——— GLOUCESTER, HEREFORD, AND WORCESTER, Cirencester, Cheltenham, Stroud, Tewkesbury, Leominster, Ross, Malvern, Kidderminster, Dudley, Bromsgrove, Evesham. Map. Post 8vo. 9s.

——— CATHEDRALS of Bristol, Gloucester, Hereford, Worcester, and Lichfield. With 50 Illustrations. Crown 8vo. 16s.

——— NORTH WALES, Bangor, Carnarvon, Beaumaris, Snowdon, Llanberis, Dolgelly, Cader Idris, Conway, &c. Map. Post 8vo. 7s.

——— SOUTH WALES, Monmouth, Llandaff, Merthyr, Vale of Neath, Pembroke, Carmarthen, Tenby, Swansea, and The Wye, &c. Map. Post 8vo. 7s.

HAND-BOOK—CATHEDRALS OF BANGOR, ST. ASAPH, Llandaff, and St. David's. With Illustrations. Post 8vo. 15*s.*

——— DERBY, NOTTS, LEICESTER, STAFFORD, Matlock, Bakewell, Chatsworth, The Peak, Buxton, Hardwick, Dove Dale, Ashborne, Southwell, Mansfield, Retford, Burton, Belvoir, Melton Mowbray, Wolverhampton, Lichfield, Walsall, Tamworth. Map. Post 8vo. 9*s.*

——— SHROPSHIRE, CHESHIRE AND LANCASHIRE—Shrewsbury, Ludlow, Bridgnorth, Oswestry, Chester, Crewe, Alderley, Stockport, Birkenhead, Warrington, Bury, Manchester, Liverpool, Burnley, Clitheroe, Bolton, Blackburn, Wigan, Preston, Rochdale, Lancaster, Southport, Blackpool, &c. Map. Post 8vo. 10*s.*

——— YORKSHIRE, Doncaster, Hull, Selby, Beverley, Scarborough, Whitby, Harrogate, Ripon, Leeds, Wakefield, Bradford, Halifax, Huddersfield, Sheffield. Map and Plans. Post 8vo. 12*s.*

——— CATHEDRALS of York, Ripon, Durham, Carlisle, Chester, and Manchester. With 60 Illustrations. 2 Vols. Crown 8vo. 21*s.*

——— DURHAM AND NORTHUMBERLAND, Newcastle, Darlington, Gateshead, Bishop Auckland, Stockton, Hartlepool, Sunderland, Shields, Berwick-on-Tweed, Morpeth, Tynemouth, Coldstream, Alnwick, &c. Map. Post 8vo. 9*s.*

——— WESTMORLAND AND CUMBERLAND—Lancaster, Furness Abbey, Ambleside, Kendal, Windermere, Coniston, Keswick, Grasmere, Ulswater, Carlisle, Cockermouth, Penrith, Appleby. Map. Post 8vo. 6*s.*

*** MURRAY'S MAP OF THE LAKE DISTRICT, on canvas. 3*s.* 6*d.*

——— SCOTLAND, Edinburgh, Melrose, Kelso, Glasgow, Dumfries, Ayr, Stirling, Arran, The Clyde, Oban, Inverary, Loch Lomond, Loch Katrine and Trossachs, Caledonian Canal, Inverness, Perth, Dundee, Aberdeen, Braemar, Skye, Caithness, Ross, Sutherland, &c. Maps and Plans. Post 8vo. 9*s.*

——— IRELAND, Dublin, Belfast, Donegal, Galway, Wexford, Cork, Limerick, Waterford, Killarney, Munster, &c. Maps. Post 8vo. 12*s.*

——— FAMILIAR QUOTATIONS. From English Authors. *Third Edition.* Fcap. 8vo. 5*s.*

HORACE; a New Edition of the Text. Edited by DEAN MILMAN. With 100 Woodcuts. Crown 8vo. 7*s.* 6*d.*

——— Life of. By DEAN MILMAN. Illustrations. 8vo. 9*s.*

HOUGHTON'S (LORD) Monographs, Personal and Social. With Portraits. Crown 8vo. 10*s.* 6*d.*

HUME'S (The Student's) History of England, from the Invasion of Julius Cæsar to the Revolution of 1688. Corrected and continued to 1868. Woodcuts. Post 8vo. 7*s.* 6*d.*

HUTCHINSON (GEN.), on the most expeditious, certain, and easy Method of Dog-Breaking. *Fifth Edition.* With 40 Illustrations. Crown 8vo. 9*s.*

HUTTON'S (H. E.) Principia Græca; an Introduction to the Study of Greek. Comprehending Grammar, Delectus, and Exercise-book, with Vocabularies. *Sixth Edition.* 12mo. 3*s.* 6*d.*

IRBY AND MANGLES' Travels in Egypt, Nubia, Syria, and the Holy Land. Post 8vo. 2*s.*

JACOBSON'S (BISHOP) Fragmentary Illustrations of the History of the Book of Common Prayer; from Manuscript Sources (Bishop SANDERSON and Bishop WREN). 8vo. 5*s.*

JAMES' (REV. THOMAS) Fables of Æsop. A New Translation, with Historical Preface. With 100 Woodcuts by TENNIEL and WOLF. *Sixty-fourth Thousand.* Post 8vo. 2*s.* 6*d.*

c

HOME AND COLONIAL LIBRARY. A Series of Works adapted for all circles and classes of Readers, having been selected for their acknowledged interest, and ability of the Authors. Post 8vo. Published at 2s. and 3s. 6d. each, and arranged under two distinctive heads as follows:—

CLASS A.

HISTORY, BIOGRAPHY, AND HISTORIC TALES.

1. SIEGE OF GIBRALTAR. By JOHN DRINKWATER. 2s.
2. THE AMBER-WITCH. By LADY DUFF GORDON. 2s.
3. CROMWELL AND BUNYAN. By ROBERT SOUTHEY. 2s.
4. LIFE OF SIR FRANCIS DRAKE. By JOHN BARROW. 2s.
5. CAMPAIGNS AT WASHINGTON. By REV. G. R. GLEIG. 2s.
6. THE FRENCH IN ALGIERS. By LADY DUFF GORDON. 2s.
7. THE FALL OF THE JESUITS. 2s.
8. LIVONIAN TALES. 2s.
9. LIFE OF CONDÉ. By LORD MAHON. 3s. 6d.
10. SALE'S BRIGADE. By REV. G. R. GLEIG. 2s.
11. THE SIEGES OF VIENNA. By LORD ELLESMERE. 2s.
12. THE WAYSIDE CROSS. By CAPT. MILMAN. 2s.
13. SKETCHES OF GERMAN LIFE. By SIR A. GORDON. 3s. 6d.
14. THE BATTLE OF WATERLOO. By REV. G. R. GLEIG. 3s. 6d.
15. AUTOBIOGRAPHY OF STEFFENS. 2s.
16. THE BRITISH POETS. By THOMAS CAMPBELL. 3s. 6d.
17. HISTORICAL ESSAYS. By LORD MAHON. 3s. 6d.
18. LIFE OF LORD CLIVE. By REV. G. R. GLEIG. 3s. 6d.
19. NORTH - WESTERN RAILWAY. By SIR F. B. HEAD. 2s.
20. LIFE OF MUNRO. By REV. G. R. GLEIG. 3s. 6d.

CLASS B.

VOYAGES, TRAVELS, AND ADVENTURES.

1. BIBLE IN SPAIN. By GEORGE BORROW. 3s. 6d.
2. GYPSIES OF SPAIN. By GEORGE BORROW. 3s. 6d.
3 & 4. JOURNALS IN INDIA. By BISHOP HEBER. 2 Vols. 7s.
5. TRAVELS IN THE HOLY LAND. By IRBY and MANGLES. 2s.
6. MOROCCO AND THE MOORS. By J. DRUMMOND HAY. 2s.
7. LETTERS FROM THE BALTIC. By a LADY. 2s.
8. NEW SOUTH WALES. By MRS. MEREDITH. 2s.
9. THE WEST INDIES. By M. G. LEWIS. 2s.
10. SKETCHES OF PERSIA. By SIR JOHN MALCOLM. 3s. 6d.
11. MEMOIRS OF FATHER RIPA. 2s.
12 & 13. TYPEE AND OMOO. By HERMANN MELVILLE. 2 Vols. 7s.
14. MISSIONARY LIFE IN CANADA. By REV. J. ABBOTT. 2s.
15. LETTERS FROM MADRAS. By a LADY. 2s.
16. HIGHLAND SPORTS. By CHARLES ST. JOHN. 3s. 6d.
17. PAMPAS JOURNEYS. By SIR F. B. HEAD. 2s.
18. GATHERINGS FROM SPAIN. By RICHARD FORD. 3s. 6d.
19. THE RIVER AMAZON. By W. H. EDWARDS. 2s.
20. MANNERS & CUSTOMS OF INDIA. By REV. C. ACLAND. 2s.
21. ADVENTURES IN MEXICO. By G. F. RUXTON. 3s. 6d.
22. PORTUGAL AND GALLICIA. By LORD CARNARVON. 3s. 6d.
23. BUSH LIFE IN AUSTRALIA. By REV. H. W. HAYGARTH. 2s.
24. THE LIBYAN DESERT. By BAYLE ST. JOHN. 2s.
25. SIERRA LEONE. By A LADY. 3s. 6d.

*** Each work may be had separately.

JAMESON'S (MRS.) Lives of the Early Italian Painters—and the Progress of Painting in Italy—Cimabue to Bassano. *New Edition.* With 60 Portraits. Post 8vo. 12s.

JENNINGS' (L. J.) Eighty Years of Republican Government in the United States. Post 8vo. 10s. 6d.

JERVIS'S (REV. W. H.) Gallican Church, from the Concordat of Bologna, 1516, to the Revolution. With an Introduction. Portraits. 2 Vols. 8vo. 28s.

JESSE'S (EDWARD) Gleanings in Natural History. Fcp. 8vo. 3s. 6d.

JOHNS' (REV. B. G.) Blind People; their Works and Ways. With Sketches of the Lives of some famous Blind Men. With Illustrations. Post 8vo. 7s. 6d.

JOHNSON'S (DR. SAMUEL) Life. By James Boswell. Including the Tour to the Hebrides. Edited by MR. CROKER. *New revised Library Edition.* Portraits. 4 Vols. 8vo. [*In Preparation.*

——— Lives of the most eminent English Poets, with Critical Observations on their Works. Edited with Notes, Corrective and Explanatory, by PETER CUNNINGHAM. 3 vols. 8vo. 22s. 6d.

JUNIUS' HANDWRITING Professionally investigated. By Mr. CHABOT, Expert. With Preface and Collateral Evidence, by the Hon. EDWARD TWISLETON. With Facsimiles, Woodcuts, &c. 4to. £3 3s.

KEN'S (BISHOP) Life. By a LAYMAN. Portrait. 2 Vols. 8vo. 18s.

——— Exposition of the Apostles' Creed. 16mo. 1s. 6d.

KERR'S (ROBERT) GENTLEMAN'S HOUSE; OR, HOW TO PLAN ENGLISH RESIDENCES, FROM THE PARSONAGE TO THE PALACE. *Third Edition.* With Views and Plans. 8vo. 24s.

——— Small Country House. A Brief Practical Discourse on the Planning of a Residence from 2000*l*. to 5000*l*. With Supplementary Estimates to 7000*l*. Post 8vo. 3s.

——— Ancient Lights; a Book for Architects, Surveyors, Lawyers, and Landlords. 8vo. 5s. 6d.

——— (R. MALCOLM) Student's Blackstone. A Systematic Abridgment of the entire Commentaries, adapted to the present state of the law. Post 8vo. 7s. 6d.

KING EDWARD VITH'S Latin Grammar. *Seventeenth Edition.* 12mo. 3s. 6d.

——— First Latin Book. *Fifth Edition.* 12mo. 2s. 6d.

KING GEORGE IIIRD'S CORRESPONDENCE WITH LORD NORTH, 1769-82. Edited, with Notes and Introduction, by W. BODHAM DONNE. 2 vols. 8vo. 32s.

KING'S (R. J.) Sketches and Studies; Historical and Descriptive. 8vo. 12s.

KIRK'S (J. FOSTER) History of Charles the Bold, Duke of Burgundy. Portrait. 3 Vols. 8vo. 45s.

KIRKES' Handbook of Physiology. Edited by W. MORRANT BAKER, F.R.C.S. *Eighth Edit.* With 240 Illustrations. Post 8vo. 12s. 6d.

KUGLER'S Handbook of Painting.—The Italian Schools. *Fourth Edition.* Revised and Remodelled from the most recent Researches. By LADY EASTLAKE. With 140 Illustrations. 2 Vols. Crown 8vo. 30s.

——— Handbook of Painting.—The German, Flemish, and Dutch Schools. *Third Edition.* Revised and in part re-written. By J. A. CROWE. With 60 Illustrations. 2 Vols. Crown 8vo. 24s.

LANE'S (E. W.) Account of the Manners and Customs of Modern Egyptians. *New Edition.* With Illustrations. 2 Vols. Post 8vo. 12s.

LAWRENCE'S (SIR GEO.) Reminiscences of Forty-three Years' Service in India; including Captivities in Cabul among the Affghans and among the Sikhs, and a Narrative of the Mutiny in Rajputana. Edited by W. EDWARDS, H.M.C.B.S. Crown 8vo. 10s. 6d.

LAYARD'S (A. H.) Nineveh and its Remains. Being a Narrative of Researches and Discoveries amidst the Ruins of Assyria. With an Account of the Chaldean Christians of Kurdistan; the Yezedis, or Devil-worshippers; and an Enquiry into the Manners and Arts of the Ancient Assyrians. *Sixth Edition.* Plates and Woodcuts. 2 Vols. 8vo. 36*s.*

*** A POPULAR EDITION of the above work. With Illustrations. Post 8vo. 7*s.* 6*d.*

———— Nineveh and Babylon; being the Narrative of Discoveries in the Ruins, with Travels in Armenia, Kurdistan and the Desert, during a Second Expedition to Assyria. With Map and Plates. 8vo. 21*s.*

*** A POPULAR EDITION of the above work. With Illustrations. Post 8vo. 7*s.* 6*d.*

LEATHES' (STANLEY) Practical Hebrew Grammar. With the Hebrew Text of Genesis i.—vi., and Psalms i.—vi. Grammatical Analysis and Vocabulary. Post 8vo. 7*s.* 6*d.*

LENNEP'S (REV. H. J. VAN) Missionary Travels in Asia Minor. With Illustrations of Biblical History and Archæology. With Map and Woodcuts. 2 Vols. Post 8vo. 24*s.*

LESLIE'S (C. R.) Handbook for Young Painters. With Illustrations. Post 8vo. 7*s.* 6*d.*

———— Life and Works of Sir Joshua Reynolds. Portraits and Illustrations. 2 Vols. 8vo. 42*s.*

LETTERS FROM THE BALTIC. By a LADY. Post 8vo. 2*s.*

———— MADRAS. By a LADY. Post 8vo. 2*s.*

———— SIERRA LEONE. By a LADY. Post 8vo. 3*s.* 6*d.*

LEVI'S (LEONE) History of British Commerce; and of the Economic Progress of the Nation, from 1763 to 1870. 8vo. 16*s.*

LEWIS'S (M. G.) Journal of a Residence among the Negroes in the West Indies. Post 8vo. 2*s.*

LIDDELL'S (DEAN) Student's History of Rome, from the earliest Times to the establishment of the Empire. With Woodcuts. Post 8vo. 7*s.* 6*d.*

LINDSAY'S (LORD) Lives of the Lindsays; Memoir of the Houses of Crawfurd and Balcarres. With Extracts from Official Papers and Personal Narratives. 3 Vols. 8vo. 24*s.*

———— Etruscan Inscriptions. Analysed, Translated, and Commented upon. 8vo. 12*s.*

LLOYD'S (W. WATKISS) History of Sicily to the Athenian War; with Elucidations of the Sicilian Odes of Pindar. With Map. 8vo. 14*s.*

LISPINGS from LOW LATITUDES; or, the Journal of the Hon. Impulsia Gushington. Edited by LORD DUFFERIN. With 24 Plates. 4to. 21*s.*

LITTLE ARTHUR'S HISTORY OF ENGLAND. By LADY CALLCOTT. *New and Cheaper Edition, continued to* 1872. With Woodcuts. Fcap. 8vo. 1*s.* 6*d.*

LIVINGSTONE'S (DR.) Popular Account of Missionary Travels and Researches in South Africa. Illustrations. Post 8vo. 6*s.*

———— Narrative of an Expedition to the Zambezi and its Tributaries, with the Discovery of the Lakes Shirwa and Nyassa. Map and Illustrations. 8vo. 21*s.*

———— Last Journals in Central Africa, from 1865 to his Death. Continued by a Narrative of his last moments and sufferings. By Rev. HORACE WALLER. Maps and Illustrations. 2 Vols. 8vo. 28*s.*

LIVONIAN TALES. By the Author of "Letters from the Baltic." Post 8vo. 2*s.*

LOCH'S (H. B.) Personal Narrative of Events during Lord Elgin's Second Embassy to China. *Second Edition.* With Illustrations. Post 8vo. 9*s.*

LOCKHART'S (J. G.) Ancient Spanish Ballads. Historical and Romantic. Translated, with Notes. *New Edition.* With Portrait and Illustrations. Crown 8vo. 5*s.*

———— Life of Theodore Hook. Fcap. 8vo. 1*s.*

LONSDALE'S (BISHOP) Life. With Selections from his Writings. By E. B. DENISON. With Portrait. Crown 8vo. 10*s.* 6*d.*

LOUDON'S (MRS.) Gardening for Ladies. With Directions and Calendar of Operations for Every Month. *Eighth Edition.* Woodcuts. Fcap. 8vo. 3*s.* 6*d.*

LUCKNOW: A Lady's Diary of the Siege. Fcap. 8vo. 4*s.* 6*d.*

LYELL'S (SIR CHARLES) Principles of Geology; or, the Modern Changes of the Earth and its Inhabitants considered as Illustrative of Geology. *Eleventh Edition.* With Illustrations. 2 Vols. 8vo. 32*s.*

———— Student's Elements of Geology. *Second Edition.* With Table of British Fossils and 600 Illustrations. Post 8vo. 9*s.*

———— Geological Evidences of the Antiquity of Man, including an Outline of Glacial Post-Tertiary Geology, and Remarks on the Origin of Species. *Fourth Edition.* Illustrations. 8vo. 14*s.*

———— (K. M.) Geographical Handbook of Ferns. With Tables to show their Distribution. Post 8vo. 7*s.* 6*d.*

LYTTELTON'S (LORD) Ephemera. 2 Vols. Post 8vo. 19*s.* 6*d.*

LYTTON'S (LORD) Memoir of Julian Fane. With Portrait. Post 8vo. 5*s.*

McCLINTOCK'S (SIR L.) Narrative of the Discovery of the Fate of Sir John Franklin and his Companions in the Arctic Seas. *Third Edition.* With Illustrations. Post 8vo. 7*s.* 6*d.*

MACDOUGALL'S (COL.) Modern Warfare as Influenced by Modern Artillery. With Plans. Post 8vo. 12*s.*

MACGREGOR'S (J.) Rob Roy on the Jordan, Nile, Red Sea, Gennesareth, &c. A Canoe Cruise in Palestine and Egypt and the Waters of Damascus. *Cheaper Edition.* With Map and 70 Illustrations. Crown 8vo. 7*s.* 6*d.*

MACPHERSON'S (MAJOR) Services in India, while Political Agent at Gwalior during the Mutiny. Illustrations. 8vo. 12*s.*

MAETZNER'S ENGLISH GRAMMAR. A Methodical, Analytical, and Historical Treatise on the Orthography, Prosody, Inflections, and Syntax of the English Tongue. Translated from the German. By CLAIR J. GRECE, LL.D. 3 Vols. 8vo. 36*s.*

MAHON (LORD), see STANHOPE.

MAINE'S (SIR H. SUMNER) Ancient Law: its Connection with the Early History of Society, and its Relation to Modern Ideas. *Fifth Edition.* 8vo. 12*s.*

———— Village Communities in the East and West. *Second Edition.* 8vo. 9*s.*

———— Early History of Institutions. 8vo. 12*s.*

MALCOLM'S (SIR JOHN) Sketches of Persia. Post 8vo. 3*s.* 6*d.*

MANSEL'S (DEAN) Limits of Religious Thought Examined. *Fifth Edition.* Post 8vo. 8*s.* 6*d.*

———— Letters, Lectures, and Papers, including the Phrontisterion, or Oxford in the XIXth Century. Edited by H. W. CHANDLER, M.A. 8vo. 12*s.*

———— Gnostic Heresies of the First and Second Centuries. With a sketch of his life and character. By Lord CARNARVON. Edited by Canon LIGHTFOOT. 8vo. 10*s.* 6*d.*

MANUAL OF SCIENTIFIC ENQUIRY. For the Use of Travellers. Edited by SIR J. F. HERSCHEL & REV. R. MAIN. Post 8vo. 3*s.* 6*d.* (*Published by order of the Lords of the Admiralty.*)

MARCO POLO. The Book of Ser Marco Polo, the Venetian. Concerning the Kingdoms and Marvels of the East. A new English Version. Illustrated by the light of Oriental Writers and Modern Travels. By COL. HENRY YULE. *New Edition.* Maps and Illustrations. 2 Vols. Medium 8vo. 42*s.*

MARKHAM'S (MRS.) History of England. From the First Invasion by the Romans *to* 1867. Woodcuts. 12mo. 3*s.* 6*d.*

——— History of France. From the Conquest by the Gauls *to* 1861. Woodcuts. 12mo. 3*s.* 6*d.*

——— History of Germany. From the Invasion by Marius *to* 1867. Woodcuts. 12mo. 3*s.* 6*d.*

——— (CLEMENTS R.) Travels in Peru and India. Maps and Illustrations. 8vo. 16*s.*

MARRYAT'S (JOSEPH) History of Modern and Mediæval Pottery and Porcelain. With a Description of the Manufacture. *Third Edition.* Plates and Woodcuts. 8vo. 42*s.*

MARSH'S (G. P.) Student's Manual of the English Language. Post 8vo. 7*s.* 6*d.*

MATTHIÆ'S GREEK GRAMMAR. Abridged by BLOMFIELD, *Revised* by E. S. CROOKE. 12mo. 4*s.*

MAUREL'S Character, Actions, and Writings of Wellington. Fcap. 8vo. 1*s.* 6*d.*

MAYNE'S (CAPT.) Four Years in British Columbia and Vancouver Island. Illustrations. 8vo. 16*s.*

MEADE'S (HON. HERBERT) Ride through the Disturbed Districts of New Zealand, with a Cruise among the South Sea Islands. With Illustrations. Medium 8vo. 12*s.*

MELVILLE'S (HERMANN) Marquesas and South Sea Islands. 2 Vols. Post 8vo. 7*s.*

MEREDITH'S (MRS. CHARLES) Notes and Sketches of New South Wales. Post 8vo. 2*s.*

MESSIAH (THE): The Life, Travels, Death, Resurrection, and Ascension of our Blessed Lord. By A Layman. Map. 8vo. 18*s.*

MILLINGTON'S (REV. T. S.) Signs and Wonders in the Land of Ham, or the Ten Plagues of Egypt, with Ancient and Modern Illustrations. Woodcuts. Post 8vo. 7*s.* 6*d.*

MILLS' (REV. JOHN) Three Months' Residence at Nablus, with an Account of the Modern Samaritans. Illustrations. Post 8vo. 10*s.* 6*d.*

MILMAN'S (DEAN) History of the Jews, from the earliest Period down to Modern Times. *Fourth Edition.* 3 Vols. Post 8vo. 18*s.*

——— Early Christianity, from the Birth of Christ to the Abolition of Paganism in the Roman Empire. *Fourth Edition.* 3 Vols. Post 8vo. 18*s.*

——— Latin Christianity, including that of the Popes to the Pontificate of Nicholas V. *Fourth Edition.* 9 Vols. Post 8vo. 54*s.*

——— Annals of St. Paul's Cathedral, from the Romans to the funeral of Wellington. *Second Edition.* Portrait and Illustrations. 8vo. 18*s.*

——— Character and Conduct of the Apostles considered as an Evidence of Christianity. 8vo. 10*s.* 6*d.*

——— Quinti Horatii Flacci Opera. With 100 Woodcuts. Small 8vo. 7*s.* 6*d.*

——— Life of Quintus Horatius Flaccus. With Illustrations. 8vo. 9*s.*

——— Poetical Works. The Fall of Jerusalem—Martyr of Antioch—Balshazzar—Tamor—Anne Boleyn—Fazio, &c. With Portrait and Illustrations. 3 Vols. Fcap. 8vo. 18*s.*

——— Fall of Jerusalem. Fcap. 8vo. 1*s.*

——— (CAPT. E. A.) Wayside Cross. Post 8vo. 2*s.*

MICHIE'S (ALEXANDER) Siberian Overland Route from Peking to Petersburg. Maps and Illustrations. 8vo. 16*s*.

MODERN DOMESTIC COOKERY. Founded on Principles of Economy and Practical Knowledge. *New Edition.* Woodcuts. Fcap. 8vo. 5*s*.

MONGREDIEN'S (AUGUSTUS) Trees and Shrubs for English Plantation. A Selection and Description of the most Ornamental which will flourish in the open air in our climate. With Classified Lists. With 30 Illustrations. 8vo. 16*s*.

MOORE & JACKMAN on the Clematis as a Garden Flower. Descriptions of the Hardy Species and Varieties, with Directions for their Cultivation. 8vo. 10*s*. 6*d*.

MOORE'S (THOMAS) Life and Letters of Lord Byron. *Cabinet Edition.* With Plates. 6 Vols. Fcap. 8vo. 18*s*.; *Popular Edition*, with Portraits. Royal 8vo. 7*s*. 6*d*.

MOSSMAN'S (SAMUEL) New Japan; the Land of the Rising Sun; its Annals and Progress during the past Twenty Years, recording the remarkable Progress of the Japanese in Western Civilisation. With Map. 8vo. 15*s*.

MOTLEY'S (J. L.) History of the United Netherlands: from the Death of William the Silent to the Twelve Years' Truce, 1609. *Library Edition.* Portraits. 4 Vols. 8vo. 60*s*. *Cabinet Edition.* 4 Vols. Post 8vo. 6*s*. each.

——— Life and Death of John of Barneveld, Advocate of Holland. With a View of the Primary Causes and Movements of the Thirty Years' War. Illustrations. 2 Vols. 8vo. 28*s*.

MOUHOT'S (HENRI) Siam, Cambojia, and Lao; a Narrative of Travels and Discoveries. Illustrations. 2 vols. 8vo.

MOZLEY'S (CANON) Treatise on Predestination. 8vo. 14*s*.

——— Primitive Doctrine of Baptismal Regeneration. 8vo. 7*s*.6*d*.

MUNDY'S (GENERAL) Pen and Pencil Sketches in India. *Third Edition.* Plates. Post 8vo. 7*s*. 6*d*.

MUNRO'S (GENERAL) Life and Letters. By REV. G. R. GLEIG. Post 8vo. 3*s*. 6*d*.

MURCHISON'S (SIR RODERICK) Russia in Europe and the Ural Mountains. With Coloured Maps, &c. 2 Vols. 4to. 5*l*. 5*s*.

——— Siluria; or, a History of the Oldest Rocks containing Organic Remains. *Fifth Edition.* Map and Plates. 8vo. 18*s*.

——— Memoirs. With Notices of his Contemporaries, and Rise and Progress of Palæozoic Geology. By ARCHIBALD GEIKIE. Portraits. 2 Vols. 8vo.

MURRAY'S RAILWAY READING. Containing:—

WELLINGTON. By LORD ELLESMERE. 6*d*.
NIMROD ON THE CHASE. 1*s*.
MUSIC AND DRESS. 1*s*.
MILMAN'S FALL OF JERUSALEM. 1*s*.
MAHON'S "FORTY-FIVE." 3*s*.
LIFE OF THEODORE HOOK. 1*s*.
DEEDS OF NAVAL DARING. 3*s*. 6*d*.
THE HONEY BEE. 1*s*.
ÆSOP'S FABLES. 2*s*. 6*d*.
NIMROD ON THE TURF. 1*s*. 6*d*.
ART OF DINING. 1*s*. 6*d*.
MAHON'S JOAN OF ARC. 1*s*.
HEAD'S EMIGRANT. 2*s*. 6*d*.
NIMROD ON THE ROAD. 1*s*.
CROKER ON THE GUILLOTINE. 1*s*.
HOLLWAY'S NORWAY. 2*s*.
MAUREL'S WELLINGTON. 1*s*. 6*d*.
CAMPBELL'S LIFE OF BACON. 2*s*. 6*d*.
THE FLOWER GARDEN. 1*s*.
TAYLOR'S NOTES FROM LIFE. 2*s*.
REJECTED ADDRESSES. 1*s*.
PENN'S HINTS ON ANGLING. 1*s*.

MUSTERS' (CAPT.) Patagonians; a Year's Wanderings over Untrodden Ground from the Straits of Magellan to the Rio Negro. *2nd Edition.* Illustrations. Post 8vo. 7*s*. 6*d*.

NAPIER'S (SIR CHAS.) Life, Journals, and Letters. *Second Edition.* Portraits. 4 Vols. Post 8vo. 48*s*.

——— (SIR WM.) Life and Letters. Portraits. 2 Vols. Crown 8vo. 28*s*.

——— English Battles and Sieges of the Peninsular War. *Fourth Edition.* Portrait. Post 8vo. 9*s*.

NAPOLEON AT FONTAINEBLEAU AND ELBA. A Journal of Occurrences and Notes of Conversations. By SIR NEIL CAMPBELL, C.B. With a Memoir. By REV. A. N. C. MACLACHLAN, M.A. Portrait. 8vo. 15*s.*

NASMYTH AND CARPENTER. The Moon. Considered as a Planet, a World, and a Satellite. With Illustrations from Drawings made with the aid of Powerful Telescopes, Woodcuts, &c. *Second Edition.* 4to. 30*s.*

NAUTICAL ALMANAC (THE). (*By Authority.*) 2*s.* 6*d.*

NAVY LIST. (Monthly and Quarterly.) Post 8vo.

NEW TESTAMENT. With Short Explanatory Commentary. By ARCHDEACON CHURTON, M.A., and ARCHDEACON BASIL JONES, M.A. With 110 authentic Views, &c. 2 Vols. Crown 8vo 21*s. bound.*

NEWTH'S (SAMUEL) First Book of Natural Philosophy; an Introduction to the Study of Statics, Dynamics, Hydrostatics, Optics, and Acoustics, with numerous Examples. Small 8vo. 3*s.* 6*d.*

——— Elements of Mechanics, including Hydrostatics, with numerous Examples. *Fifth Edition.* Small 8vo. 8*s.* 6*d.* Cloth.

——— Mathematical Examinations. A Graduated Series of Elementary Examples in Arithmetic, Algebra, Logarithms, Trigonometry, and Mechanics. *Third Edition.* Small 8vo. 8*s.* 6*d.* each.

NICHOLLS' (SIR GEORGE) History of the English, Irish and Scotch Poor Laws. 4 Vols. 8vo.

NICOLAS' (SIR HARRIS) Historic Peerage of England. Exhibiting the Origin, Descent, and Present State of every Title of Peerage which has existed in this Country since the Conquest. By WILLIAM COURTHOPE. 8vo. 30*s.*

NIMROD, On the Chace—Turf—and Road. With Portrait and Plates. Crown 8vo. 5*s.* Or with Coloured Plates, 7*s.* 6*d.*

NORDHOFF'S (CHAS.) Communistic Societies of the United States; including Detailed Accounts of the Shakers, The Amana, Oneida, Bethell, Aurora, Icarian and other existing Societies; with Particulars of their Religious Creeds, Industries, and Present Condition. With 40 Illustrations. 8vo. 15*s.*

OLD LONDON; Papers read at the Archæological Institute. By various Authors. 8vo. 12*s.*

ORMATHWAITE'S (LORD) Astronomy and Geology—Darwin and Buckle—Progress and Civilisation. Crown 8vo. 6*s.*

OWEN'S (LIEUT.-COL.) Principles and Practice of Modern Artillery, including Artillery Material, Gunnery, and Organisation and Use of Artillery in Warfare. *Second Edition.* With Illustrations. 8vo. 15*s.*

OXENHAM'S (REV. W.) English Notes for Latin Elegiacs; designed for early Proficients in the Art of Latin Versification, with Prefatory Rules of Composition in Elegiac-Metre. *Fifth Edition.* 12mo. 3*s.* 6*d.*

PALGRAVE'S (R. H. I.) Local Taxation of Great Britain and Ireland. 8vo. 5*s.*

——— NOTES ON BANKING IN GREAT BRITAIN AND IRELAND, SWEDEN, DENMARK, AND HAMBURG, with some Remarks on the amount of Bills in circulation, both Inland and Foreign. 8vo. 6*s.*

PALLISER'S (MRS.) Brittany and its Byeways, its Inhabitants, and Antiquities. With Illustrations. Post 8vo. 12*s.*

——— Mottoes for Monuments, or Epitaphs selected for General Use and Study. With Illustrations. Crown 8vo. 7*s.* 6*d.*

PARIS' (DR.) Philosophy in Sport made Science in Earnest; or, the First Principles of Natural Philosophy inculcated by aid of the Toys and Sports of Youth. *Ninth Edition.* Woodcuts. Post 8vo. 7*s.* 6*d.*

PARKMAN'S (FRANCIS) Discovery of the Great West; or, The Valleys of the Mississippi and the Lakes of North America. An Historical Narrative. Map. 8vo. 10*s.* 6*d.*

PARKYNS' (MANSFIELD) Three Years' Residence in Abyssinia: with Travels in that Country. *Second Edition*, with Illustrations. Post 8vo. 7*s*. 6*d*.

PEEK PRIZE ESSAYS. The Maintenance of the Church of England as an Established Church. By REV. CHARLES HOLE—REV. R. WATSON DIXON—and REV. JULIUS LLOYD. 8vo. 10*s*. 6*d*.

PEEL'S (SIR ROBERT) Memoirs. 2 Vols. Post 8vo. 15*s*.

PENN'S (RICHARD) Maxims and Hints for an Angler and Chess-player. Woodcuts. Fcap. 8vo. 1*s*.

PERCY'S (JOHN, M.D.) Metallurgy. Vol. I., Part 1. Fuel, Wood, Peat, Coal, Charcoal, Coke, Refractory Materials, Fire-Clays, &c. *Second Edition*. With Illustrations. 8vo. 24*s*.

——— Vol. I., Part 2. Copper, Zinc, Brass. *Second Edition*. With Illustrations. 8vo. (*In the Press.*)

——— Vol. II. Iron and Steel. *New Edition*. With Illustrations. 8vo. (*In Preparation.*)

——— Vol. III. Lead, including Desilverization and Cupellation. With Illustrations. 8vo. 30*s*.

——— Vols. IV. and V. Gold, Silver, and Mercury, Platinum, Tin, Nickel, Cobalt, Antimony, Bismuth, Arsenic, and other Metals. With Illustrations. 8vo. (*In Preparation.*)

PERSIA'S (SHAH OF) Diary during his Tour through Europe in 1873. Translated from the Original. By J. W. REDHOUSE. With Portrait and Coloured Title. Crown 8vo. 12*s*.

PHILLIPS' (JOHN) Memoirs of William Smith. 8vo. 7*s*. 6*d*.

——— Geology of Yorkshire, The Coast, and Limestone District. Plates. 4to.

——— Rivers, Mountains, and Sea Coast of Yorkshire. With Essays on the Climate, Scenery, and Ancient Inhabitants. *Second Edition*, Plates. 8vo. 15*s*.

——— (SAMUEL) Literary Essays from "The Times." With Portrait. 2 Vols. Fcap. 8vo. 7*s*.

PICK'S (DR.) Popular Etymological Dictionary of the French Language. 8vo. 7*s*. 6*d*.

POPE'S (ALEXANDER) Works. With Introductions and Notes, by REV. WHITWELL ELWIN. Vols. I., II., VI., VII., VIII. With Portraits. 8vo. 10*s*. 6*d*. each.

PORTER'S (REV. J. L.) Damascus, Palmyra, and Lebanon. With Travels among the Giant Cities of Bashan and the Hauran. *New Edition*. Map and Woodcuts. Post 8vo. 7*s*. 6*d*.

PRAYER-BOOK (ILLUSTRATED), with Borders, Initials, Vignettes, &c. Edited, with Notes, by REV. THOS. JAMES. Medium 8vo. 18*s*. *cloth*; 31*s*. 6*d*. *calf*; 36*s*. *morocco*.

PRINCESS CHARLOTTE OF WALES. A Brief Memoir. With Selections from her Correspondence and other unpublished Papers. By LADY ROSE WEIGALL. With Portrait. 8vo. 8*s*. 6*d*.

PUSS IN BOOTS. With 12 Illustrations. By OTTO SPECKTER. 16mo. 1*s*. 6*d*. Or coloured, 2*s*. 6*d*.

PRINCIPLES AT STAKE. Essays on Church Questions of the Day. 8vo. 12*s*. Contents:—

Ritualism and Uniformity.—Benjamin Shaw.
The Episcopate.—Bishop of Bath and Wells.
The Priesthood.—Dean of Canterbury.
National Education.—Rev. Alexander R. Grant.
Doctrine of the Eucharist.—Rev. G. H. Sumner.
Scripture and Ritual.—Canon Bernard.
Church in South Africa.—Arthur Mills.
Schismatical Tendency of Ritualism.—Rev. Dr. Salmon.
Revisions of the Liturgy.—Rev. W. G. Humphry.
Parties and Party Spirit.—Dean of Chester.

PRIVY COUNCIL JUDGMENTS in Ecclesiastical Cases relating to Doctrine and Discipline. With Historical Introduction, by G. C. BRODRICK and W. H. FREMANTLE. 8vo. 10s. 6d.

QUARTERLY REVIEW (THE). 8vo. 6s.

RAMBLES in the Syrian Deserts. Post 8vo. 10s. 6d.

RANKE'S (LEOPOLD) History of the Popes of Rome during the 16th and 17th Centuries. Translated from the German by SARAH AUSTIN. *Third Edition.* 3 Vols. 8vo. 30s.

RASSAM'S (HORMUZD) Narrative of the British Mission to Abyssinia. With Notices of the Countries Traversed from Massowah to Magdala. Illustrations. 2 Vols. 8vo. 28s.

RAWLINSON'S (CANON) Herodotus. A New English Version. Edited with Notes and Essays. *Third Edition.* Maps and Woodcut. 4 Vols. 8vo.

——— Five Great Monarchies of Chaldæa, Assyria, Media, Babylonia, and Persia. *Third Edition.* With Maps and Illustrations. 3 Vols. 8vo. 42s.

——— (SIR HENRY) England and Russia in the East; a Series of Papers on the Political and Geographical Condition of Central Asia. Map. 8vo.

REED'S (E. J.) Shipbuilding in Iron and Steel; a Practical Treatise, giving full details of Construction, Processes of Manufacture, and Building Arrangements. With 5 Plans and 250 Woodcuts. 8vo. 30s.

——— Iron-Clad Ships; their Qualities, Performances, and Cost. With Chapters on Turret Ships, Iron-Clad Rams, &c. With Illustrations. 8vo. 12s.

REJECTED ADDRESSES (THE). By JAMES AND HORACE SMITH. *New Edition.* Woodcuts. Post 8vo. 3s. 6d.; or *Popular Edition*, Fcap. 8vo. 1s.

RENNIE'S (D. F.) British Arms in Peking, 1860. Post 8vo. 12s.

——— Narrative of the British Embassy in China. Illustrations. 2 Vols. Post 8vo. 24s.

——— Story of Bhotan and the Doear War. Map and Woodcut. Post 8vo. 12s.

RESIDENCE IN BULGARIA; or, Notes on the Resources and Administration of Turkey, &c. By S. G. B. ST. CLAIR and CHARLES A. BROPHY. 8vo. 12s.

REYNOLDS' (SIR JOSHUA) Life and Times. By C. R. LESLIE, R.A. and TOM TAYLOR. Portraits. 2 Vols. 8vo.

RICARDO'S (DAVID) Political Works. With a Notice of his Life and Writings. By J. R. M'CULLOCH. *New Edition.* 8vo. 16s.

RIPA'S (FATHER) Thirteen Years' Residence at the Court of Peking. Post 8vo. 2s.

ROBERTSON'S (CANON) History of the Christian Church, from the Apostolic Age to the Reformation, 1517. *Library Edition.* 4 Vols. 8vo. *Cabinet Edition.* 8 Vols. Post 8vo. 6s. each.

——— How shall we Conform to the Liturgy. 12mo. 9s.

ROME. *See* LIDDELL and SMITH.

ROWLAND'S (DAVID) Manual of the English Constitution. Its Rise, Growth, and Present State. Post 8vo. 10s. 6d.

——— Laws of Nature the Foundation of Morals. Post 8vo. 6s.

ROBSON'S (E. R.) SCHOOL ARCHITECTURE. Being Practical Remarks on the Planning, Designing, Building, and Furnishing of School-houses. With 300 Illustrations of School-buildings in all Parts of the World, drawn to scale. Medium 8vo. 31s. 6d.

RUNDELL'S (MRS.) Modern Domestic Cookery. Fcap. 8vo. 5s.

RUXTON'S (GEORGE F.) Travels in Mexico; with Adventures among the Wild Tribes and Animals of the Prairies and Rocky Mountains. Post 8vo. 3s. 6d.

ROBINSON'S (REV. DR.) Biblical Researches in Palestine and the Adjacent Regions, 1838—52. *Third Edition.* Maps. 3 Vols. 8vo. 42s.

——— Physical Geography of the Holy Land. Post 8vo. 10s. 6d.

——— (WM.) Alpine Flowers for English Gardens. *New Edition.* With 70 Illustrations. Crown 8vo. [*Nearly ready.*

——— Wild Garden; or, our Groves and Shrubberies made beautiful by the Naturalization of Hardy Exotic Plants. With Frontispiece. Small 8vo. 6s.

——— Sub-Tropical Garden; or, Beauty of Form in the Flower Garden. With Illustrations. Small 8vo. 7s. 6d.

SALE'S (SIR ROBERT) Brigade in Affghanistan. With an Account of the Defence of Jellalabad. By REV. G. R. GLEIG. Post 8vo. 2s.

SCHLIEMANN'S (DR. HENRY) Troy and Its Remains. A Narrative of Researches and Discoveries made on the Site of Ilium, and in the Trojan Plain. Edited by PHILIP SMITH, B.A. With Maps, Plans, Views, and 500 Illustrations of Objects of Antiquity, &c. Medium 8vo.

SCOTT'S (SIR G. G.) Secular and Domestic Architecture, Present and Future. 8vo. 9s.

——— (DEAN) University Sermons. Post 8vo. 8s. 6d.

SHADOWS OF A SICK ROOM. *Second Edition.* With a Preface by CANON LIDDON. 16mo. 2s 6d.

SCROPE'S (G. P.) Geology and Extinct Volcanoes of Central France. Illustrations. Medium 8vo. 30s.

SHAW'S (T. B.) Manual of English Literature. Post 8vo. 7s. 6d.

——— Specimens of English Literature. Selected from the Chief Writers. Post 8vo. 7s. 6d.

——— (ROBERT) Visit to High Tartary, Yarkand, and Kashgar (formerly Chinese Tartary), and Return Journey over the Karakorum Pass. With Map and Illustrations. 8vo. 16s.

SHIRLEY'S (EVELYN P.) Deer and Deer Parks; or some Account of English Parks, with Notes on the Management of Deer. Illustrations. 4to. 21s.

SIERRA LEONE; Described in Letters to Friends at Home. By A LADY. Post 8vo. 3s. 6d.

SINCLAIR'S (ARCHDEACON) Old Times and Distant Places. A Series of Sketches. Crown 8vo.

SMILES' (SAMUEL) Lives of British Engineers; from the Earliest Period to the death of the Stephensons. With Portraits and Illustrations. *Cabinet Edition.* 5 Vols. Crown 8vo. 7s. 6d. each.

——— Lives of George and Robert Stephenson. *Library Edition.* With Portraits and Illustrations. Medium 8vo. 21s.

——— Lives of Boulton and Watt. *Library Edition.* With Portraits and Illustrations. Medium 8vo. 21s.

——— Self-Help. With Illustrations of Conduct and Perseverance. Post 8vo. 6s. Or in French, 5s.

——— Character. A Companion Volume to "SELF-HELP." Post 8vo. 6s.

——— Industrial Biography: Iron-Workers and Tool-Makers. Post 8vo. 6s.

——— Boy's Voyage round the World; including a Residence in Victoria, and a Journey by Rail across North America. With Illustrations. Post 8vo. 6s.

SMITH'S (Dr. Wm.) Dictionary of the Bible; its Antiquities, Biography, Geography, and Natural History. Illustrations. 3 Vols. 8vo. 105*s*.

——— Christian Antiquities. Comprising the History, Institutions, and Antiquities of the Christian Church. 2 Vols. 8vo. Vol. I. (*Nearly ready.*

——— Biography and Doctrines; from the Times of the Apostles to the Age of Charlemagne. 8vo. (*In Preparation.*

——— Concise Bible Dictionary. With 300 Illustrations. Medium 8vo. 21*s*.

——— Smaller Bible Dictionary. With Illustrations. Post 8vo. 7*s*. 6*d*.

——— Atlas of Ancient Geography—Biblical and Classical. (5 Parts.) Folio. 21*s*. each.

——— Greek and Roman Antiquities. With 500 Illustrations. Medium 8vo. 28*s*.

——— Biography and Mythology. With 600 Illustrations. 3 Vols. Medium 8vo. 4*l*. 4*s*.

——— Geography. 2 Vols. With 500 Illustrations. Medium 8vo. 56*s*.

——— Classical Dictionary of Mythology, Biography, and Geography. 1 Vol. With 750 Woodcuts. 8vo. 18*s*.

——— Smaller Classical Dictionary. With 200 Woodcuts. Crown 8vo. 7*s*. 6*d*.

——— Greek and Roman Antiquities. With 200 Woodcuts. Crown 8vo. 7*s*. 6*d*.

——— Latin-English Dictionary. With Tables of the Roman Calendar, Measures, Weights, and Money. Medium 8vo. 21*s*.

——— Smaller Latin-English Dictionary. 12mo. 7*s*. 6*d*.

——— English-Latin Dictionary. Medium 8vo. 21*s*.

——— Smaller English-Latin Dictionary. 12mo. 7*s*. 6*d*.

——— School Manual of English Grammar, with Copious Exercises. Post 8vo. 3*s*. 6*d*.

——— Primary English Grammar. 16mo. 1*s*.

——— History of Britain. 12mo. 2*s*. 6*d*.

——— French Principia. Part I. A Grammar, Delectus, Exercises, and Vocabularies. 12mo. 3*s*. 6*d*.

——— Principia Latina—Part I. A Grammar, Delectus, and Exercise Book, with Vocabularies. With the Accidence arranged for the "Public School Primer." 12mo. 3*s*. 6*d*.

——— Part II. A Reading-book of Mythology, Geography, Roman Antiquities, and History. With Notes and Dictionary. 12mo. 3*s*. 6*d*.

——— Part III. A Latin Poetry Book. Hexameters and Pentameters; Eclog. Ovidianæ; Latin Prosody. 12mo. 3*s*. 6*d*.

——— Part IV. Latin Prose Composition. Rules of Syntax, with Examples, Explanations of Synonyms, and Exercises on the Syntax. 12mo. 3*s*. 6*d*.

——— Part V. Short Tales and Anecdotes for Translation into Latin. 12mo. 3*s*.

——— Latin-English Vocabulary and First Latin-English Dictionary for Phædrus, Cornelius Nepos, and Cæsar. 12mo. 3*s*. 6*d*.

——— Student's Latin Grammar. Post 8vo. 6*s*.

——— Smaller Latin Grammar. 12mo. 3*s*. 6*d*.

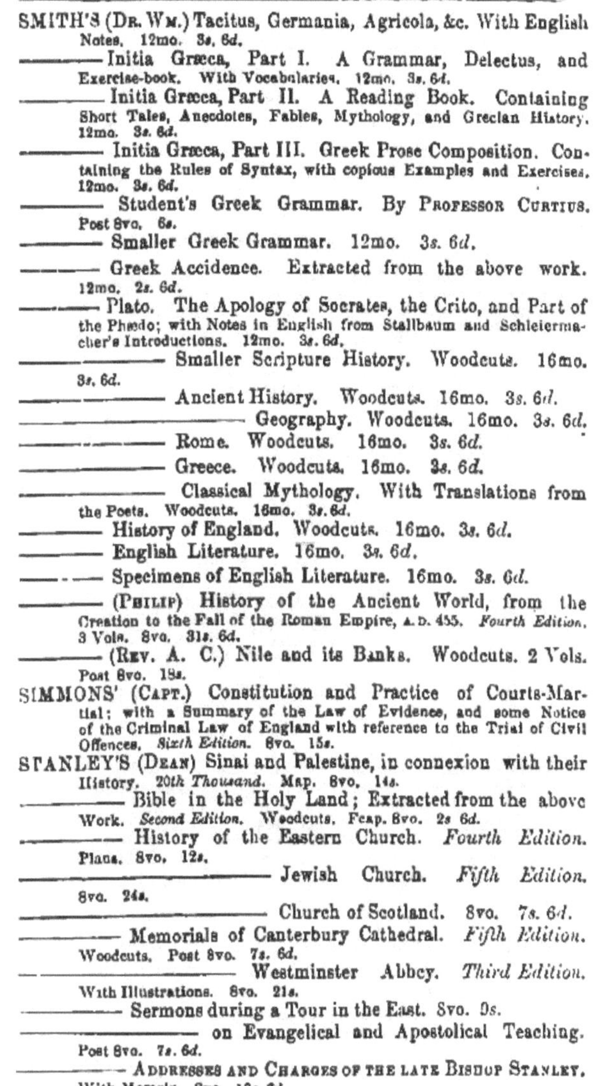

SMITH'S (DR. WM.) Tacitus, Germania, Agricola, &c. With English Notes. 12mo. 3s. 6d.

——— Initia Græca, Part I. A Grammar, Delectus, and Exercise-book. With Vocabularies. 12mo. 3s. 6d.

——— Initia Græca, Part II. A Reading Book. Containing Short Tales, Anecdotes, Fables, Mythology, and Grecian History. 12mo. 3s. 6d.

——— Initia Græca, Part III. Greek Prose Composition. Containing the Rules of Syntax, with copious Examples and Exercises. 12mo. 3s. 6d.

——— Student's Greek Grammar. By PROFESSOR CURTIUS. Post 8vo. 6s.

——— Smaller Greek Grammar. 12mo. 3s. 6d.

——— Greek Accidence. Extracted from the above work. 12mo. 2s. 6d.

——— Plato. The Apology of Socrates, the Crito, and Part of the Phædo; with Notes in English from Stallbaum and Schleiermacher's Introductions. 12mo. 3s. 6d.

——— Smaller Scripture History. Woodcuts. 16mo. 3s. 6d.

——— Ancient History. Woodcuts. 16mo. 3s. 6d.

——— Geography. Woodcuts. 16mo. 3s. 6d.

——— Rome. Woodcuts. 16mo. 3s. 6d.

——— Greece. Woodcuts. 16mo. 3s. 6d.

——— Classical Mythology. With Translations from the Poets. Woodcuts. 16mo. 3s. 6d.

——— History of England. Woodcuts. 16mo. 3s. 6d.

——— English Literature. 16mo. 3s. 6d.

——— Specimens of English Literature. 16mo. 3s. 6d.

——— (PHILIP) History of the Ancient World, from the Creation to the Fall of the Roman Empire, A.D. 455. *Fourth Edition.* 3 Vols. 8vo. 31s. 6d.

——— (REV. A. C.) Nile and its Banks. Woodcuts. 2 Vols. Post 8vo. 18s.

SIMMONS' (CAPT.) Constitution and Practice of Courts-Martial; with a Summary of the Law of Evidence, and some Notice of the Criminal Law of England with reference to the Trial of Civil Offences. *Sixth Edition.* 8vo. 15s.

STANLEY'S (DEAN) Sinai and Palestine, in connexion with their History. *20th Thousand.* Map. 8vo. 14s.

——— Bible in the Holy Land; Extracted from the above Work. *Second Edition.* Woodcuts. Fcap. 8vo. 2s 6d.

——— History of the Eastern Church. *Fourth Edition.* Plans. 8vo. 12s.

——— Jewish Church. *Fifth Edition.* 8vo. 24s.

——— Church of Scotland. 8vo. 7s. 6d.

——— Memorials of Canterbury Cathedral. *Fifth Edition.* Woodcuts. Post 8vo. 7s. 6d.

——— Westminster Abbey. *Third Edition.* With Illustrations. 8vo. 21s.

——— Sermons during a Tour in the East. 8vo. 9s.

——— on Evangelical and Apostolical Teaching. Post 8vo. 7s. 6d.

——— ADDRESSES AND CHARGES OF THE LATE BISHOP STANLEY. With Memoir. 8vo. 10s. 6d.

STUDENT'S OLD TESTAMENT HISTORY; from the Creation to the Return of the Jews from Captivity. Maps and Woodcuts. Post 8vo. 7*s*. 6*d*.

——— NEW TESTAMENT HISTORY. With an Introduction connecting the History of the Old and New Testaments. Maps and Woodcuts. Post 8vo. 7*s*. 6*d*.

——— ANCIENT HISTORY OF THE EAST; Egypt, Assyria, Babylonia, Media, Persia, Asia Minor, and Phœnicia. By PHILIP SMITH. Woodcuts. Post 8vo. 7*s*. 6*d*.

——— GEOGRAPHY. By REV. W. L. BEVAN. Woodcuts. Post 8vo. 7*s*. 6*d*.

——— HISTORY OF GREECE; from the Earliest Times to the Roman Conquest. By WM. SMITH, D.C.L. Woodcuts. Crown 8vo. 7*s*. 6*d*.

*** Questions on the above Work, 12mo. 2*s*.

——— HISTORY OF ROME; from the Earliest Times to the Establishment of the Empire. By DEAN LIDDELL. Woodcuts. Crown 8vo. 7*s*. 6*d*.

——— GIBBON'S Decline and Fall of the Roman Empire. Woodcuts. Post 8vo. 7*s*. 6*d*.

——— HALLAM'S HISTORY OF EUROPE during the Middle Ages. Post 8vo. 7*s*. 6*d*.

——— HUME'S History of England from the Invasion of Julius Cæsar to the Revolution in 1688. Continued down to 1868. Woodcuts. Post 8vo. 7*s*. 6*d*.

*** Questions on the above Work, 12mo. 2*s*.

——— HALLAM'S HISTORY OF ENGLAND; from the Accession of Henry VII. to the Death of George II. Post 8vo. 7*s*. 6*d*.

——— ENGLISH LANGUAGE. By GEO. P. MARSH. Post 8vo. 7*s*. 6*d*.

——— LITERATURE. By T. B. SHAW, M.A. Post 8vo. 7*s*. 6*d*.

——— SPECIMENS of English Literature from the Chief Writers. By T. B. SHAW, Post 8vo. 7*s*. 6*d*.

——— HISTORY OF FRANCE; from the Earliest Times to the Establishment of the Second Empire, 1852. By REV. H. W. JERVIS. Woodcuts. Post 8vo. 7*s*. 6*d*.

——— MODERN GEOGRAPHY; Mathematical, Physical, and Descriptive. By REV. W. L. BEVAN. Woodcuts. Post 8vo. 7*s*. 6*d*.

——— MORAL PHILOSOPHY. By WILLIAM FLEMING, D.D. Post 8vo. 7*s*. 6*d*.

——— BLACKSTONE'S Commentaries on the Laws of England. By R. MALCOLM KERR, LL.D. Post 8vo. 7*s*. 6*d*.

——— ECCLESIASTICAL HISTORY. A History of the Christian Church from its Foundation to the Eve of the Protestant Reformation. By PHILIP SMITH, B.A. Post 8vo. 7*s* 6*d*.

SPALDING'S (CAPTAIN) Tale of Frithiof. Translated from the Swedish of ESIAS TEGNER. Post 8vo. 7*s*. 6*d*.

STEPHEN'S (REV. W. R.) Life and Times of St. Chrysostom. With Portrait. 8vo. 15*s*.

ST. JOHN'S (CHARLES) Wild Sports and Natural History of the Highlands. Post 8vo. 3*s*. 6*d*.

——— (BAYLE) Adventures in the Libyan Desert. Post 8vo. 2*s*.

STORIES FOR DARLINGS. With Illustrations. 16mo. 5*s*.

STREET'S (G. E.) Gothic Architecture in Spain. From Personal Observations made during several Journeys. *Second Edition.* With Illustrations. Royal 8vo. 30*s*.

——— Gothic Architecture in Italy, chiefly in Brick and Marble. With Notes of Tours in the North of Italy. *Second Edition.* With 60 Illustrations. Royal 8vo. 26*s*.

STANHOPE'S (EARL) England during the Reign of Queen Anne, 1701—13. *Library Edition.* 8vo. 16s. *Cabinet Edition.* Portrait. 2 Vols. Post 8vo. 10s.

——— from the Peace of Utrecht to the Peace of Versailles, 1713-83. *Library Edition.* 7 vols. 8vo. 93s. *Cabinet Edition*, 7 vols. Post 8vo. 5s. each.

——— British India, from its Origin to 1783. 8vo. 3s. 6*d*.

——— History of "Forty-Five." Post 8vo. 3s.

——— Spain under Charles the Second. Post 8vo. 6s. 6*d*.

——— Historical and Critical Essays. Post 8vo. 3s. 6*d*.

——— Life of Belisarius. Post 8vo. 10s. 6*d*.

——— Condé. Post 8vo. 3s. 6*d*.

——— William Pitt. Portraits. 4 Vols. 8vo. 24s.

——— Miscellanies. 2 Vols. Post 8vo. 13s.

——— Story of Joan of Arc. Fcap. 8vo. 1s.

——— Addresses Delivered on Various Occasions. 16mo. 1s.

STYFFE'S (KNUTT) Strength of Iron and Steel. Plates. 8vo. 12s.

SOMERVILLE'S (MARY) Physical Geography. *Sixth Edition*, Portrait. Post 8vo. 9s.

——— Connexion of the Physical Sciences. *Ninth Edition.* Portrait. Post 8vo. 9s.

——— Molecular and Microscopic Science. Illustrations. 2 Vols. Post 8vo. 21s.

——— Personal Recollections from Early Life to Old Age. With Selections from her Correspondence. *Fourth Edition.* Portrait. Crown 8vo. 12s.

SOUTHEY'S (ROBERT) Book of the Church. Post 8vo. 7s. 6*d*.

——— Lives of Bunyan and Cromwell. Post 8vo. 2s.

SWAINSON'S (CANON) Nicene and Apostles' Creeds; Their Literary History; together with some Account of "The Creed of St. Athanasius." 8vo.

SYBEL'S (VON) History of Europe during the French Revolution, 1789—1795. 4 Vols. 8vo. 48s.

SYMONDS' (REV. W.) Records of the Rocks; or Notes on the Geology, Natural History, and Antiquities of North and South Wales, Siluria, Devon, and Cornwall. With Illustrations. Crown 8vo. 12s.

TAYLOR'S (SIR HENRY) Notes from Life. Fcap. 8vo. 2s.

THIELMAN'S (BARON) Journey through the Caucasus to Tabreez, Kurdistan, down the Tigris and Euphrates to Nineveh and Babylon, and across the Desert to Palmyra. Translated by CHAS. HENEAGE. 2 Vols. Post 8vo.

THOMS' (W. J.) Longevity of Man; its Facts and its Fiction. Including Observations on the more Remarkable Instances. Post 8vo. 10s. 6*d*.

THOMSON'S (ARCHBISHOP) Lincoln's Inn Sermons. 8vo. 10s. 6*d*.

——— Life in the Light of God's Word. Post 8vo. 5s.

TOCQUEVILLE'S State of Society in France before the Revolution, 1789, and on the Causes which led to that Event. Translated by HENRY REEVE. *2nd Edition.* 8vo. 12s.

TOMLINSON (CHARLES); The Sonnet; Its Origin, Structure, and Place in Poetry. With translations from Dante, Petrarch, &c. Post 8vo. 9s.

TOZER'S (REV. H. F.) Highlands of Turkey, with Visits to Mounts Ida, Athos, Olympus, and Pelion. 2 Vols. Crown 8vo. 24s.

——— Lectures on the Geography of Greece. Map. Post 8vo. 9s.

TRISTRAM'S (CANON) Great Sahara. Illustrations. Crown 8vo. 15*s.*

——— Land of Moab; Travels and Discoveries on the East Side of the Dead Sea and the Jordan. *Second Edition.* Illustrations. Crown 8vo. 15*s.*

TWISLETON (EDWARD). The Tongue not Essential to Speech, with Illustrations of the Power of Speech in the case of the African Confessors. Post 8vo. 6*s.*

TWISS' (HORACE) Life of Lord Eldon. 2 Vols. Post 8vo. 21*s.*

TYLOR'S (E. B.) Early History of Mankind, and Development of Civilization. *Second Edition.* 8vo. 12*s.*

——— Primitive Culture; the Development of Mythology, Philosophy, Religion, Art, and Custom. *Second Edition.* 2 Vols. 8vo. 24*s.*

VAMBERY'S (ARMINIUS) Travels from Teheran across the Turkoman Desert on the Eastern Shore of the Caspian. Illustrations. 8vo. 21*s.*

VAN LENNEP'S (HENRY J.) Travels in Asia Minor. With Illustrations of Biblical Literature, and Archæology. With Woodcuts. 2 Vols. Post 8vo. 24*s.*

WELLINGTON'S Despatches during his Campaigns in India, Denmark, Portugal, Spain, the Low Countries, and France. Edited by COLONEL GURWOOD. 8 Vols. 8vo. 20*s.* each.

——— Supplementary Despatches, relating to India, Ireland, Denmark, Spanish America, Spain, Portugal, France, Congress of Vienna, Waterloo and Paris. Edited by his SON. 14 Vols. 8vo. 20*s.* each. *** *An Index.* 8vo. 20*s.*

——— Civil and Political Correspondence. Edited by his SON. Vols. I. to V. 8vo. 20*s.* each.

——— Despatches (Selections from). 8vo. 18*s.*

——— Speeches in Parliament. 2 Vols. 8vo. 42*s.*

WHEELER'S (G.) Choice of a Dwelling; a Practical Handbook of Useful Information on Building a House. *Third Edition.* Plans. Post 8vo. 7*s.* 6*d.*

WHITE'S (HENRY) Massacre of St. Bartholomew. 8vo. 16*s.*

WHYMPER'S (EDWARD) Scrambles among the Alps. With the First Ascent of the Matterhorn, and Notes on Glacial Phenomena. *Second Edition.* Illustrations. 8vo. 21*s.*

——— (FREDERICK) Travels and Adventures in Alaska. Illustrations. 8vo. 16*s.*

WILBERFORCE'S (BISHOP) Essays on Various Subjects. 2 vols. 8vo. 21*s.*

——— Life of William Wilberforce. Portrait. Crown 8vo. 6*s.*

WILKINSON'S (SIR J. G.) Popular Account of the Ancient Egyptians. With 500 Woodcuts. 2 Vols. Post 8vo. 12*s.*

WOOD'S (CAPTAIN) Source of the Oxus. With the Geography of the Valley of the Oxus. By COL. YULE. Map. 8vo. 12*s.*

WORDS OF HUMAN WISDOM. Collected and Arranged by E. S. With a Preface by Canon LIDDON, D.D. Fcp. 8vo. 3*s.* 6*d.*

WORDSWORTH'S (BISHOP) Athens and Attica. Plates. 8vo. 5*s.*

——— Greece. Pictorial, Descriptive, and Historical. With 600 Woodcuts. Royal 8vo.

YULE'S (COLONEL) Book of Marco Polo. Illustrated by the Light of Oriental Writers and Modern Travels. With Maps and 80 Plates. 2 Vols. Medium 8vo. 42*s.*

ZINCKE'S (REV. F. B.) Winter in the United States. Post 8vo. 10*s.* 6*d.*

BRADBURY, AGNEW, & CO., PRINTERS, WHITEFRIARS.

Zeitfracht Medien GmbH
Ferdinand-Jühlke-Straße 7
99095 Erfurt, Deutschland
produktsicherheit@kolibri360.de